A Reader's Guide to W. H. Auden

A Reader's Guide to W. H. Auden

John Fuller

THAMES AND HUDSON · LONDON

FOR KATE AND ROY

Printed in Great Britain by Cox & Wyman Ltd, London, Fakenham and Reading

500 14015 4 clothbound
500 15006 0 paperbound

Contents

Part Four LATER POEMS

Foreword

This book is intended to serve primarily as a commentary on Auden's poetry and drama, taken in their chronological sequence. My main concern has been to help the reader with difficult passages and to trace some of the sources and allusions, since despite the now happily increasing volume of Auden criticism, there is still nothing quite as systematic or as detailed as the reader would like.

I have omitted unpublished and uncollected poems, translations, prose, radio scripts, and so on. But I believe that there is an advantage to be gained from concentrating on Auden's central œuvre: I have been able to give the space due to the works that the reader will wish to know most about, and I have been able to arrange the volume in such a way that it may conveniently be read in company with the *Collected Shorter Poems* (1966) and the *Collected Longer Poems* (1968).[1] This simplification will, I hope, increase the book's usefulness.

Auden's work falls into fairly well-defined periods, and I have followed his own four-part division of the 1966 *Collected Shorter Poems* in my own arrangement, too. The period 1927–32 covers his last year in Oxford, the Berlin visit and the years he spent teaching in Scotland (where *The Orators* was written). The period 1933–38 sees him teaching in Gloucestershire, working in films and in the theatre, and travelling in Belgium, Iceland, Spain and China. The years 1939–47 are the New York period, when he wrote the four long poems; he emigrated before the outbreak of war and became an American citizen in 1946. From 1948 to 1957 he began to spend the summers in Ischia, and this is the time of his greatest activity in opera and criticism. In 1957 he moved to Austria, and from 1956 to 1961 was Professor of Poetry at Oxford.

I have been concerned on the whole to acknowledge Auden's own estimate of his work, and thus to use the latest editions, for two reasons: it is handier for his readers (which is the main point, after all), and it gives Auden some overdue credit for knowing what he is doing. This is not to say that I am not sometimes disturbed by revisions and omissions (and I have felt it necessary to include a chapter on some of the famous poems at present omitted from the canon), but I do feel that Auden criticism has suffered from excessive ideological and bibliographical niggling, and that the time has come to call a slight halt.

Auden's evolution has amply displayed his many talents. He has been a brilliant undergraduate digesting Eliot and Stein; an inventive mouthpiece of the post-Freudians; a social prophet; a religious synthesizer; an aphoristic critic; and so on. For breadth, wisdom, myth, moral power and sheer technical excitement, he is for me the greatest living poet writing in English. Many would share this view, but there is no doubt that he has been under fire for a variety of reasons, and his reputation even today is uncertain. Auden is frighteningly at ease with ideas, and likes occasionally to both tease and hector his readers. He is not often emotionally demonstrative in his poetry, and is one of the most challengingly adroit versifiers there has ever been. He has been his own kind of Lawrentian, his own kind of Marxist and his own kind of Anglican. He left England for good on the eve of the Second World War. One could multiply such reasons for his alienating certain sectors of the reading public, and some of the reasons would probably not have much to do with poetry. But only a great and unignorable poet could infuriate in ways like these, and Auden is big enough to disappoint or perplex those who have expected him to stand still and perpetuate a stance.

The main accusation is that Auden lost his key subject and his emotional impetus when war at last broke out in 1939. This widely held view is considered to be almost biographically self-evident. If Auden had been a mere journalist of political doom, this would be true; but in fact his treatment of events and their implications goes deeper than this. I hope I have shown how the major works of the 'forties are, among other things, ambitious analyses of human weakness; and I hope I have shown how his work since then has built constructively upon such basic analyses a gentle and humane quest for man's positive, if limited, ideals in life. Auden's career is never quite the retreat it is accused of being: few, I agree, actually *prefer* the later work, but it is surprising, in the face of Auden's developing moral and artistic integrity, that this fact should so frequently issue in rebukes.

Auden's great theme is the integration of life, and his progress from Saga to High Table centres on this. Indeed, the progress itself is part of its meaning, since Auden has had to exorcize in his myth of the failed Leader his inherited notion of the artist as hero. This notion is a humanist one, and humanism, as Auden endlessly pointed out, has no resources against a Hitler. Thus he created for himself a viable Christian system.

His Christianity (or something like it) can be seen with hindsight to be lurking in a good deal of the very early work. Auden's mind is not the scavenging one that it superficially appears to be. He is someone who needs to be fully satisfied at any time of what he feels to be the truth, and thus many apparent contortions are giant simplifications viewed from a rather unexpected angle. In 1933, a great year for discarded neo-Marxist work, a year in which Lawrence seems to have been put behind him, and a year evidently of some artistic turmoil and choice of direction, one might well have expected a more decisive move towards a religious position. But Auden's energies in the following half-dozen years were to a great degree technical: in ideas he stood fairly still. And this is what admirers of the ballad-and-cabaret Auden tend to like. We know it now to have been only a phase, just as the early oblique poetry of disappointed love was a phase, and the middle Rilkean period of historical analysis was a phase. Throughout the most popular period, Auden was trying intermittently to resolve the central problems raised by war as the prime example of man's fallible nature. When the first real approaches to the Christian position were made in a rather personal group of poems published in the Autumn 1939 issue of *Southern Review* (see pp. 169–71), this should not have seemed surprising. I hope that my commentary will in general imply the continuity in Auden's thought throughout his career.

I have provided a comprehensive index of poems, giving titles and first lines, and referring the reader to the main treatment of each poem in the text. This main treatment in the text includes details of publishing history, given in square brackets immediately after the title of the poem. These details are not comprehensive, but do indicate first publication, alternative titles, first collected appearance, and page references in the bulkier collected editions. The abbreviations used are explained in the first part of the Bibliography on p. 271.

The second part of the Bibliography contains only a selection of useful Auden criticism. Nobody writing on Auden can fail to feel gratitude for the work of Monroe Spears and B. C. Bloomfield. I would particularly like to thank the latter for supplying me with some facts from the forthcoming second edition of his invaluable Auden *Bibliography*. For allowing me to quote from the works of W. H. Auden, I am grateful to the author himself, and to Messrs Faber and Faber, London, and Random House, New York, the publishers of the English and American editions, respectively.

J.L.F.

Part One

THE EARLY POETRY

1 Paid on Both Sides

'I have sent you the new *Criterion*,' wrote T. S. Eliot to E. McKnight Kauffer, 'to ask you to read a verse play *Paid on Both Sides*, by a young man I know, which seems to me quite a brilliant piece of work. . . . This fellow is about the best poet that I have discovered in several years.'[1] Interest in Auden's self-styled 'charade' was maintained when it was reprinted with only one small excision in the *Poems* of the same year, and it earned a respectful analysis from William Empson in *Experiment*, No. 7 (1931).

Paid on Both Sides was written in Berlin in 1928, and can be regarded jointly with Eliot's *Sweeney Agonistes* (1927) as a major influence on English poetic drama of the 'thirties. However, it owes little to Eliot's play. *Paid*, which derives from English sources like the Mummers' Play and uses dreams in the manner of contemporary German expressionism, contrasts favourably with the calculated effects of Eliot's Minstrel Show Euripides. It has not been as often produced, but this could be explained by its greater cohesion as ritual. The ideal performance of *Paid* would be by amateurs at a house party as a piece of Christmas Eve therapy, for the piece is most obviously an enigmatic and mythical evaluation of the middle-class ethos of its day. As Auden was later to write: 'Drama began as the act of a whole community. Ideally there would be no spectators. In practice every member of the audience should feel like an understudy.'[2]

In view of such Eliotelian belief, it is natural that Auden should clothe the high seriousness of the themes of his plays with informality, and with a variety of tone in action and situation. Both poets believed in the ultimate compatibility of, say, the vulgarity of the music-hall and the ritual of the Mass because these were both, simply, manifestations of that communal emotion which constitutes dramatic experience. Neither the playfulness nor the obscurity of *Paid* should, therefore, be held against it. The terse style of the poetry was developed here for urgency, and to embody the primitive menace of the Icelandic sagas upon which Auden drew for his account of a feud between two mill-owning families.

'I love the sagas,' Auden wrote in 1937, 'but what a rotten society they describe, a society with only the gangster virtues' (*Letters from Iceland,* p. 119). To the conception of the saga-hero as gangster he added that of the saga-hero as public schoolboy, an idea he seems to have derived from Christopher Isherwood (see the essay in *New Verse,* Nov. 1937, p. 5, recounting their early association). This idea thrown out by Isherwood found a full response in Auden's fusion, in an atmosphere of dark threats, practical jokes, riddles and deliberate understatements, of what is common to epic warfare and a school cadet force field-day. After all, the public school is a special kind of microcosm of the society anatomized in the play, and no matter how much else Auden might add by way of allusiveness, this central fact could not be altered. For example, the setting is patently English,[3] but the names of the characters indicate a German–Jewish conflict (the Nowers are Kurt, Walter, Zeppel, etc; the Shaws, Aaron, Seth, etc). And again, in a further attempt at universalization, Anne's father is called Red Shaw, indicating that the family's biblical names are also appropriately those of American hillbillies, and invoking the classic feud of the Martins and the Coys. But none of this is more than a connotative crust to the essential tone of the play, whose most natural dialogue settles comfortably (and near-satirically) at the clubhouse level.

What are the 'sides' of the play (apart from the term's obvious relevancy to a 'charade')? It is clear that there is no suggestion of Disraeli's Two Nations in the actual conflict: the social parity of the Nowers and Shaws is stressed throughout, even though the play is critical of capitalist morality. The key to the play (and to the meaning of the title) lies in seeing the society that Auden portrays as an allegory also of an individual psyche, sick and irrevocably divided.

In Berlin, Auden became interested in the theory of the moral and spiritual origins of illness put forward by the psychologist Homer Lane. Like D. H. Lawrence, Lane taught that the real desires of men are good and must not be repressed; that there is only one sin, and that is disobedience to the inner law of our own nature. The central episodes of the play, in particular, involve an identification on John Nower's part of the division between the families as a spiritual division in himself. As we shall see, psychological malaise is attributed to the influence of the mother, and the terms are by implication sexual. John nearly breaks the feud by marrying Anne Shaw, but Anne's mother revives it, and John dies. Social unity is thus in effect a psychiatric objective, the point being that no one side can really win: one side's defeat is the defeat of the other.

There has been some confusion about the doubling of parts, marked in the cast list by asterisks, which has been further complicated by a misprint in CSP50. In all earlier texts, Trudy had three asterisks, the only character so indicated. Now the doubling works, although the Chief Guest could hardly double with the Butler. I see little point in the doubling, except possibly in the case of Stephen and the Doctor's Boy, both parts of boyish insouciance familiar in the Auden plays (e.g. David Gunn in *The Ascent of F6*).

The play begins with news of John's father's death in a Shaw ambush (p. 12). John is as yet unborn, but the shock of the bad news brings on his premature birth. The condensed time-scale of these first scenes puts the feud into perspective, but it also gives an opportunity to show how the Nowers have already begun to try to break out of the feud pattern. John's father was ambushed on his way to speak with 'Layard'. This is an important clue to the real meaning of the play, since it was through John Layard that Auden had been introduced to Lane's psychological theories (see *Lions and Shadows,* 1938, p. 299) and though the reference seems very private, it can only mean that Nower senior was trying to arrive at a true understanding of his predicament by consulting this disciple of Lane's at the time of his death. By contrast, Joan's following speech, addressed to the body of her dead husband and the baby John, is an oblique

and sinister call to arms, hypnotic and insidious after the deliberately breezy clichés of the Doctor ('My God, I'm thirsty after all
that. Where can I get a drink?'). This is the kind of transition that the
audience, or reader, has to become accustomed to: the effect is
finely condensed and propulsive.

From the stage recess, Joan contrasts the living with the dead in
the first quatrain of her speech (pp. 12–13). There is an interesting
ambiguity here, for both husband and son are 'new ghost' and
neither is able from a former state to learn anything about his
present one: both are novices. This is self-evident, but the repetition
and incantation lend Joan's words the wisdom of sensed power. In
effect she is saying that the dead are now irrelevant, and that the new
spirit (ghost = *geist*) must be instructed by the 'old termers', those
experienced in their quest for life's meaning. In the next quatrain
she says that everyone ('Who's' refers back to the 'new ghost')
grows to be resentful of youth ('his latest company'), a resentment
that only death can end; the 'new ghost' glosses over the fact of
death (its plain unconnectedness with life mentioned in the first
quatrain) by concentrating on the aspects that make it an occasion
for grief and regret ('sorrow'). We may imagine her pointing ironically at the corpse as she says 'sorrow is sleeping thus'. The third
quatrain develops her hard, realistic view of life and death by reference to the feud. Remembering, or being mindful, is not merely
nostalgia ('Unforgetting is not today's forgetting/For yesterday')
or the petulance of the old ('not bedrid scorning'), but a determination to preserve the continuity of unyielding resolution ('But a
new begetting/An unforgiving morning').

In other words, Joan is saying that life and traditions must continue as they have begun. It is an appeal in generalized terms to the
preservation of a social order. At this point the baby squeals, and
Joan is reminded, in the midst of her generalizations, of the actual
situation. The baby's cry seems to symbolize his virility, and Joan,
like a latterday Volumnia, relishes the day when John will be old
enough to take active part in the feud. The whole speech is difficult
and gnomic in the manner that Auden seems to have picked up from
Laura Riding (see p. 36), but it is not crabbed: the measured elegiac
tone is maintained, and the theme of the feud subtly advanced.

The following chorus (p. 13) seems to respond to Joan's authoritarian challenge by acknowledging that the young desire to succeed and to be approved. They perform for their elders but discover no social cohesion ('We were mistaken, these faces are not ours'). In a plainly Shakespearean image, Auden shows that the body which has performed all these feats is simply not to be trusted by a mind which (in the final stanza, p. 14) acknowledges a greater power, a 'watcher in the dark' who arouses the desire to awake to a different order of reality, and who proposes clear standards of morality and humility lacking in the 'old systems which await/The last transgression of the sea'. If this is not God, it is something very like God, certainly something more like God than it is like John Layard (cf. the Witnesses in *The Dog Beneath the Skin*). But Auden is here merely exposing the heroic ethos, where the young are instructed 'to point/ To jump before ladies' and, like Coriolanus, 'to show our scars'. The invocation of the last stanza thus can easily carry the suggestion that what is most naturally opposed to Public School Bloody is Public School Pi: it reads in this context as an unconscious parody of an Anglican prayer. The chorus is not Auden himself, but a Sophoclean voice of an only tentative wisdom.

Now John is grown up, and the real action of the play begins. Dick proposes to emigrate. It may be that the docks which he proposes to sail from symbolize a specific political commitment, since John later seems to be avoiding such commitment when he talks of 'boy's voice among dishonoured portraits/To dockside barmaid speaking/Sorry through wires, pretended speech' (p. 25); but perhaps he is referring to some purely personal betrayal. Dick's emigration, however, is one obvious way out of the feud, and is not a way that Layard would have approved.

Meanwhile John is continuing the feud, and in the following scenes plans to ambush Red Shaw at Brandon Walls. The interlude in the bar offers an opportunity for the recording of some inane contemporary slang and sporting talk. Much of this material is reminiscent of Isherwood's verbatim jottings in the Isle of Wight (see *Lions and Shadows,* p. 244) and might have been borrowed from him. A piece of automatic writing that Isherwood produced in the summer of 1928 oddly refers to one of the characters in this scene: 'ah yes, ah no, ah, ah, far car, stop that, Trudy, drop it or I shoot' (*Lions and Shadows,* p. 276). Similarly, the name 'Basley' in a later chorus of *Paid* (p. 31) is the name of the boy who takes up with Victor Page at school in Isherwood's *All the Conspirators* (also 1928). One needn't presume any kind of collaboration, but some affinity between the work of Auden and Isherwood certainly already exists at this time (cf. Isherwood's school-saga experiment, 'Gems of Belgian Architecture', in *Exhumations,* 1966, p. 176).

Trudy's speech (p. 17) expresses a Shakespearean dissatisfaction with the state of feud. It is full of images of monstrous birth, and 'He's trash, yet if I cut my finger it bleeds like his' is very like Shylock's 'If you prick us, do we not bleed?' Walter's reply has an elegiac tone strongly echoing certain Old English poems. Compare, for instance, 'Often the man, alone shut . . .' with the opening of *The Wanderer:* 'Oft him anhaga . . .' (*Exeter Book,* ed. G. P. Krapp and E. V. K. Dobbie, 1936, p. 134). The mood of this elegy, with its lament for lost friends, is maintained, while the line 'Spring came, urging to ships, a casting off' seems to be suggested by *The Seafarer,* 11. 48–51 (*Exeter Book,* p. 144):

> Bearwas blostmum nimað, byrig fægriað
> wongas wlitigiað, woruld onetteð;
> ealle þa gemoniað modes fusne
> sefan to siþe, þam þe swa þenceð
> on flodwegas feor gewitan.

> 'The woods blossom, the towns become fair, fields look more than beautiful, the world revives; all these fire the spirit of the eager-minded man, who therefore decides to travel far on the paths of the ocean.'

The point is, of course, that John has not left, but at that very moment is preparing to ambush Red Shaw at Brandon Walls. The alienation of the elegiac personae of these and other Old English poems was to become a potent mood in later work of Auden's (e.g. 'The Wanderer', CSP, p. 51).

The ambush is then related in a highly formalized four-stress metre by John Nower, George and Sturton (p. 18). The general reliance of the speech on the narrative formulae of Old English heroic poems like *Beowulf* or *The Battle of Maldon* underlines John's feelings at this point that he must accept the feud and avenge his father's death. Stephen's tipsy behaviour after his successful baptism of fire ('Don't go, darling') is appropriate to the emotional tenor of the heroic *comitatus*: together with the praise of courage and athletic achievement (already expounded in the bar scene) comes mere boyish affection and silliness.

At this point, the Spy (a son of Red Shaw) is found, led out and plainly shot (p. 19). This is the occasion for the central and most important section of the play, five pages of expressionistic fantasy in which John's state of mind is openly allegorized. On the surface, the reason is easy to see: to have the Spy shot is to perpetuate the feud beyond the immediate purpose of revenge. When John exclaims 'I'll destroy the whole lot of you', it would seem that he is already beyond redemption.

John's soliloquy ('Always the following wind of history', p. 19) recognizes this evil, returning to the play's earlier theme of the endless perpetuation of education in the sterile traditions of his class. The initial metaphor is of sailing or gliding: the wind of tradition supports us until we encounter those air-pockets of experience where there is no precedent to rely on and we are thrown on our own resources. The superficial routine of the athletic and imperialist middle-classes simply does not allow for the higher ideals of love or philosophy, and therefore stunts their growth ('to gaze longer and delighted on/A face or idea be impossible'). John wants to have lived in an innocent age ('Could I have been some simpleton') before society reached this stage of corruption and disintegration ('disaster' sends 'his runners' like a conquering general exploring territory) and decides that even worms must suffer in this way. He would have been happier, he concludes, as some form of inorganic life.

The chorus (p. 20) then elaborates upon the traditions in which John finds himself trapped, in a beautifully paced survey of capitalist society. Auden is being ingenious here. 'Spring unsettles sleeping partnerships' because at the end of the financial year the partner with the money but with no active interest in the firm may merely find that he has lost his money; foundries and shops improve and expand. Auden brilliantly suggests in these opening lines that the capitalist process is also a natural one, since Spring is traditionally the season of love. Thus marriages ('sleeping partnerships') become unsettled by recurring sexual desire, children are conceived ('Foundries improve their casting process') and new generations born ('shops/Open a further wing'). The irony of these double meanings takes a further point from their contrast with John's previous desire for the landscape to appear 'sterile as moon': by a hideous inversion of values, only capitalism appears to be fruitful.

However, as the chorus continues, it soon becomes apparent that disaster is in store: gears rust, land is forfeited. The chorus breaks into a lament for the whole condition of man, who does not choose to be born ('The body warm but not/By choice') and whose one desire is for a happier, more primitive social organization. Man 'learns, one drawn apart, a secret will/Restore the dead', alluding to Confirmation and the gospel of the Resurrection, but the sensational promise of religion leads nowhere: men die (as in the First World War) in millions. Thus the after-life is a cheat, man's moral vows melt like ice ('the most solid wish he tries to keep/His hands show through') and therefore, considering his suffering, he really had, as John had wished, better be a stone.

Both of these last speeches indicate the range of ideas and meaning that lies behind John's inherent defeatism and depression, and prepare one for the faster pace and more elusive symbols of the following scenes (pp. 20–25). These scenes are complex and difficult, not only because they rely on some very obscure sources, but because here Auden is trying to get across a psychological theory in terms of grotesque knockabout humour. As a dramatic experiment it is interesting and novel in its intensity, but it has proved a stumbling-block to appreciation of the play.

Homer Lane had spoken out against repression of our real desires. He also pointed out that much of our behaviour stems from our earliest experiences of fear and punishment, that the child's play is often a dramatized rebellion against parental authority. Thus it is that at this point of *Paid* the feud comes to represent just such a pattern of human behaviour, especially inasmuch as it was observed to derive from the profound experience of weaning from the mother's breast. In the fantasy of John's interrogation of the Spy, it is plain that accuser and accused are to be identified (the Spy is 'really' dead), since it is John's mother who threatens the Spy with a giant feeding-bottle.

Before this interpretation can be pursued, however, it is necessary to look at the form and characters of the scenes. Many of these are taken from the old Mummers' Play, which Auden must have read in R. J. E. Tiddy's *The Mummers' Play* (1923). There is also an account of a performance in Hardy's *The Return of the Native*.

Father Christmas is the traditional Presenter of the Mummers' Play. Bo conceivably might derive from Sambo, also a Mummers' character. The Man–Woman seems to be an imaginative misunderstanding of the phrase used by Tiddy to describe the character in his introduction: 'It has been suggested that the man–woman is the survival of an endeavour to promote fertility by the mere fact of wearing a woman's clothes.' In fact the role was usually a mute one: the character merely came in wielding a broom. Auden turns it into something much more significant.

Finally, the major borrowing from the Mummers' Play is the scene of the Doctor and his Boy (pp. 23–24). A number of parallel extracts from Tiddy may be compared with this scene:

Fool. Five pounds for a doctor.
Another Person. Ten pounds to stop away. (Tiddy, p. 246)

*   *   *

John Finney. Hold him yourself then.
Doctor. What's that, you saucy young rascal?
John Finney. Oh, I hold him, sir, etc. (Tiddy, pp. 165–6)

*   *   *

Father Christmas. Pray, Doctor, what can you cure?
Doctor. Oh, all sorts of diseases,
    Whatever my physick pleases,
    If it's the itch, the pitch, the palsy & the gout,
    If the devil is in, I can fetch him out. (Tiddy, p. 162)

*   *   *

Jack brings the implements, consisting of hammer, saw, files, pincers, etc. and throws them on the ground.   (Tiddy, p. 177)

*   *   *

Ladies and gentlemen, all this large wolf's tooth has been growing in this
man's head ninety-nine years before his great grandmother was born: if it
hadn't have been taken out today, he would have died yesterday. . . . Rise up,
bold fellow, and fight again.   (Tiddy, p. 166)

How is it that John and the Spy are to be identified? The Nower–
Shaw feud represents a psychic split in one individual. When the
Spy groans at the revelations of the Man–Woman, John cannot
bear it, and shoots him (p. 23). This suggests, by the evident theme
of sexual repression, that John represents the repressive Censor, and
the Spy the repressed natural drives – the Ego and the Id respectively.
In *The Orators* (p. 43) spying is identified with introversion.

The trial scene is based, curiously enough, on a dream reported
and analysed by the psychiatrist W. H. R. Rivers in his book
Conflict and Dream (1923, pp. 22ff). This is the dream of a medical
Captain who had served in France during the First World War. His
experiences (especially those centring on the death of a French
prisoner mortally wounded during his escape from the German
lines) made him reluctant to return to the practice of his profession.
Rivers concludes after a careful analysis: 'The interpretation has
shown that the dream was the transformed expression of a wish to
commit suicide in order to escape from a conflict which was becoming intolerable' (Rivers, p. 28).

In his dream, the Captain finds himself giving a patriotic speech
at a London theatre, the Golders Green Empire. As he mounts the
stage, his place in the audience is filled by his double, who suffers
in agony as he speaks. The Captain feels the strong desire to put him
out of his misery by shooting him. As recounted, the dream is a
fascinating and dramatic account of mental disturbance. Clearly
Auden used it both to suggest that John envisages the Spy's death as
a form of suicide, and also to underline a meaning already introduced in the play, that his state of mind is itself a result of the decline
of Western civilization, represented in this instance by the horrors
of the First World War, the war that Auden's generation felt so much
guilt about because they were too young to take part in it.

John is the accuser (p. 21), but when called to give evidence can
only make a jingoistic speech closely similar in tone and content to

the Captain's in his dream: 'We must continue the struggle to the last man. Better let us die than lose our manhood and independence and become the slaves of an alien people? . . . I know . . . that we have suffered and are all suffering dreadful agony. . . . There must be no surrender. We must not give in' (Rivers). This is simply the automatic response, perpetuating the feud.

The following speech of Bo implies (elliptically, I agree) that some break is possible. The first four lines seem imitative of the last section of *The Waste Land,* and the remainder of the speech, continuing the military imagery, elaborates the possibility of a change of heart. Decision, action and conviction are, it seems to say, still possible. But the Spy groans, as the Captain's double groans in the dream. Compare Joan with her feeding-bottle ('Be quiet, or I'll give you a taste of this') with the Canadian (representing the Captain's in-laws) who is standing at the exit of the Golders Green Empire ('Silence there . . . or I'll deal with you . . . I'll give you a taste of this'). In *Paid* it is not a proposed return to the Front which has caused the mental disorder, but the domination of the Mother and the sensual deprivation of weaning (see *Lions and Shadows,* p. 193, for a contemporary joke of Auden's about insufficient weaning: 'I must have something to *suck'*): hence the feeding-bottle.

Po's speech (p. 21) produces the alternative to ambiguous action: a nostalgic, introverted self-regard. The successful middle-class administrator finds at last only a furtive hoarded love, a love which is no better than the mother's patient, possessive fidelity to the long-departed son. The Spy groans again (cf. Rivers: 'the man in my chair . . . groaned aloud in agony'), so John produces a revolver, saying that it is better to get it over. Joan's words 'This way for the Angel of Peace' are taken verbatim from the Captain's dream. In the dream they are spoken by a doctor who, like the Canadian, is guarding one of the exits to the theatre, and refer to the solution of suicide. Father Christmas's words are almost exactly paralleled by Rivers, who himself appears in his patient's dream at this point, saying: 'Don't do it . . . the man is ill, but he will get well.'

Here the Man–Woman appears (significantly 'a prisoner of war'), representing the real victim of the feud: love. It is evident that war has no place for love, but in terms of the psychic fantasy we see that the equilibrium of this function is disturbed also by a matriarchal tyranny. Lawrence had much to say about the possessive demands of the mother in his *Fantasia of the Unconscious* (1922), a work that greatly influenced the early Auden, especially in *The Orators*. The half-rhymed couplets of the Man–Woman's speech are remarkably similar in tone not only to those of the choruses – 'The Spring unsettles sleeping partnerships' (p. 20) and 'To throw away the key and walk away' (p. 27) – but also to those of the early poem 'Venus Will Now Say a Few Words' (CSP, p. 33). The similarity is striking enough to suggest a common origin, perhaps a planned long poem. (Cannibalization of shorter poems appears in two other choruses, a speech of Anne's and a speech shared by John and Anne; see below.)

It is tempting to see the Man–Woman as an ambiguous symbol representing the homosexual's predicament (a Cocteauesque *truc* like the hermaphrodite in *Le Sang d'un Poète*) and to relate him to a later Auden character, Baba the Turk, Rakewell's bearded wife in *The Rake's Progress*. Auden has denied such a reading of this latter work as 'obscene',[4] but it is at least clear that the figure in each case represents the hero's repression of natural sexual love: in *Paid*, Oedipal narcissism, experiment, fear, sexual self-consciousness; in the opera, an *acte gratuit*. But even if the Man–Woman's significance is less precise than this (though the character's mistaken development from Tiddy's remark is interesting in this connection), he is at least a kind of daemon of John's maladjustment, representing his inability to achieve a natural and spontaneous love relationship. The Spy is the accused, and all these are prosecution witnesses; but this has meaning only if we remember all the time that the real function of John's fantasy is to probe his own internal predicament.

The Man–Woman (p. 22) tells him that there is now no second chance. He has been educated to believe that love is purely scandal and romance: through his reading ('traffic in memoirs') he takes it that love is achieved by romantic protestation. This futile day-dream is continued in the next three lines in a Robin Hood metaphor: John had his 'orders to disband', but 'remained in woods'. His real emotional and sexual needs remained unfulfilled, so that love 'went/ Hearing you call for what you did not want.' The remainder of the Man–Woman's speech elaborates the frigid sexual resources that follow from such false attitudes: masturbation and nerve-racked, calculated attempts at sexual gratification. Here we see how the rationalizing Ego has taken over. The Man–Woman says:

> I tried then to demand
> Proud habits, protestations called your mind
> To show you it was extra, but instead
> You overworked yourself, misunderstood,
> Adored me for the chance.

Love, in other words, gives the intellectual some justification for preferring the spirit to the body: sex can come to seem an 'extra'. Love *is* spiritual, but the chance to feel that the body is distinct from the mind is eagerly taken up by the compulsive verbalizer. This is Lawrence's sex in the head. Love can't be followed now, because he is going where 'all talking is forbidden'.

The shooting is now repeated in the fantasy (p. 23), and the comic Mummers' Play Doctor is called for. The Doctor is more than merely comic, however. He is a Homer Lane figure who is required to resurrect the shot Spy (i.e. the repressed Id) and who actually does succeed.

Much of this scene is a simple dramatic borrowing from Tiddy (see above), but the rest is intended to suggest the kind of healing powers the Doctor possesses. He says that he has discovered the origin of life, but makes it plain that he does not refer to mere physical life, for death is an incontrovertible fact to him: he will leave his head for medical analysis at his death, but 'the laugh will be gone and the microbe in command'. John tries to see what the Doctor is doing as he takes the circular saws, bicycle-pumps and so on from his bag, ready to examine the Spy's body, but the Doctor pushes him away. John is a 'war-criminal' and his evidence is valueless: in other words, the Ego is to blame, and is thus powerless to assist in restoring the psychic health of the individual. The Doctor examines the body and blames 'the conscious brain' which, more effectively than the Devil, 'advances and retreats under control and poisons everything round it'. The cure is effected by the traditional withdrawal of a gigantic tooth.

John's anxiety remains, however: he still seeks the Spy like a train he is late for. In the end they are reunited, and plant a tree together (a private allusion, possibly, to the poet's patron saint, St Wystan, who planted a stick which grew into a tree?). Their words here indicate yet again the play's theme that the past is irrevocably lost. John says (p. 25):

> Sametime sharers of the same house,
> We know not the builder nor the name of his son.

The 'same house' in terms of the play's meanings can be both 'society' and 'womb'. The middle-class boy's background is both betrayed ('dishonoured portraits') by the actual situation, and a cause of its betrayal ('pretended speech'). The dockside barmaid is evidently a symbol of a social and sexual adventure which fails. The Spy's speech, with its imagery of war refugees, underlines the alienation of the split psyche (the rootlessness of the *déclassé* artist, perhaps: 'We stay and are not known'). They are sharers of the same house, 'attendants on the same machine' (the body), and are yet divided.

The central fantasy of the play ends here, and it ends pretty inconclusively, it might be said. But a dramatic development has taken place, and after the scene in which the emigrating Dick takes his leave (pp. 25–26), John is in the position to examine his predicament rationally.

In his soliloquy (p. 26) he discovers the importance of love, its social and personal healing power. He equates his life with a city. Now, he says, he has an understanding of himself that leaves him 'lighted and clean', instead of dark and dirty like the slum he had previously made of his life. He has been proud and indifferent: his 'streets' have witnessed the conveniently arranged 'accidents' of the rich. Now love, 'sent east for peace/From tunnels', perhaps like the revolutionary Andrei Zhelyabov who assassinated Alexander II in 1881, 'feels morning streaming down/Wind from the snows'. The Russian allusion seems to be maintained in the last stanza: love is no longer uncommitted ('Nowise withdrawn by doubting flinch'), nor yet committed to any rigid programme ('belief's firm flange'), but rejoices in the new fruitful life indicated by the Eisensteinian montage of 'The tugged-at teat/The hopper's steady feed, the frothing leat'.

John is thus led to contemplate intermarriage with the Shaws as a way out of both feud and emotional sterility. He asks his servant to fetch his horse.

The next chorus (p. 27) is perhaps the most important in the play. It had already appeared as a poem in its own right in Auden's *Poems* (1928), No. xx, but in the new context its meaning is immeasurably opened up. If the Nowers and the Shaws are essentially alike, the feud exists only on its own terms. In some kinds of charade both 'sides' act simultaneously, and to the difficulty of guessing is added the difficulty of finding the chance to act out your meaning. Auden means to suggest that these compulsive social forms are a kind of game which may be 'won'. To avoid the inherited state of feud between the sides, one can emigrate, like Dick, or one can marry, like John and Anne Shaw; but to do this is really to spoil the game and not to solve it. The chorus suggest that to be an 'abrupt exile' in this way is evasive. Somehow one should stay in the charade and try to guess the answer. Or, in political terms, change spiritually and realize one's true nature, not alter the forms of society by violence. Rather than revolution there must be a psychologically understood adjustment to social disease:

> The future shall fulfil a surer vow,
> Not smiling at queen over the glass rim,
> Nor making gunpowder in the top room,
> Not swooping at the surface still like gulls
> But with prolonged drowning shall develop gills.

The whole chorus seems to imply that the historical process must be respected.[5] 'All pasts/Are old past now', it says, and 'although some posts/Are forwarded', 'these [a reading from P28] are still to tempt; areas not seen'. In other words, an existentialist solution is offered: the future will be arduous, and is described in terms of the Wanderer following a misleading signpost in a snow-storm. The future is not predictable, even when its 'guessed at wonders would be worth alleging', and the Wanderer will 'receive no normal welcome'. But this is the only way in which the true meaning of the charade may be discovered.

A brief scene shows that the feud is still in full swing (pp. 27–28), and this is followed by the announcement of John's engagement to

Anne Shaw. The two families mix, but Seth talks about getting a chance for revenge.

The following scene between John and Anne (pp. 29–31), which consists largely of four poems from the 1928 *Poems* (Nos. XIX, XVIII, XIII and XVII in that order), provides a lyrical and elegiac investigation into the nature of love, and of the old world and the new. John is so conditioned by the school-saga ethos that love seems strange to him, he says. The passage 'Some say that handsome raider still at large' elaborates the idea that only the first-hand experience of love will do: what others tell us is no use to us.[6] The Yeatsian trimeter of 'The summer quickens all' is a common form in *Poems* (1928) and beautifully points the ephemerality of their love: disaster will surely come. At this point Anne tries to persuade John to join Dick abroad, but John says that he has decided to stay. Anne appears to presume that John is being faithful to the memory of the dead. She says that the dead, despite their astonishing deaths, have no moral power over the living: 'The too-loved clays . . . shall not speak/Out of that grave [,] stern on no capital fault'. If John escapes now, he need not have regrets or any desire to make up for committed violence: he will only have 'lightly touched the unworthy thing'. John replies: 'We live still', meaning that their continued good fortune is itself reproached by those who have suffered. Anne says that the dead forget. John's rather elliptic reply suggests, I think, that he feels the failings of the dead to be eternal qualities, recurrent in themselves, 'echoes . . . what dreams or goes masked . . . touches of the old wound' (original sin).

The chorus (p. 31) concurs, or at least implies that the system is hardly likely to change as a result of a single perception of its rottenness: the defeated factory-owner and the wounded outlaw are at the mercy of cyclical change ('Spring' = history), and the individual who has made an advance beyond the present conditions of his society finds only an 'alone success'. He is again aligned with the Old English Wanderer figure through an echo of the 'Hwaer cwom' passage in that poem (11. 92ff). John and Anne go inside, and the chorus asks 'For where are Basley who won the Ten,/Dickon so tarted by the House,/Thomas who kept a sparrow-hawk?' The implication is that John has lost the friendship of his feud comrades as the Wanderer had lost his 'seledreamas', his joy in the communal life of the hall. The tongue is ashamed, 'deceived by a shake of the hand', because John really regrets the lost fellowship, or was mistaken about the degree of its emotional meaning for him. His predicament has been subtly delineated throughout the play: guilt and division, alternating hope for the future and regret for the past, a feeling that he cannot and should not escape, a search for love, a carrying of old weaknesses. The play now moves swiftly to his death.

At the marriage party (p. 32) Mrs Shaw reproaches Seth for complying with the truce, and reminds him of his brother's (the Spy's) death. In a brief soliloquy, remarkably similar in style to some of Isherwood's interior monologues in *All the Conspirators* (1928), Seth thinks of his brother as a blubbing coward, and resolves to be 'a stern self-ruler' and kill John as his mother has instructed. John is killed, and we are led to believe that the feud will continue.

In a final Sophoclean chorus, Auden suggests that in a society like this 'no man is strong'. Probably his reading of Malinowski and other anthropologists gave him the idea of putting an Oedipal conflict into a matrilineally organized society. John cannot 'bring home a wife' because in a matrilocal marriage he would have to live with the bride's family (i.e. at Nattrass); and, as is emphasized, at the wedding he is only a guest in the Shaw house. To preserve her ascendancy (as well as to perpetuate the feud), Mrs Shaw is obliged to have John killed: 'His mother and her mother won.' The predicament is to reappear in Auden's work, notably in *The Orators, The Ascent of F6* and *The Bassarids*. What it really 'means' is that maternal possessiveness can produce emotional disaster in the son, with the result that he finds himself divided, perpetuating social violence, only able through conscious effort to achieve a normal love relationship. Auden has an amusing early poem, hitherto unpublished (B M Notebook Add. MS. 52430, fol. 8):

> Tommy did as mother told him
> Till his soul had split:
> One half thought of angels
> And the other half of shit.

The accusations of the Man–Woman provide a more circumstantial version of this sorry tale.

2 Poems 1927–1932

This period roughly covers Auden's last year at Oxford, the Berlin visit of 1928–29 and the years he spent teaching in Scotland, at Larchfield Academy, Helensburgh. He is not much concerned yet with large public themes: this is a poetry of oppressive family and social ties, of unrequited love and psychological cure and of isolation and uncertain heroism. These are themes of youth, but Auden's style is already superbly authoritative. The oblique energy of his work is sharpened by a beautifully underplayed perceptiveness and by rich feelings which underwrite even the most elusive meaning.

In 'The Letter' [P28; P30, P33; CP, p. 44: 'The Love Letter'; CSP50; CSP, p. 19] the new valley is a new love, the season Spring, the sun unaccustomed, making the poet frown. But already the year has passed, and he finds himself sheltering behind a sheep-pen during a storm, reflecting on love's restlessness, its endless cycle of erotic desire. The lovers have seen Spring and Autumn, and these will be seen again, but for these particular lovers the future is not assured. Waiting for the poet when he returns is his lover's letter, which makes him frown again ('to interrupt the homely brow'), disturbing his peace of mind, which had warmed 'through and through' as his body had done after the rain-storm. The letter breaks off the affair: 'Speaking of much but not to come' means either that his lover is merely analysing the past with no thought of a future relationship, or that his lover is full of other thoughts, and will not now be joining him. The break in the poem, in the middle of a couplet, seems to represent the break in the relationship that the letter signifies (though in *Poems,* 1928, the break came at the turning of a page, and may thus have been introduced later in a transcription from the earlier volume).

In the last lines the poet pretends to accept the situation because of its familiarity: it seems appropriate to him to change as the seasons change. In the poet's rueful nod and smile the 'country god' shows his approval: the reticence means that romantic protestation is superfluous if you accept that love is a natural seasonal process. The god might also be Pan, traditional protector of flocks, living in mountains, caves and lonely places, for this is appropriate to the Lake District setting of the poem. 'Love's worn circuit' in line 9, really an image from electricity, also suggests the idea of love as a chase like Keats's urn, and thus brings the consolation of art to the lover who can't run fast enough (Pan and Syrinx). The stone smile is undeniably chilly. The poet accepts the letter's message, but this does not make him brood ('Nor speech is close'). There is an undeniable protest lurking in the wry understatement that love 'not seldom' receives an unjust answer, and we note that the nod and the smile contain a *fear* of making any commitment: perhaps, we feel, some greater commitment should be made. Perhaps love is something more than a worn circuit, and could itself rise above seasonal change.

'Taller To-day' [P28; P30, P33; CP, p. 113: 'As Well as Can Be Expected'; CSP50; CSP, p. 20] acts, in its imagery and conclusions, as a kind of companion piece to 'The Letter'. The first was a poem of separation, while the second is a poem of union, however precarious. The lovers are 'no nearer each other', but together they are happy: their emotional bond is deeper than on the 'similar evenings' of childhood. Now they are alert to all that threatens love. They are like the fruit of the orchard irrigated by a brook whose source is a glacier: its coldness and remoteness lie on one side, while on the other are the windy headlands where the dead howl. Between (like Bede's sparrow flying through the lighted hall, the Old English symbol of human life) is 'this peace'. It will not last (earlier readings of the penultimate line make this clearer), but the mere fact of its existing is important, meaning that the moment (call it love or not, call it 'loved' or merely 'endured') has achieved its fulfilment. The

'Adversary' of line 6 may be compared with the 'supreme Antagonist' of 'Consider' (CSP, p. 49). Like the Hopkinsian address to
God as 'Sir' in *Poems,* 1930, No. xxx, this oblique reference to the
Devil implies a respectful reappraisal of the Christian terms. Two
omitted stanzas from the poem may be noted. The first (despite the
celebrated Captain Ferguson[1]) did not advance the poem's argument. The second contained material similar to that in *The Orators,*
I, iii, and was perhaps better omitted.

'Missing' [P30, P33; CP, p. 43; CSP50; CSP, p. 20] introduces a
theme of some importance in Auden's early poetry. What is heroism,
he asks? The conclusion is simple: heroism does not lie in acts of
bravery but in endurance, in 'resisting the temptations/To skyline
operations'. The skyline operations are visualized in the first section
of the poem, and evoke the feuding world of *Paid on Both Sides.*
The landscape of these saga-heroes may be disciplined and austere;
the leader may be 'unwounded'; but the little band are 'doomed':
today the tourists come with guide-books to reconstruct the sagas
in what is merely a holiday environment providing a spuriously
exciting contrast to the bland elegance of the capital.

Some critics believe that this argument is contradicted by the line
' "Leave for Cape Wrath to-night" ' and feel that this is a romantic
celebration of saga-heroism (e.g. Spears, 1963, p. 43). This can
hardly be so: the host is seen waiting for his guest, who does not
arrive. He passes 'alive' into the house, in evident contrast to the
guest who may be presumed dead as a result of his journey to Cape
Wrath. (We remember that 'bravery is now,/Not in the dying
breath' but in a deliberate refusal to fight merely 'for no one's sake'.)
It is a simple enough interpretation, but does depend upon an
admitted obscurity in the Cape Wrath line. Its source lies in an
account by Isherwood in *Lions and Shadows* (pp. 265–70) of a
drunken journey north in Bill Scott's car. They have no idea where
they are going, only that they have to keep on the move. 'These
suddenly undertaken excursions exactly suited my escapist tempera-
ment,' Isherwood wrote. He had already (pp. 207–8) elaborated the
conception of the Truly Strong Man and the Truly Weak Man,
which he shared with Auden. The Truly Strong Man has no need to
prove himself. Only the Truly Weak Man finds himself undertaking

absurd heroics in an effort to master his real nature. The drunken journey in *Lions and Shadows* is just such an effort, and its climax is suitably melodramatic: 'We drove on, across the misty bog-plains, striped black where peat had been cut, in the direction of Cape Wrath. The coast was gashed into jagged fjords: under the cliffs, the water lay like ebony, with vivid jade shallows. The mountains were piled up in the west against an angry sunset' (p. 269). Isherwood realizes how mad it all is ('One always has to go back, I thought, at the end of these little escapades') and soon afterwards makes his decision to study medicine. Auden's reference is inescapably ironic: Cape Wrath is an illusion, an unresisted temptation of the wrong sort.

Lines 6–14, and the final line and a half, are taken from *Poems* (1928), No. II.[2] I find this a rather significant piece of cannibalization for several reasons: first, in the earlier poem he talks with friends about 'that severe Christopher', evidently Isherwood himself. Second, the conversation turns to love, and his friends 'both dropped silent in/The contemplation of/A singular vision/And sceptical beholder', indicating that the poet is again adopting the practical 'country god' attitude to love of 'The Letter'. This attitude is supported by the rest of the poem, where he thinks 'how everyman/Shall strain and be undone,/Sit, querulous and sallow/Under the abject willow'. Third, the identical endings of the poems show that the 'host' of 'Missing' is really the poet himself. All this amounts to a powerful suggestion that the heroism discussed in 'Missing' is in one sense a metaphor for love: certainly this interpretation enormously enlarges the impact of the poem. The waiting 'host' becomes, like the poet moving 'decent with the seasons' in 'The Letter', a figure of stoical realism, abandoned by his lover. Thus the subject of the poem, the hero, the loved one, is 'missing' both in the military sense, and in the sense of 'being missed': a masterful ambiguity.

'The Secret Agent' [P28; P30, P33; CP, p. 29; CSP50; CSP, p. 22] is an unrhymed sonnet, simple enough in surface meaning, but which has proved troubling to explicators because of its supposed lack of context. But enough 'context' is provided by an unnoticed allusion in the last line, one which Auden, fresh from the Oxford English School, had every reason to believe would be understood.

The line is taken from the Old English poem 'Wulf and Eadwacer', which is the monologue of a captive woman addressed to her out-lawed lover (she is on one island, he on another). The line is: 'þaet mon eaþe tosliteð þaette naefre gesomnad waes' ('They can easily part that which was never joined together', *Exeter Book*, p. 180).

Thus the situation is one of unconsummated love. The spy represents the individual's emotional urge to make contact with another human being ('this new district'); he is forced to act as a secret agent because the individual does not consciously recognize his love (the spy) and represses it. 'They', who ignore his wires, and eventually shoot him, represent the conscious will, the Censor, which represses the individual's emotional desires. Like John Nower in *Paid on Both Sides,* 'they' shoot the spy because they are unwilling to face the truth about the situation which he reveals. A later sonnet, 'Meiosis' (CSP, p. 77), works by a very similar allegory, and acts as a useful gloss on the unbuilt bridges (sexual contact). The trouble is not entirely 'their' fault, of course. The spy is betrayed by his own 'side', but also walks into a trap. The 'old tricks' which seduce him are, I think, the limiting social conventions external to the divided individual, but hardly less responsible for his inability to make human contact.

'The Watershed' [P28; P30, P33; CP, p. 175; CSP50; CSP, p. 22] seems to represent in subject-matter an early interest of Auden's. He had already written extensively about the arduous life of lead-miners in an early uncollected poem, 'Lead's the Best' (*Oxford Outlook,* VIII [1926], 119), a poem with very much the same scenery as this one.[3] 'The Watershed' is a self-addressed warning that this kind of life may be observed but not really understood. It can in no sense become an integral part of the experience ('accessory content') of a young middle-class poet who merely happens to be 'rather there than here'. In 'Lead's the Best' a similar feeling is expressed in the final lines, in which the 'bleak philosophy of Northern ridges/Harsh afterglow of an old country's greatness' becomes merely 'Themes for a poet's pretty sunset thoughts'. But if the idea is similar, it has immeasurably matured in perception in the later poem. Innocent delight in the achievements of the miners has been replaced by a more pervasive sense of symbolic portent in the pathos of their forgotten lives. The industrial landscape is 'dismantled', 'comatose', 'ramshackle'. The poet is not even allowed to indulge in nostalgia, but is warned away as if from a present danger. And in the brilliant image of the startled hare in the last lines, this danger is shown to work both ways: there are two worlds here, in imminent collision.

'No Change of Place' [P33; CP, p. 176; CSP50: 'Better Not'; CSP, p. 23] is based on the paradox that the improved communications of modern industrial society have in fact brought about a state of affairs where no one can any longer communicate except at a distance. Emotional energy is expended on the anticipation of love letters not on human contact, spring flowers arrive smashed, and the impersonality of the telephone reduces human sympathy to a merely functional response (pity is 'flashed', not, I think, like a morse signal, but like a pass or badge: it has become a shibboleth).

Auden intends the images in lines 4–9 to suggest, not *ennui* or anxiety, but a kind of vegetative calm. The greater perception and understanding of life that will result from 'journey from one place to another' is simply not being risked: nothing better is known. The mood of Eliot's *Prufrock* is strongly present in this stanza. In the third stanza, the 'professional traveller' is contrasted with those suffering from accidie: by making the journey, he has discovered some truth about life which they have not. He has nothing to say to them which they would understand, and their maps seem to bear no relationship to any reality they know (thus perhaps the professional traveller represents the writer, and maps represent modern literature?).

The final stanza develops this theme by indicating that the knowledge which the 'professional traveller' may have acquired has something to do with a possible change of social forms. The capital is waiting for conversion (perhaps this is a financial pun, too), but since nobody travels, nobody finds out: 'no one goes/Further than railhead' (cf. 'had they pushed the rail/Some stations nearer' in 'The Secret Agent', CSP, p. 22). The hint of decadence in the capital ('brilliant') is matched by corruption in the shires. The village band celebrates the 'ugly feast' of an aristocracy whose hirelings protect their privileges by force ('gaitered gamekeeper with dog and gun').

The point of the poem is simple, but decisively and dramatically put: the retreat from life lived at first hand conspires to perpetuate the stagnation and corruption of political life.

'Let History Be My Judge' [P30, P33; CP, p. 156; CSP50; CSP, p. 24] proposes, with all the deadly reasoning of a self-righteous counter-revolutionary, a justification of repression and control by authority in the face of developing resistance to it. The 'situation' might be a generalized version of the General Strike: at least, there is some kind of emergency presented in the first two stanzas, which the speaker presumes is a challenge to a whole way of life, and must be met by force. Whose fault is this emergency? Stanzas 5 and 6 suggest that those in precarious control do have some inkling that the seeds of disruption are contained in the basic nature of the society ('possibilities of error/At the very start'), so that finally the speaker is left clinging only to his self-respect and vested interests. After that, it appears, anything might happen.

'Never Stronger' [P30, P33; CP, p. 5: 'Two's Company'; CSP50; CSP, p. 25] shows how the weak are again and again attracted to mere talk about love, instead of to the real thing. They may in conversation feel that they have grasped what it is all about, but this is imaginary. Gossip about other people's love affairs doesn't tell them how to embark on one themselves. They may leave the talkers and try to act, but out of timidity they usually return, because although they may seem to be defying their real natures by returning, they can escape judgment: at the heart of a hurricane there is always a womb-like calm ('the centre of anger/Is out of danger') in which they can hide.

Auden's early reviewers noted that his syntax and absence of visual imagery in many poems recalled the work of Laura Riding (see, for instance, Michael Roberts in *Adelphi,* December 1930). The evident debt has nowhere been more tendentiously expressed than by Robert Graves in *The Crowning Privilege* (1955, p. 130): 'During 1928–9,' he writes, 'I was printing books by hand, and he subscribed to them. I had to suggest that the half-guinea he paid for Laura Riding's *Love as Love, Death as Death* gave him no right to borrow half-lines and whole lines from them for insertion in his own verse.' Graves does not quote any whole lines borrowed (Miss Riding's lines are

not anyway long), but certainly the influence is marked. 'This
Loved One' [P30, P33; CP, p. 19: 'This One'; CSP50; CSP, p. 26]
is a particularly notable example. Compare:

> And smiling of
> This gracious greeting,
> 'Good day. Good luck',
> Is no real meeting,
> But instinctive look,
> A backward love.

with the following from Miss Riding's book (*Love as Love, Death as
Death,* 1928, pp. 19 and 57):

> The standing-stillness,
> The from foot-to-foot,
> Is no real illness,
> Is no real fever.
>
> *   *   *
>
> We shall say, love is no more
> Than waking, smiling,
> Forcing out 'good morning'.

Miss Riding's style here owed something to E. E. Cummings, as
Edgell Rickword's parody in 'Twittingpan' (*Collected Poems,*
1947, p. 59) shows. The parody comes near to early Auden, too, but
on the whole Auden jettisons the quaintness while preserving the
edgy dignity and dark wisdom of the Riding manner. In 'This
Loved One' heredity is seen as all-powerful: the thought that all this
has happened before would not normally affect the lover; but,
combined with a decline in the fortunes of the family, the endless
cycle of love seems inevitably tainted and selfish.

'Easy Knowledge' [P33; CP, p. 22: 'Make up your Mind';
CSP50; CSP, p. 27] is another poem in the Riding manner, though
it begins with an apparent echo of Eliot's *The Hollow Men*. Love is
assailed by indecisiveness (the CP title, as so often, makes the point
of the poem clear), and the lover's behaviour seems merely absurd
and embarrassing. The examples of the hesitant lover's oafishness
are borrowed from poems in the 1928 volume (11. 16–17 from
No. XII and 11. 18–21 from No. IX). The 'snub-nosed winner' is

'snub-nosed Gabriel Carritt' of *Letters from Iceland,* p. 254, as the
BM Notebook, fol. 65, makes clear.[4] The second part of the poem
typically uses the image of the loved one as a town to be visited: the
lover loses his way, has to ask for directions. Again, love is talked
about and rationalized ('registering/Acreage, mileage') but not felt
('the divided face/Has no grace').

'Too Dear, Too Vague' [P30, P33; CP, p. 78; CSP50; CSP,
p. 281] skilfully maintains the Ridingesque lyrical-didactic by suggesting that only our efforts to understand love taunt us with the
possibility of its perfection and finality. We define it into yes and no –
into, that is, reciprocated and unreciprocated love – as though these
clear alternatives solved anything. Auden shows that love can
destroy itself, whatever its circumstances: our insistent rationalizations are irrelevant to it. The second part of the poem carries
echoes of Lawrence's arguments about 'sex in the head', and Auden
may have in mind, in his lines about leaving 'the North in place/
With a good grace', Lawrence's elaboration of his theory about the
four poles of the dynamic psyche (see *Fantasia of the Unconscious,*
pp. 100ff).[5]

'Between Adventure' [P30, P33; CP, p. 151: 'Do be Careful';
CSP50; CSP, p. 29], with its injunction 'On narrowness stand, for
sunlight is/Brightest only on surfaces' (an image that suggests
military training), has a slight overtone of the *Paid* myth as it
appears in Auden's early poems, but no more than that. The rhymes
slow down the verse and cleverly mimic the cautiousness advocated
for the lover: friendship is safe; it avoids a decision. On either side
of its knife-edge lies commitment or rejection, each involving the
world of emotion which is being avoided.

'A Free One' [P30, P33; CP, p. 152: 'We all Make Mistakes';
CSP50; CSP, p. 29] parallels the careful lover of 'Between Adventure' by a more dramatically caricatured member of the emotionally
constipated middle-classes. Though 'the beggar's envy', he is not
free: the country-house routine, like the undemonstrative *camera-
derie* of 'Between Adventure' is 'the longest way to an intrinsic
peace'. The Yeatsian penultimate stanza proposes (vaguely) a solution: the 'buried' life, the 'warning' of war (compare 'iron wood'
with Pope's 'iron harvests' in his *Essay on Man,* IV, 12) are the

symptoms of capitalist decadence, and would be healed by 'the song, the varied action of the blood'. Instead, we have the formalized gestures of the imperialist class, based at several removes upon the heroes they no longer resemble, now merely inflexible and evasive.

'Family Ghosts' [P30, P33; CP, p. 132; CSP50; CSP, p. 30] seems to be acknowledging the poet's predictable role as a converter of emotion into art. The actual feelings of love are seen as an excuse by poets to invoke the Muse (strings = bowels, drum = heart), who should actually ignore the irrelevance of what they have to say to real life ('loquacious when the watercourse is dry'). The third stanza seems to acknowledge, too, that the poet is as moss-grown as everybody else, and is merely deluded by the power of love, by 'ghost's approval of the choice'. In yet another use of the metaphor of siege for being in love, Auden proposes that out of the poet's emotional timidity comes the power and pressure of art ('speeches at the corners, hope for news'), and that the characteristic images of great poets of the past have been conditioned by real emotions like his own: Pope's insecurity in the image of the satirist swooping on his prey; Donne's grief in the image of tears as tides drawn by the moon ('lunatic'); and perhaps the blind Milton's lost Paradise in the image of the Golden Age which has become an Age of Ice. The poet adopts these images and affirms (with some irony) his kinship with all poets: art itself is born of sterility.

'The Questioner Who Sits So Sly' [P30, P33; CP, p. 177; CSP50; CSP, p. 31] is addressed to those members of society who have perceived its malaise, but are too weak to do anything about it. The tone of the opening question should reflect a certain measure of derision ('How can you possibly . . .?'), and the title (first used in CP) reinforces this with its allusion to Blake's 'Auguries of Innocence':

> The Questioner who sits so sly
> Shall never know how to reply.

Obviously, the 'questioner' is the enlightened but passive intellectual who is being addressed. He must do more than question, or he himself will not be able to stand interrogation (i.e. the poem). The implication throughout is that if he can see why the rich are behaving as they are, he ought to act to cure them: i.e. he ought to wear a 'ruffian badge'. The rich are seen as totally conditioned by their psychological state of mind, according to the theories of Homer Lane and John Layard. Compare, for instance, the 'stork-legged heaven-reachers' with Auden's reported comment, as he expounded his newly discovered Lane doctrine, on Stephen Spender in 1928: 'Stephen's different. You know why he's so tall? He's trying to reach Heaven!' (*Lions and Shadows,* p. 303). 'Death' in stanzas 5–8 represents this overriding wish of a society to destroy itself (as in *The Dance of Death*) and is personified as hypochondriac, eccentric, and possibly homosexual. Stanzas 8–10 give examples of the paradoxical position into which the sly questioner is forced (the infinitives are all dependent on 'Hard' in 1. 31), and the conclusion is that there is no reward for his attitude: the immediate result of such compromise is apparent failure, though to his descendants ('later other') the compromise might seem honourable. The poem succeeds by virtue of its curiously suggestive imagery rather than by its point or argument, and much of its persuasiveness lies in the half-rhymes.

'Venus Will Now Say a Few Words' [P30, P33; CP, p. 109; CSP50; CSP, p. 33] shows more clearly the origin of these half-rhymes in the half-rhymed couplets of Owen's 'Strange Meeting' (several speeches in *Paid on Both Sides* use them too). They produce a more formalized but no less compulsive and insidiously muted address. Here Nature explains to the happy games-playing lover how he represents only a momentary stage in her evolutionary plans, and how earlier forms of life, like his, were experimental and doomed to extinction. It is clear that the lover is being accused of selfishness. Compare 'Remembering everything you can confess' with 'Hushed for aggression/Of full confession' in 'Too Dear, Too Vague' (CSP, p. 28). And compare 'Relax in your darling's arms like a stone' with 'Stop behaving like a stone' in *Poems* (1930), No. XXII. This phrase is explained by a note in the BM Notebook, fols. 11–12: 'That which desires life to itself, to arrest growth, is behaving like a stone and casts itself like Lucifer out of heaven.' The self, yet again like a besieged town, will starve. If the lover turns to religion, this merely means that the life force has moved on to another evolutionary stage, perhaps his son: and even he will be treated in the same way, 'tipped' (to win?) and later 'topped' (hanged?). The cycle seems inevitable.

'1929' [P 30, P 33; CP, p. 62; CSP 50; CSP, p. 34], in its length, variety of detail and autobiographical realism, breaks new ground (elsewhere in *Poems, 1930,* only 'The Letter' and 'Family Ghosts' use a reliably personal 'I'). It elaborates in an organized meditative framework, with its four parts corresponding roughly with the four seasons, Auden's central theory of social and psychological death and rebirth. It is, in this sense, as the first line indicates, very much an Easter poem: when the poet remembers in Part I 'all of those whose death/Is necessary condition of the season's putting forth,/ Who, sorry in this time, look only back/To Christmas intimacy', it seems inescapable that he has the Christian story somewhere in his mind; and some allusions at the end of the poem support this. In fact, since he needs to suggest a mysterious interrelationship of various cycles of change, personal, bodily, social and psychological, it is small wonder that the Resurrection, too, finds a place.

But it is not stressed: rather, the contrasted recent particulars are the ones which seem most important. Here, we feel, is a 'homesick foreigner' in Germany, sizing up his own position and observing society from a distance. He is hopeful for the future, but reminded of the present. There is on his arm 'A fresh hand with fresh power' (Isherwood had joined Auden in Berlin in March 1929), but he encounters 'solitary man . . . weeping on a bench', and the generalizing power of his omitted articles elevates this image into a symbol of human despair. The friend who analyses his own failure is contrasted with two German friends, happy because unselfconscious. Part I ends with a strikingly metaphorical evocation of the peaceful natural scene before him: it is so natural that 'choice' (i.e. the efforts of the analysers and of the 'unforgiving' in Part II to rationalize their divided selves) seems inevitably mistaken. The odd word 'sessile' was probably borrowed from Alexander Hume's 'Of The Day Estivall', stanza 22.

In Part II this instinctive natural life is embodied in the ducks which the poet observes in the harbour. They find the 'luxury' of the summer sun enough, and do not know the 'restlessness of intercepted growth' (see above, p. 40, for BM Notebook, fols. 11–12, which explains this). In the fourth stanza Auden elaborates this idea of arrested growth by giving a rather laconic Lawrentian account of the birth and growth of the individual (the central chapters of *Psychoanalysis and the Unconscious* seem relevant here). The failure is sexual failure: 'Body reminds in him to loving,/Reminds but takes no further part'. In other words, reason and instinct are divided. As Auden himself comments: 'Body and mind are distinct but neither can exist alone, nor is there rightly a rivalry between them. Attempts to turn body into mind (Manicheeism) or mind into body (Arianism) lead to disease, madness, and death' (BM Notebook, fol. 13). This is, of course, Lane's doctrine, too. And the concluding urgency 'To love my life' is given added significance by the setting of this part of the poem in a time of political disturbance. The poet is naturally distressed to hear of police brutality, but says he is pleased because this will accelerate the revolution (just as the Crucifixion is at once painful and joyful to a Christian, so the girl of nineteen shot through the knees takes on a significance that transcends the particular circumstances).

In Part III the divided individual is seen desperately doing what he can to alleviate his loneliness. Auden provides a rather facetious framing reference to his travelling here (to timetables, and so on); but perhaps he is merely trying to reinforce the general feeling in these stanzas of the only half-consciously perceived passing of events. Time irrevocably propels us along, and leaves us no idea whether what we cling to belongs to the past or to the future. It seems probable, however, that life will change, and in the last stanza Auden is clear that seasonal experience does prepare us for change, and for 'new conditions'. A couple of borrowings from the remarkably Eliotelian No. IC in *Poems* (1928) gives a clue as to the kind of 'death' that Auden means here (see p. 56).

In Part IV the impending winter underlines the final decadence of society and the final madness of the psychologically ill, and at this moment of crisis the country-house guest and the closeted maniac can hardly be distinguished. Children playing in a depressing industrial environment are sensitive to the critical change: it is more than the year that is dying. The 'enemy' and the 'dragon' are natural forces, too, but they are also supernatural ones, borrowed from fairy-tales and bearing an uncomfortable amount of weight (cf. the climax of *The Ascent of F6*). More convincing (and supported in the original *Poems* text by sixteen omitted lines) is the idea that real love needs death, too. Not the love of the 'frightened soul' in Part III, who does not know if love 'be seed in time to display/ Luxuriantly in a wonderful fructification', but a love completely reborn.

Auden takes up this idea of love as a seed in the phrase 'death of the grain', referring to John xii. 24: 'Except a corn of wheat fall into the ground and die, it abideth alone: but if it die, it bringeth forth much fruit.' The allusion in Auden's phrase also introduces Gide's autobiography, *'Si le Grain ne Meurt'*. The Christian sense of life-in-death is provided in the same line by an echo of Eliot's 'Journey of the Magi' published a couple of years before: compare 'death, death of the grain, our death' with Eliot's 'This Birth was/Hard and bitter agony for us, like Death, our death.'

Though 'death of the old gang' (i.e. of the die-hard Tories) seems merely to be thrown in for good measure, the poem ends by prophesying the burial of these beautifully selected representatives of their social class, 'The hard bitch and the riding-master'. But though they are 'stiff' underground, the last figure, the bridegroom, is 'lolling', and he is lolling 'deep in clear lake'. Now it seems clear from a later poem ('A Misunderstanding', CSP, p. 77) that the bridegroom is in fact a healing or revolutionary figure. I tentatively suggest that the unrigid, 'lolling bridegroom' in this poem is therefore a periphrasis for the dead Christ (the bride would be the Church), who is particularly *not* 'forgotten in the spring' (i.e. Easter), but is equally dead, 'necessary condition of the season's putting forth'. The accumulation of images here, however obscure, is none the less marvellously convincing.

'The Bonfires' [P33; CP, p. 77; CSP50; CSP, p. 39], through also ultimately obscure, does with deliberation set its scene dramatically and fantastically by an ironically self-questioning use of heroic and surrealist props. The point would seem to be that the lovers ('we') are not simple like heroes, and cannot cope with the usual trials and terrors (such phrases as 'glaciers calving' and the Popean 'hedgehog's gradual foot,/Or fish's fathom' preserve a mocking tone). Instead they sit indoors smouldering with desire like the garden bonfires (irony is preserved in the cliché) and are satisfied if they can 'time the double beat' of their hearts.

'On Sunday Walks' [P30, P33; CP, p. 92: 'Such Nice People'; CSP50; CSP, p. 40], a casually assured portrait of the managerial class, is very characteristic of Auden's ability to combine generalized insight and acute detail with a strengthening lightness of tone. The way a word like 'conquerors' goes beyond irony into myth is typical, too, of his infallible verve with his material. The managers 'know what to know', but are visited by nightmares about tigers and bishops (the dreamlike atmosphere helped along by the half-rhymes). Their traditions are handed on, and hereditary rights observed, but, like lingering superstitions, their original virtues have dwindled to the forms of ceremony, 'all glory and all story,/Solemn and not so good'. Typically, the mother is given a large share of responsibility (1. 36).

'Shorts' [No. 8: P30, P33; Nos. 9 and 10: O; CSP, p. 42], all twelve of them, may be found in the BM Notebook, fols. 4, 4v, 25, 38, 41v, 54, 55 and 85.[6] 'Pick a quarrel, go to war' is a simple exposition of the Auden-Isherwood theory of the Truly Strong Man, who has no need for bravado, but 'sits drinking quietly in the bar' (*Lions and Shadows,* p. 207). Auden's account of the same theory may be found in his review of Liddell Hart's book on T. E. Lawrence (*Now and Then,* No. 47, Spring 1934). Most of the remaining shorts rather patly illustrate Homer Lane's theory of psychosomatic illness, though 'I'm beginning to lose patience' turns the despondency of the lavish and unsuccessful wooer into a memorably wry witticism. 'Let us honour if we can' was the dedicatory quatrain of *Poems* (1930). The vertical man is alive, the horizontal one dead. The resurrection of these gnomic and comic marginalia should at last dispel the accusations of middle-aged triviality that greeted the clerihews in *Homage to Clio:* Auden has been writing this kind of thing all along.

'Happy Ending' [P30, P33; CP, p. 125; CSP50; CSP, p. 43] is in an equally gnomic style. Auden is himself a youngest son, and has even said that he tends to look upon himself as the youngest person in any room (*The Review,* No. 11/12, p. 8). It is the youngest son who is successful in fairy tales, where it is also a good thing to have obscure origins (cf. stanza 3). But although success is possible in life, this does not seem to include success in love. The odd syntax of the last stanza yields alternative interpretations, of which the likeliest would seem to be: 'It is simple to prove that deeds *can* succeed in life, but it is only love which can succeed in love, and only "tales" (i.e. art) which can be said to be achieving anything in tales of a world in which *no one* fails.'

'This Lunar Beauty' [P30, P33; CP, p. 134: 'Pur'; CSP50: 'Like a Dream'; CSP, p. 44] seems to be 'about' a photograph of the loved-one as a child. Certainly such an interpretation would help to explain the obscure CP title, and the poem makes sense in this light. Isherwood quoted the last two lines as evidence of the influence of Emily Dickinson (*New Verse,* Nov. 1937), and the poem's tone is indeed abstract, delicate, evanescent, with a strong whiff of poignant mortality.

'The Question' [P33; CP, p. 141: 'What Do You Think?'; CSP50: 'The Hard Question'; CSP, p. 45] returns to the mode of Riding and Graves. Trivial and conventional salutations like 'Where are you going?' or 'How do you do?' are here seen by Auden to contain real and difficult questions which the individual cannot answer, because he does not know anything about himself or his future. Since he is 'Afraid/To remember what the fish ignored' (i.e. how to evolve from his environment), he puts himself in the same category as the fish, and forfeits the memory of evolution which, as a human being, he might have had. So his progress is slow and painful. Instead of learning, remembering and developing, he longs, like the cowardly bird, for 'windy skies'; like the cold fish, for water; like the obedient sheep, for a master. In the last stanza, Auden hopes that love will have the power to restore to man his awareness of his inner nature, for it is love ('dark and rich and warm all over') which restores to him the condition of the womb in which he began his personal evolution.

'Five Songs': No. 1: 'What's in your mind, my dove, my coney' [P33; CP, p. 239; CSP50; CSP, p. 46] is a bold sexual invitation which exposes the emotional limitations of the person addressed. In the first stanza love is sarcastically linked with materialism and acquisitiveness: this is sterile sex in the head. 'Do thoughts grow like feathers, the dead end of life' implies that rationalized love may, like plumage, be beautiful or protective, but is actually dead not living (cf. Lawrence's 'The mind is the dead end of life', *Psychoanalysis and the Unconscious*, p. 239). The loved one is then urged to become really aware through sight and touch of what love is about, until the phallic serpent rises, and sexual urgency takes over. The phrase 'great big serpent' is taken from Baudelaire (*Intimate Journals*, tr. Isherwood, p. 44), who comments: 'Such caprices of language, too often repeated, with an excessive use of animal nicknames, testify to a Satanic aspect in love.'

No. II: 'That night when joy began' [LS; CP, p. 229; CSP50; CSP, p. 46] yields, in twelve brief lines, a most ingenious metaphor. Night is associated with sexual tumescence ('narrowest veins'), morning with the end of love (and, by extension, of the love affair). The lovers expect to be challenged by the morning as by a sentry, but peace has been made: now they can see no end to their love.

No. III: 'For what as easy' [*New Signatures*, 1932: 'Poem'; CP, p. 42: 'To You Simply'; CSP50; CSP, p. 47] is an oblique lyric whose deliberately stumbling mode of expression recreates a sense of instinctive gratitude for a happy love affair. Sex is seen as a necessary exchange (the inevitability is suggested by the curiously tautologous 'data given'), and a couple of lines in the first version, subsequently omitted, underlined this Donnean theme in the final stanza. As it now stands, the poem stresses the unchanging nature of feeling.

No. IV: 'Seen when the nights are silent' is from *The Dog Beneath the Skin*, and No. V: ' "O where are you going?" said reader to rider' is from *The Orators*.

'Uncle Henry' [CSP, p. 48] was first published in 1966, with minor changes, from the B-M Notebook, fol. 70. Uncle Henry is the airman's homosexual uncle in *The Orators*, his 'true ancestor'. He is portrayed here, however, as a lisping, upper-class pederast, who, following Wilde and Gide, scours North Africa for 'a fwend,/don't you know, a charmin' cweature'. This certainly conflicts with his role in *The Orators*, where he is presented seriously. The poem is an exercise in English Sapphics.

'Consider' [P30, P33; CP, p. 27; CSP50; CSP, p. 49] shows the sick society 'as the hawk sees it or the helmeted airman'. Auden presents the cigarette-end smouldering on the border, the international set in the winter sports hotel, the farmers in the stormy fens and so on, cinematically, 'as the hawk sees the one concentrated spot where beats the life-heart of our prey' (Lawrence, *Fantasia of the Unconscious,* p. 62). The cinema was doubtless an influence in this kind of panoramic view, but there are literary parallels, too. For instance, Auden had first read Hardy in the summer of 1923, and later admitted: 'What I valued most in Hardy, then, as I still do, was his hawk's vision, his way of looking at life from a very great height, as in the stage directions of *The Dynasts,* or the opening chapter of *The Return of the Native'* (*Southern Review,* Vol. VI, Summer 1940). The images are also linked in other ways (the guests at the garden party 'pass on' too, going south in the winter, and the playboys listen to the same band as the lonely farmers), and the political implications in this nexus and its language ('smouldering', 'dangerous', 'stormy') are tense and unignorable.

Critics take the 'supreme Antagonist' to be death, but the tautology implicit in death making the highborn mining-captains 'wish to die' seems clumsy. Both the Old English *Bestiary* and *Paradise Lost* (I, 200) compare the whale with Satan, as, I believe, Auden is doing. In Auden's glossary of Christian and psychological terms (BM Notebook, fol. 44) Satan is seen as the Censor, responsible for repressing man's natural instincts and bringing about that self-consciousness which separates him from the rest of the animal kingdom. It is this division in men and society, keeping them from their 'real desires, that Auden is anatomizing in the poem. The Antagonist's admirers, the ill, are in ascendancy and are themselves responsible for the malaise, the 'immeasurable neurotic dread', which conditions them.

Auden has omitted from the beginning of the final section eight lines in P30 attacking financiers, dons and clergy. This strengthens the poem, though it does play down the sense of impending social revolution implicit in the fates of the selfish which accumulate in the last lines. These fates take the form of psychological illnesses, and can all be found expounded in William McDougall's *An Outline of Abnormal Psychology* (1926). 'Fugues' (McDougall, p. 257) are a form of amnesia involving compulsive travel; 'irregular breathing' is a symbolic symptom in abnormal psychology (McDougall, p. 278); 'alternate ascendancies' (McDougall, pp. 483ff) are cases of alternating personalities with reciprocal amnesia like fugues; while for the 'explosion of mania' the reader may refer to McDougall's explanation (p. 360) of anger as a secondary feature of mania.

'The Wanderer' [*New Signatures*, 1932: 'Chorus from a Play'; P33; CP, p. 34: 'Something is Bound to Happen'; CSP50; CSP, p. 51] may have been intended for *Paid on Both Sides*, with which it shares its mood of elegiac stoicism: the original title suggests a dramatic origin. The present title stresses the Old English likeness further, and the poem's central part may be compared with lines 37–48 of the Old English poem *The Wanderer*, itself also echoed in *Paid* (see p. 18). The first line is actually taken from a Middle English homily, *Sawles Warde:* 'Ha beoð se wise þat ha witen alle godes reades. his runes ant his domes þe derne beoð ant deopre þen ani sea dingle' ('They are so wise that they know all God's counsels, his mysteries and his judgments, which are secret and deeper than any sea dingle'). 'Doom' is thus really the judgment of God. The Wanderer's compulsive exile also suggests Bunyan's Christian ('No cloud-soft hand can hold him, restraint by women'), though this rejection is present in *Sawles Warde* as well. Auden maintains the Old English mood with a minimum of the appropriate technical devices. There are kennings like 'houses for fishes', along the lines of 'hwaeles eþel' in *The Seafarer*, 1. 60; 'unquiet' is reminiscent of the Old English 'unstille' (in the *Maxims*); and there are one or two alliterating lines. However, the mood of the poem is largely created by the movement and cadence of the irregular verse, and by the ambiguity of its subject. Is this a lordless warrior or the emergent adolescent of the Prologue to *The Orators?* Is the exile an evasion of responsibility or a Quest? Is the doom a punishment or a providential directive? The suggestive vagueness of the poem's message is a large part of its strength.

'The Watchers' [*New Country*, 1933: 'A Happy New Year'; LS; CP, p. 83: 'Not All The Candidates Pass'; CSP50; CSP, p. 52] is an extreme example of the pruning process which some of Auden's poems have undergone. Originally it formed the second part of a sixty-two-stanza fantasy somewhat in the vein of lampooning topical extravaganza found in the third Ode in *The Orators*. The whole poem has never been reprinted, and 'The Watchers' itself has lost ten stanzas which located the meditation decisively in the Scottish school in which Auden was teaching at the time, and which made it clear that the poet's concern in the poem is for the boys in his care and what is going to become of them (originally the rather un-convincing line about the 'near-by families' read: 'The jets in both the dormitories are out'). The revisions have made a neater poem, but one regrets the loss of the personal element.

Other poems of Auden's in *New Country* represented a conscious flirtation with Communism: here the prospect of revolution is con-sidered more sceptically. The Great Bear 'hangs as a portent over Helensburgh', probably as a symbol of Soviet Russia (an omitted stanza immediately goes on to refer to 'China's drum' as another portent ignored by 'the blood [moving] strangely in its moving home'). Auden makes his appeal, however, to the 'Lords of Limit', who, like the Witnesses in *The Chase* (see p. 80) and, more mar-ginally, those in *The Dog Beneath the Skin,* represent at this period his version of God or Fate. The appellation 'Lords of Limit' may derive from Blake, in whose system the Limits of Opacity and Contraction (Satan and Adam) were 'fixed as an act of mercy by the divine Saviour, to put bounds to error.' However, in Auden's system at this time (as sketched in BM Notebook, fol. 44), the duality they represent is symbolic of man's divided nature ('setting a tabu 'twixt left and right'), itself to be equated with the Fall of Man, and with the appearance of class distinction ('From whom all property begins'). They represent the very precariousness of man's condition. Their 'sleepless presences endear/Our peace to us with a perpetual threat', and their control over man's life cannot be avoided except by 'a trick'. In other words, by a paradox not unlike the conventional Christian *felix culpa,* they are ultimately benign.

In the final stanzas the political theorist ('starving visionary') has prophesied the Marxist revolution ('seen/The carnival within our gates,/Your bodies kicked about the streets'), but Auden views this outcome as a disaster to his impulsive and vulnerable pupils, and appeals to the Lords of Limit to use their power to prevent chaos and violence. If this reading is valid, the poem is interestingly quietist and religious, and in its original form contrasted with the surrealist hilarity of the longer initial narrative section, creating a profoundly suggestive tension.

'Adolescence', 'The Exiles', 'The Decoys' and 'Have a Good Time' are from *The Orators,* and are discussed in the next chapter. The previously uncollected 'Half Way' [*Cambridge Left,* No. 1, Summer 1933: 'Interview'; CSP, p. 58], both by its position in CSP and by its subject-matter (the surrealist briefing of a defecting enemy), also seems to be a fragment intended for *The Orators.* It is a high-spirited piece, though slight enough (its level is indicated, for instance, by the comic conflation of *Julius Caesar* and free-masonry ritual in 'Your public refusal of a compass/Is fixed for to-morrow'). An omitted stanza helped, with its schoolboy nick-names, to identify both the humour and the imagery as essentially that of the school world. 'Ode' is also from *The Orators.* 'Legend' and 'The Witnesses' are from *The Dog Beneath the Skin,* and are discussed in Chapter 4.

3   The Orators

The Orators[1] was the work which set the seal on Auden's early reputation. Subtitled 'An English Study', it forms among other things a surrealist anatomy of a country in crisis. The conception is large-scale, the tone exuberantly varied and experimental. Though there is much in the work which is direct and satirical, the predominant allegiance evoked is to the European avant-garde of the 'twenties, to the prose of Stein, Joyce and Wyndham Lewis, to the lingering influence of Baudelaire and Rimbaud, and to more recent poets like St-J. Perse. Many reviewers emphasized its obscurity, but most came out in the work's favour. Bonamy Dobrée was enthusiastic in The Spectator (20 Aug. 1932) and even included passages from it in his Modern Prose Style (1934). The ultimate accolade came almost from the throne-room itself when in October 1932 John Hayward wrote in The Criterion: 'I have no doubt that it is the most valuable contribution to English poetry since The Waste Land.'

Unlike Eliot, Auden was not concerned to purify the dialect of the tribe, but to restore its flavour. And it is certainly a brilliant performance. Without the threads of fiction which Book II directs forcefully into our reading of the work, it might arguably be seen to be more of a 'notebook' conglomeration than the coherent whole that it has succeeded in being. But it is also true that the discrete prose and verse items of the other two books have the most individual impact: the parodies of the Anglican responses, the prize-day speech and the middlebrow romance; the fastidious prosody of the second Ode, the satiric vigour of the third or the absurd hymn-syntax of the

fifth (the various Odes have different numbers in the earlier editions);
these are the remembered successes of the work, and they indicate a
widening of range in Auden's writing at a point of vital importance
to his stature.

Auden has supplied a preface which directly confronts the frequent
charges of unconscious fascism levelled at the work: 'My name on
the title-page,' he says, 'seems a pseudonym for someone else,
someone talented but near the border of sanity, who might well, in a
year or two, become a Nazi.' In the 'thirties he said that he opposed
fascism because he knew from his experience of school what a fascist
state was like.[2] As a schoolmaster at the time of writing *The Orators,*
his opposition thus assumed the status of espionage, a prominent
theme of the work. But the spy is shown to be an introvert and a
failure ('Which Side Am I Supposed To Be On?'), incapable of
serious political action. Much of the work is certainly about the
need for revolution in 'this country of ours where nobody is well',
but is concerned with revolution according to Blake, Baudelaire or
Homer Lane, not according to Marx, whose insistence on its proletarian character is effectively denied both by Auden's messianic
mythologizing and (in the third Ode) by his direct Skeltonic sneers
at the working class.

But if he is more concerned with Leadership than with Communism, one must be clear that the concern is based firmly on the
psychology of the individual, and in many places is expressed with
an ironical sense of the individual's weakness. Indeed, one important
theme of the book is the need for group organization, even though
this seems sometimes to work at the level of Moral Rearmament.
Many of the passages omitted from earlier editions would soften
what might seem too programmatic. A smokescreen has been drawn
in front of the autobiographical elements (Gabriel, Uncle Wiz,
'Derek my chum', the Essay Club and so on), and other discarded
pieces maintained the personal context. For instance, the omitted
Ode to the rugger fifteen (originally Ode Two) was delightful
Hopkins parody:

> Defeats on them like lavas
> Have fallen, fell, kept falling, fell
> On them, poor lovies . . .

But it was more than just this, for it brought the half-mystical Lawrentian *Wandervögel* sentiments of the work directly and comfortingly into line with public-school hero-worship. Later on, of course, Auden was highly critical of both Fascist and Lawrence-influenced educational practice (see *Education Today and Tomorrow*, 1939, p. 38).

The work's title and subtitle indicate the area of its concern: the characters and personae orate, but do not act; they live in a fantasy world, perceiving the need for a new life but secretly in love with the old. And this is 'an English study', a portrait of a culture sketched both by social and political allusion, and by a conscious exercise of its literary forms. The orators are compulsive verbalizers, all with some apprehension of the malaise, some with a felt need for spiritual leadership; but all bound by their own social and psychological conditioning, and all doomed to failure. The Ciceronian political ideal, mirrored in the British educational and diplomatic system, may have provided an ironical structure for the work, with parallels to be found in the three-part form between *De Oratore*, on the orator's training, and Book I ('The Initiates'); between *Brutus* and Book II ('Journal of an Airman'); and between *Orator*, partly autobiographical and concerned with the ideal orator, and Book III ('Five Odes'). By his virtuoso range of parody and stylistic allusion, Auden shows that he is as much concerned with rhetoric as with politics; and of course the whole work shows a powerful interest in education. Indeed, the training of the ruling class provides an ambience of homoerotic *Kameradschaft* which on a number of occasions appears in itself to be spiritually regenerating.

The dedicatory verse to Stephen Spender may be found, together with a large number of other unpublished gnomic poems, in the BM Notebook, fol. 55, and is a neat variation on the old proverb: 'Fools' names and fools' faces/Are often seen in public places.' Auden's point is that society's health depends on the sum of the health of its members, not upon the rigidity and efficiency of its forms. It suggests, with memorable concreteness, that the community will benefit more from contributions from individuals than it will from an organized bureaucracy. It may also contain a sly apologia for the private references in the work.

The 'Prologue', entitled 'Adolescence' in separate printings in CP and CSP, presents in miniature the half-hidden message of the whole work: that the introverted adolescent is obsessed and motivated by mother love, unable to free himself from it, deriving his neurosis from her and yet accused by her of it. The adolescent (like the Airman of Book II, and like John Nower in *Paid on Both Sides* and Michael Ransom in *The Ascent of F6*) is driven to his exploits by his mother, and yet is ultimately destroyed by her. In Auden's mythology she becomes the Enemy, the Dragon, and in this 'Prologue', though she is first seen as a mammary landscape to which the adolescent is devoted, by the end of the poem she has become a shuffling giantess, crying 'Deceiver'. Her son is a deceiver because, like Nower perpetuating the feud or Ransom climbing F6, he believed that he undertook his quest out of bravery, whereas it was really to please his mother.

Moreover, it is only the Truly Weak Man (see p. 32) who has to satisfy his weakness in this way. His Quest lends him a quasi-divinity as the biblical allusions in the second stanza imply, but he is no Jove, and his swan-like beauty is impotent, 'worshipping not lying', whispering in girls' ears rather than going to bed with them (secondary sexual meanings of 'beak' and 'concha' reinforce what might have been). He does understand that life should be natural and instinctive, lying not worshipping, unselfconscious as the roots of trees that the summer bands tell him about, but he does not put his knowledge into action. He tells others about it. He is, in fact, an 'orator'. The metaphor of the tree-roots in the third stanza probably derives from Lawrence: 'A huge, plunging, tremendous soul. I would like to be a tree for a while. The great lust of roots. Root-lust. And no mind at all' (*Fantasia of the Unconscious*, p. 39). The adolescent has too much of a mind, represented perhaps by the 'finest of mapping pens' with which he compulsively annotates a landscape as familiar to him as life itself. It is for this reason that though his Quest has taken him quite a long way, 'this prophet . . . receives odd welcome from the country he so defended'. This further biblical allusion shows why: 'A prophet is not without honour, save in his own country, and in his own house' (Matthew xiii. 57). It is precisely 'in his own house' that his weakness lies, a weakness which is to be explored in Book II of *The Orators*.

Book I ('The Initiates') is largely about how the 'orators', with their varying degrees of perception and evasiveness, are trained in the specious rhetoric of self-justification. In Part I ('Address for a Prize-Day') we see psychological Phariseeism in a school; in Part II ('Argument') we see an adolescent day-dream about an imaginary Leader, and the sanctimonious prayers which he inspires; in Part III ('Statement') we see a display of prophetic fatalism; and in Part IV ('Letter to a Wound') we see a secret devotion to the very illness which is sapping the individual's strength. The twin triumph of this four-part book is its stylistic virtuosity and its generous irony: like Swift's *Tale of a Tub* it presents us with an ever-shifting viewpoint in which, though the writer *in propria persona* is not present, many of his attitudes are. To a certain extent Auden is melodramatizing aspects of his own intellectual beliefs: the analysis in the prize-day speech of the kinds of defective love, for example, or the fantastic catalogues of 'Statement', these are in a basic sense obviously 'Auden'. Perhaps the point is simply that Auden, as a radical intellectual schoolmaster, is himself an orator.

The speaker at the prize day[3] has the right ideas (Homer Lane's), but ends in mere incoherence (he has a train to catch), urging the boys to bullying and persecution. Auden was to develop the monologue as a form with some deftness (in the Vicar's Sermon in *The Dog Beneath the Skin,* for example, or in the cabaret sketch *Alfred*), so that in spite of its persona and occasion, it became primarily a vehicle for the ideas contained in it rather than an expression of character. In this case, the speaker's main purpose is to elaborate Dante's division of the sinners in *Purgatorio,* XVII, into 'those who have been guilty in their life of excessive love towards themselves or their neighbours, those guilty of defective love towards God and those guilty of perverted love'. His elaboration ascribes, on Lane's principles, various physical symptoms to each category, a procedure which Auden undertook in greater clinical detail in a diagram in the BM Notebook, fol 48. A comparison of this preliminary plan with the 'Address' will reveal the strength of Auden's suggestive inventiveness and imagery in the course of composition:

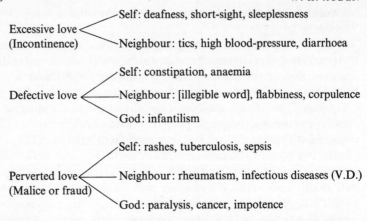

Excessive love (Incontinence)
- Self: deafness, short-sight, sleeplessness
- Neighbour: tics, high blood-pressure, diarrhoea

Defective love
- Self: constipation, anaemia
- Neighbour: [illegible word], flabbiness, corpulence
- God: infantilism

Perverted love (Malice or fraud)
- Self: rashes, tuberculosis, sepsis
- Neighbour: rheumatism, infectious diseases (V.D.)
- God: paralysis, cancer, impotence

There are similarities in the 'Address' to images in the early poems. Compare, for instance, 'Have you never noticed in them the gradual abdication of central in favour of peripheral control?' (p. 16) with 'central anguish felt/For goodness wasted at peripheral fault' in 'Venus Will Now Say a Few Words' (CSP, p. 33). These terms are part of a system that Auden is in the process of creating: the surface mannerisms of his old schoolmaster are a comic literary safety-valve.

The second part of Book I, 'Argument', begins with an arresting epic 'Lo!' (cf. Old English 'Hwaet!'), and images of birth introduce the theme – evidently derived from Perse's *Anabase*, recently translated by Eliot – of the establishment of a new order by a mysterious Leader. Certain images and phrases (that of the 'stranger', for instance), and much that is oblique, exotic and liturgical in this and the following part, seem inspired by *Anabase*. The speaker is affected, apparently in a dream, by the idea of the cycle of seasonal change, of death and life. The image of the skull forced out of the dyke by the growing bulbs is borrowed from an earlier poem (*Poems*, 1928, No. IC):

> In Spring we saw
> The bulb pillow
> Raising the skull,
> Thrusting a crocus through clenched teeth.

The image is familiar from Eliot's 'Whispers of Immortality'.

The Leader (capitalized pronouns suggest divinity) is, like Jesus, imagined as organizing a secret group of resistance ('Their annual games . . . their day . . . their women' vaguely sketches in the Enemy at this stage). It is all very like Buchman's Group Movement (Moral Rearmament), which had been Oxford-based when Auden was an undergraduate and was rapidly expanding at the time *The Orators* was written.[4] A similar Buchmanite role is predicted for the infant John Warner in the third Ode (p. 92):

> The gauche and the lonely he will introduce of course
> To the smaller group, the right field of force.

Although they still hand round tea, these young men become strangers to their parents by virtue of their secret understanding with their Leader, and feel themselves akin to the crofter 'working in sweat and weathers' (compare the third Ode, p. 92: 'All of the women and most of the men/Shall work with their hands and not think again').[5]

The passage on page 21 suggests that all this is still a dream of the speaker, who in his suburban home ('the laurelled drive') imagines, with the resources of a boy's adventure story, how the group will move into action to serve its Leader. Auden uses a complex of images here, some of which turn up elsewhere and would seem to have a significance not available to the reader. Compare 'At the frontier getting down, at railhead drinking hot tea waiting for pack-mules, at the box with the three levers watching the swallows' with 'On the frontier at dawn getting down,/Hot eyes were soothed with swallows' (*Poems,* 1928, No. v). Compare these swallows and the next sentence but one ('The young mother in the red kerchief suckling her child in the doorway, and the dog fleaing itself in the hot dust') with 'Westland swallows swooped in and out of the eaves overhead. In a doorway opposite, a young mother looked down at her suckling babe with ineffable Westland tenderness' (*The Dog Beneath the Skin,* p. 70). Moreover, a little further on in this last passage is a reference to new-mown hay, which also turns up in the *Orators* section (bottom of p. 20).

What do these images mean? Getting down (from a train) at the frontier obviously provides a moment in the journey to the new life for appraisal of what is to come. The swallows and the suckling child symbolize the fruitfulness of the new life, the 'idea of building' which governs the whole section. None the less the images are personal, perhaps derived from Auden's visit to Germany: these, and the whole paragraph on pages 20–21, elaborate the imaginary world of the small group waiting for action, a world familiar in its outlines from *Paid on Both Sides*. But the paragraph following shows that it is all conditional. The absurd hero-worship and self-sacrifice are all in the mind of the speaker. It is the 'world of the Spider, not Him', and those who desire the new life are reduced to superstitious ritual. 'Resurgam' is the cry, but it is expressed by urinating in a patch of snow, a strange device with a stranger banner.

The passage beginning on page 23 describes a journey, but it is not clear that the journey is likely to accomplish anything ('Is it wise, the short adventure on the narrow ship?'). The images of the dew-wet hare and the emmet are borrowed from *Poems* (1928), No. ıh. The horns in the spring are reminiscent of *The Waste Land,* line 197. Women are tender in the spring, but the group must leave them (compare 'The Wanderer', CSP, p. 51) because 'it is your art just now against the inner life'. In other words, it is the women who are preventing the new life from coming about and must be abandoned. The group are obedient to His will, but it is not clear that they really know what they are up to.

The second section of 'Argument' (p. 24) consists of the group's prayers, a parody of the Anglican responses. Prayer for delivery from various forms of neurotic illness is made to detectives of fiction, and prayer on behalf of defective lovers is made to a series of pubs: *private* detectives and *public* houses is, I think, the thematic joke. Most of the material here is plain enough. 'The drought that withers the lower centres' (p. 24) is the mother's inhibiting love.[6] The 'two against one' (p. 25) is illuminated by a couplet in the BM Notebook, fol. 43:

> There are two kinds of friendship even in babes
> Two against one and seven against Thebes.

In other words, exclusiveness is not required (cf. p. 20: 'Our bond, friend, is a third party'). The source of the phrase may be an Icelandic proverb: 'Two are an army against one.'[7] Auden has omitted an invocation to Ferrers Locke for delivery from, among other things, 'the death-will of the Jews', which probably seems (*pace* Miss Arendt) a little tasteless now.

The third section of 'Argument' (p. 27) contains more than the usual share of writing that seems impenetrably stream-of-consciousness. Again Auden uses passages from early poems. Compare 'Shutting the door on the machines, etc.' with 'The Engine House' (*Lions and Shadows*, p. 186). 'Love, that notable forked one, etc.' is adapted from *Poems* (1928), No. IX. The section appears to describe a time of crisis in the absence of the Leader, and it strongly evokes the meetings with Christ before the Resurrection ('Catching sight of Him on the lawn with the gardener. . . . Hysterical attempts of two women to reach Him'). 'We who on the snow-line were in love with death, despised vegetation, we forgot His will' may allude to Eliot's 'Journey of the Magi', 11. 21–22: 'Then at dawn we came down to a temperate valley,/Wet, below the snow line, smelling of vegetation.' The magi were similarly confused about the meaning of Christ, similarly involved with death, and are also alluded to at the end of Auden's early poem '1929' (see p. 43). The Leader appears to have vanished as mysteriously as he came (or did he ever come?), leaving only legend behind him, and a stone whose inscription playing children ignore. The Christian implications of 'Argument' are no doubt fully intended by Auden to derive from its speaker. The final sentence appears to deliver a judgment upon his motivation and imagination: 'The priest's mouth opens in the green graveyard, but the wind is against it.'

The third part of Book I, 'Statement' (p. 30), consists largely of laconic catalogues and gnomic observations which underline the idea of fate. The use of Perse continues (compare 'Summon. And there passed such cursing his father, and the curse was given him' with 'Stranger. Who passed, etc.' in Eliot's translation of *Anabase*, p. 15), but the basic debt is to Old English poetry. The three sections of 'Statement' are each built around a fairly direct pastiche of an Old English poem: the first uses *The Gifts of Men*, the second *The Fortunes of Men*, and the third *Maxims*. These three poems appear in different parts of the *Exeter Book*, but are printed together in

R. K. Gordon's *Anglo-Saxon Poetry* (1926), which Auden had probably used. *The Gifts of Men* introduces the 'sum' formula. Compare (in Gordon's translation):

He who has power of judgment scatters variously to dwellers throughout this world the bodily powers of men. To one on earth here He grants goods, wordly treasures. One is poor, an unfortunate man; yet he is wise in arts of the mind. One receives more bodily strength. One is beautiful, fair in form. One is a poet skilled in songs. One is eloquent in words. One is a pursuer in hunting of glorious beasts, etc.

Auden has converted the Old English ascription of men's gifts to God's providence into a purely materialistic and utilitarian generalization: 'To each an award, suitable to his sex, his class and the power.' The resemblance of this to the famous dictum of Karl Marx is probably not accidental. In elaborating the catalogue, Auden may have been inspired by Perse (cf. p. 65, the passage about 'all conditions of men') or by Whitman's *Song of Myself,* but the 'sum' formula crops up in many places, in the *Iliad,* XIII, 726–34, for instance, and in Corinthians.

Auden also cannibalizes, as usual, from earlier poems. Compare, for instance, 'one is skilful at improvising a fugue; the bowel tremors at the pedal-entry' with 'That pedal-entry in the fugue/ Roared in, swept soul and knees away' ('In Due Season', *Oxford Outlook,* Dec. 1926). The effect of this section is a marvellously concrete evocation of the potential and variety of the human condition, which is quickly dispelled by the following section's parallel itemizing of the disaster and illness which befall individuals. The conclusion is appropriate: 'Have seen the red bicycle [of the telegraph messenger bringing fatal news] leaning on porches and the cancelling out was complete.'

The final section of 'Statement' (p. 33) accentuates the inevitability of the process it has described so far. It describes the plenitude and continuity of life: 'Nothing is being done but something being done again by someone.' The first paragraph is a pastiche of Gertrude Stein (compare her *Useful Knowledge,* 1929, p. 1), whom Auden admired while he was at Oxford.[8] In the following paragraph, the Old English *Maxims* is pastiched. Compare 'Fate is strongest.

Winter is coldest; spring most frosty. . . . The bird shall sport in the air. The salmon shall go darting in the pool, etc.' (Gordon, pp. 313–14). Auden used his image of the salmon again in *The Dog Beneath the Skin,* p. 33: 'Salmon leaping the ladder'. 'The belly receives; the back rejects' is reminiscent of Blake's 'Proverbs of Hell' ('The Cistern contains; the fountain overflows'). The third paragraph, while continuing to follow the Old English at random though sometimes closely (compare 'Two are consorts. A woman and a man shall bring a child into the world by birth', Gordon, p. 309), introduces some of Lawrence's educational ideas. When Auden wrote (p. 34) 'The boy and the girl shall not play together; they shall wait for power', he was probably thinking of something like 'Then keep the girls apart from any familiarity or being "pals" with the boys. The nice clean intimacy which we now so admire between the sexes is sterilizing. It makes neuters. Later on, no deep, magical sex-life is possible' (*Fantasia of the Unconscious,* p. 84). Such injunctions (and the Old English 'sceal' formula which binds them) seem to suggest that fate has better things in store. The final paragraph, reminiscent of 'The Watchers' (CSP, p. 52), corroborates this by implying that out of the endless battle of contraries comes eventual good, 'Good against evil, youth against age, life against death, light against darkness', as the Old English puts it (Gordon, p. 314). Its terms are those of Lawrence's theory of the cosmological duality of life (*Fantasia of the Unconscious,* pp. 150ff) and it is an implication that Blake would have understood.

The fourth part of Book I, 'Letter to a Wound' (p. 35), provides an ingenious portrait of one who is 'in love with death'. His wound represents his psychological illness, and he writes a love letter to it rather in the manner of Groddeck, because he is unwilling to be cured. Indeed, the surgeon has no hope. ('Gangle' suggests Lawrence's ganglia, the four great nerve centres.) The wound enables him to understand various other forms of perverted love (p. 38), such as that between the disgustingly named Offal and Snig, 'the partners in the hardware shop on the front'. The intimate, coy tone of the letter is cleverly observed, though Auden has no hesitation in introducing his friends into it – Gabriel Carritt, Olive Mangeot and Margaret Marshall ('Margaret the brazen leech' of *Poems,* 1928, No. II) – in such a way as to tease us with the thought that the writer of the letter is himself, and the wound something more particularly identifiable.

Book II, 'Journal of an Airman', contains the central action of the whole work. We have already seen how hard it is for the individual to break with his illness and embrace the new life, and we have seen how the mystique of a powerful leader affects those who are thus divided. Now we have an account by such a leader of his understanding of the forces which prevent spiritual regeneration ('the enemy') and his programme of combat against them. But it transpires that this Truly Strong Man is a Truly Weak Man, his programme misconceived and doomed to failure. Beach points out (*The Making of the Auden Canon*, p. 80) that the Yiddish *Luftmensch* means something like 'Johnny Head-in-Air'; on the other hand, the helmeted airman had turned up earlier in Auden's poetry as a clinical observer (CSP, p. 49). Auden's own comment, made later, is probably the most helpful: 'The closest modern equivalent to the Homeric hero is the ace fighter pilot' (*The Portable Greek Reader*, 1948, p. 18). It is a wholly appropriate choice.

The airman's pseudo-scientific observations about the enemy do establish the basic fact that their activities hinder the natural development of society and of the individual, but there is a nervous, evasive tone about all these analogies drawn from physics, biology and psychiatry, as though the airman, by seeking to establish an objective view of the enemy, is avoiding a subjective understanding. The airman notes that an organically developing society must be based on the healthy self-sufficiency of the individual (self-care) and is weakened by the selfish demands of the neurotically introverted (self-regard). Self-regard is a sex-linked disease, he says (p. 42), thus invoking the Mendelian theory of inheritance, where incidence of the characteristic is largely restricted to one sex. Other sex-linked diseases include night-blindness, colour-blindness and various ocular defects: this explains the diagrams that then follow. If you suspect someone of self-regard, you can give him an ocular test of the kind used for colour-blindness. If he picks out an unusual shape, it is, as the airman observes (p. 43), 'wiser to shoot at once'; for his selection represents his division of 'the unity of passion' (p. 48). In the case of this sex-linked disease, man is the sufferer, woman the

carrier: ' "What a wonderful woman she is!" Not so fast: wait till
you see her son.' The thematic outline of the 'Prologue' is already
being filled in.

On pages 43–44, Auden elaborates the airman's idea of his role
as an agent of love ('central awareness'). The metaphor of the circles,
and the relationships between circumferences and centres, refers to
Lawrence's upper and lower centres of awareness respectively. The
enemy's disturbance of these relationships (in the individual, and
between individuals) represents, as we shall see, not only the divided
psyche of the spiritually ill, but also the mother's 'partial priority',
her love for the son which strangles the deeper sensual centres (cf.
Fantasia of the Unconscious, p. 119). The airman explores the
relationship of the circles in time according to the Mendelism which
he has already introduced, discovering that 'the true ancestral line
is not necessarily a straight or continuous one'. His diagram, with
the circle representing the zygote, the half-circles the gametes, and
F_1, F_2 and F_3 the various filial generations, demonstrates the basic
Mendelian conclusion that where the inheritance of an alternative
pair of characters is concerned, the effect of the cross in successive
generations is to produce only three different sorts of individuals,
viz: dominants which breed true, dominants which give both
dominant and recessive offspring in the ratio of $3:1$, and recessives
which always breed true. Thus the airman is forced to conclude that
his true ancestor is his uncle or great-grandfather.

Now the airman has two uncles: Uncle Sam, who arranges sing-
songs 'with all the assurance of a non-airman' (p. 48), and Uncle
Henry, who committed suicide and appears to have been a homosexual (see pp. 58 and 60, and the poem 'Uncle Henry' in CSP,
p. 48). The airman, fresh from his Mendelian charts, has a moment
of doubt (p. 49: 'Uncle Sam, is he one too? He has the same back-
ward-bending thumb that I have' refers to the tell-tale sucked
thumb indicating deprivation of the breast at weaning), but he does
assume that it is Uncle Henry who is his true ancestor. For this
reason, the aeroplane becomes associated with homosexuality, and
flying seems an unnatural activity: 'My mother's dislike of my
uncle, the people's satisfaction at crashes. "If the Lord had intended
people to fly He'd have given them wings" ' (pp. 44–45). But the

airman is still primarily an agent of love, the central awareness: homosexuality is an enemy-created bogey, irrelevant to the main problem of healing the individual and society, and the airman notes (p. 45) that the aeroplane is really only 'a guarantee of good faith to the people, frightened by ghost stories, the enemy's distorted vision of the airman's activities'.

As the airman begins to look for bases from which to conduct his heroic campaign against the enemy, he has an inkling that his role may involve self-deception. Watching skuas (a kind of gull) he reflects:

> You are a man, or haven't you heard
> That you keep on trying to be a bird?

We are reminded of Auden's adoption of Lane's theories as reported by Isherwood in *Lions and Shadows,* page 303: 'epilepsy . . . was an attempt to become an angel, and fly'. Isherwood himself pointed this out, in *New Verse,* November 1937. There is no doubt that the airman is in fact ill. He is probably a kleptomaniac, though his remarks about this frequently suggest masturbation (see pp. 49, 57, 61, 72 and 74), and it is his weakness (like Nower and Ransom) which forces him to his exploits.

The airman then goes on (p. 45) to talk of the enemy as a philosopher who treats 'intellect-will-sensation' as separate entities. In a splendid interpretation of the sestina which follows (called 'Have a Good Time' in CP), John Blair shows how these three faculties correspond allegorically to the bay, the clock and the wood which appear in the poem. Blair, I think rightly, also interprets the vats as 'dyer's vats, which serve as an allegorical representation of art', and shows how the whole poem serves to describe the poet's (and by extension the airman's) education and setting-out in life, and his attempts to integrate intellect, will and sensation.[9]

The enemy are above all, and in a limiting way, rational ('Their extraordinary idea that man's only glory is to think'), and their private and fixed associations need to be upset by practical jokes which are contradictory and public (p. 48). Their 'terrible rat-courage' (p. 47) is borrowed from 'The Watchers' (CSP, p. 52), where it is a characteristic of the sick trying to evade the power of the

Lords of Limit who control their fate. Meanwhile the airman is gathering his forces at a hotel, where he begins his compulsive stealing (p. 49).

The airman's alphabet is modelled directly on the Icelandic Runic Poem. Compare:

> Wealth = source of discord among kinsmen
> and fire of the sea
> and path of the serpent.

> Shower = lamentation of the clouds
> and ruin of the hay-harvest
> and abomination of the shepherd, etc.[10]

The alphabet is fairly straightforward, though it is suggestively erotic.

The following definitions of the enemy (pp. 52–54) are largely social and psychological. Auden wittily adapts the ninth-century Irish triad[11] to produce a comically elaborated list of personal *bêtes noires* reminiscent of Apollinaire's *merde/rose* or Wyndham Lewis's Blasting and Blessing. The general picture that emerges is of the comfortable, cautious and stuffy bourgeoisie.

The airman's continued preparations and agitation are revealed by the week's timetable which follows, mentioning 'The Hollies', the house which becomes the centre of his operations. It appears that the 'E' who lives there is loved by the airman, but is in danger because of this, and must be given up (pp. 57, 59, 67 and 73: E's sex has been changed since the first edition). Other allies of the airman appear in the following dozen or so pages: A, a scout; B, an indecisive and sceptical ally; Derek, a particular friend, killed through sabotage; and so on. The feuding atmosphere of *Paid on Both Sides* is evoked ('A tells me they have been in Kettlewell and most of the outlying farms', p. 55), and there are a number of philosophical jottings, lists of armaments, reported dreams, etc. On page 58, the metaphor of 'drawing the line' is derived from Dedekind's Section, the method of defining irrational or transcendental numbers devised by the mathematician Dedekind. The passage about Uncle Henry on the same page explains his influence over the airman. Auden may have got ideas about the influence of uncles from explanations of 'swustersunu' (sister's son) at line 115 of *The Battle of Maldon*, since he quotes this Old English poem later in *The Orators;* or it may be that he was struck by the role they play in matrilineal societies like that of the Trobriand Islanders described by Bronislaw Malinowski in his *The Father in Primitive Psychology* (1927), a work with which we know he was familiar. Uncle Henry is clever and dissolute, feared and denigrated by the mother whose comfortable bourgeois standards he appears to threaten. He is the wicked bachelor who invites the sixteen-year-old nephew to his flat and gives him champagne for dinner. In the airman's anxiety dream (pp. 59–60) he appears as someone who has made a journey that the airman is unable to make, even to save his loved one from a terrible danger. The journey turns out to be suicide, but the airman does not realize the significance of this until later.

The airman appears at The Hollies (p. 60), drawn to the games-playing life of leisure that goes on there, but more and more uncertain as to his real position. Are the people that he meets on his side or not? He visits in order to 'acquire their ruses', and imagines that 'the spies have gone to phone for their police'. His kleptomania returns, and he has more bad dreams. The following half-dozen pages, in terms of the dramatic shape of the 'Journal', are merely marking time, and Auden fills them with a variety of thematic material employing the usual devices. There are fragments from early uncollected poems (e.g. the worrying mower on p. 60 from 'Chloe to Daphnis in Hyde Park', *Oxford Outlook*, viii [1926], p. 209); instances of obscure slang (p. 61: 'gonsil' and 'first-of-May' are both cant words meaning a young tramp; cf. 'The Duet', CSP, p. 228) and suggestive newspaper headlines (p. 62: 'Hearts humbled by Queens' – football teams); allusions to Baudelaire's *Intimate Journals*, recently translated by Isherwood (e.g. p. 62, on hygiene); allusions to *All the Conspirators* ('Allen and Page' on p. 64 are probably Allen Chalmers and Victor Page, major characters from Isherwood's novel); and a good deal of what looks like automatic writing. This last may look like the harassed explicator's excuse, but in the summer of 1928 Isherwood and Edward Upward were practising automatic writing (*Lions and Shadows*, p. 276), and the similarities become striking at times. Compare the following from *The Orators,* p. 63:

In the greenhouse they loiter, imagine coiled shapes, malignant, phosphorescent, in the zinc darkness of a tank. Come on you chaps! After their change of heart, a desert silence, shadows of wool-white clouds. A caterpillar, lacking compass or guides, crosses the vast uplands of his shoe, whom bees ignore. They have all gone in to tea.

with Upward's reported exercise in *Lions and Shadows:*

Rubber statuary in gardens of ice-cream roses bearing every imprint of foot and belly. Kissing beneath the jangling clock before the cinema doors are opened. Plush seats unbarred between, mumbling hands convolved in calico. Steady, chaps, go slow. Where were we?

This kind of writing does have a kind of internal coherence, but it is difficult to say exactly what it means. Much in *The Orators* might be ascribed to this method, since Isherwood's piece of automatic writing contains a reference to a character in *Paid on Both Sides,* and *The Orators* contains allusions to characters in Isherwood's and Upward's Mortmere stories (Moxon and Miss Belmairs on p. 92). When, in the preface to his *Collected Poetry,* Auden spoke of *The Orators* as 'a case of the fair notion fatally injured', he may well have thought the fatal injury arose from the obscurity of such surrealist passages. As early as June/July 1936 in *New Verse* he was expressing pseudonymous 'Honest Doubts' about surrealism.

The airman, then, feels that he is likely to be exposed (the poem 'There are some birds in these valleys', called 'The Decoys' in CP, bears this out), and that his weaknesses are betraying his uncle. Sure enough, he learns that the enemy are going to attack (p. 67), forcing him to set in motion his plan for a twenty-eight day mobilization. This alludes to the mobilization of the German army in preparation for the First World War, as recounted in General Ludendorff's *The Coming War* (1931), pp. 70ff: '[The Army] was able . . . at the beginning of the fourth week after the commencement of mobilization, as a result of several great victorious actions, to force its way into France' (p. 71). Auden, however, conflates this historical mobilization with Ludendorff's eccentric, doom-laden account of what he saw as the probable mobilization *against* Germany of a

Franco–Italian alliance.[12] The tone of this latter account is recognizably a model for this part of the 'Journal': 'All payments from public funds, including of course unemployment benefits, pensions and salaries are suspended. Wages very soon cease to be paid and distress begins to stalk through the land' (Ludendorff, p. 105). Hair-raising enough in Ludendorff, with its allusions to a Jewish-Jesuit-Freemason conspiracy, this mobilization is given a Bosch-like, apocalyptic turn by Auden that is directly reminiscent of Isherwood's and Upward's Mortmere stories, which they themselves recognized as a 'special brand of medieval surrealism' and an indulgent escape from reality. Similarly, in the 'Journal' the anarchy described is really too comic to be very disturbing: 'All menstruation ceases. Vampires are common in the neighbourhood of the Cathedral, epidemics of lupus, halitosis, and superfluous hair' (p. 71).

It is at this climactic point that the airman realizes the significance of his earlier dream (p. 59). His uncle had not failed after all, because he had perceived a truth about the enemy which enabled him to pass beyond the vain struggle that the airman is undertaking. At the centre of the enemy's world stands the mother, the bearer of the disease from which the hero suffers. As we have seen, D. H. Lawrence had said that the love-sympathy between parent and child aroused the deeper sensual centres but provided no outlet for them. This spiritual mothering is responsible for introversion and masturbation, 'enemy' traits which have been sublimated in the airman as spying and as kleptomania, the latter being a subconscious cry for help ('They stole to force a hearing', p. 72) which seems to be his eventual undoing. The comfortable conventionalized world of the mother stifles, not because it is bourgeois ('our homes and duty'), but simply because it is the mother's. It is the black-sheep uncle who has overcome this stifling by accepting it and by embracing his real nature ('self care'), rather than by trying to fight it as the airman has been doing. Thus the sacrificed uncle becomes quasi-divine ('Uncle, save them all, make me worthy', p. 73), for his way out was to see that there is no way out. The airman has learned that:

1. The power of the enemy is a function of our resistance, therefore
2. The only efficient way to destroy it – self-destruction . . .

This really only makes sense if we see it as the airman's resistance to his mother-induced neurosis: the enemy is not an external enemy at all, but is to be found within himself, a part of his own nature. His exploits cannot lift him beyond his emotional crippling (as the 'Prologue' puts it, 'The giantess shuffles nearer, cries "Deceiver" ' ; one simply cannot deceive oneself into thinking that one can escape this early conditioning).

On the last page of the 'Journal' (p. 74) we leave the airman about to make his final decision on the day fixed for the attack. I think we are meant to feel, in the ambiguous ending, that he accepts his death as a necessary condition for future understanding and new life. After a list of readings from his instruments as he guides his machine at 10,000 feet, comes the phrase 'Hands in perfect order'. This implies that his weakness has disappeared, but it is also an interesting allusion to a phrase of Wilfred Owen's in a letter to Sassoon (which Owen repeated in a letter to his mother): 'The Battalion had a sheer time last week. I can find no better epithet; because I cannot say I suffered anything, having let my brain grow dull. That is to say, my nerves are in perfect order.'[13] It is likely that Isherwood's 'Test' complex, ingenuously and sympathetically expounded in *Lions and Shadows* (see especially pp. 77–78) as being overtly about the missed 1914 war and covertly about sex, had its lasting effect upon others of his generation. Ending the 'Journal' with this allusion to Owen, himself a victim of the airman-type, serves to throw the whole fantasy of guilt into a sharper relief.

Book III consists of 'Five Odes', patently a group of substantial poems that Auden happened to have ready at the time. But despite the occasional nature of some of them, all are relevant to the theme of the whole work: the quest for social and spiritual health. The first (called 'January 1, 1931' in CP) recounts a dream in which the events of the previous year are weighed and found wanting. It is a very personal poem (the 'savers, payers, payees' in the first stanza were originally 'Wystan, Stephen, Christopher'), establishing a mysterious connection between the poet's operation and the death of D. H. Lawrence (on 2 March 1930) and referring to various European adventures of 'Pretzel' (Stephen Spender) and 'Maverick' (Isherwood). 'The drunken Scotsman' might refer to Hugh Mac-

Diarmid's *A Drunk Man Looks at the Thistle,* which was published in
1926. The alliteration and the strange seasonal metaphors maintain a
familiar tone of fatalism and compulsion: what the poet sees in his
dream is a world of self-regard waiting for a spiritual leader. His
reticence about proposing himself as one is justified by the troop of
healers who in fact rush forward (including, in an earlier text, 'loony
Layard'), creating a chaos which breaks his dream. In the early
morning he reflects upon the relative value of a psychological
revolution and a political one, implying (rarely for Auden) that it is
time for a firm decision about the latter. The beggar (the working
class?) wants to be told why the solution to the problem is not
Communism, whose success is described metaphorically in the progress of constitutional democracy in Ancient Greece, reference
being made to the overthrow of the Corinthian tyranny in the sixth
century BC and the later ascendancy of the 'brilliant' democracy of
Athens.[14]

The second Ode (p. 81, called 'The Exiles' in CP, and dedicated to
Upward, drawing attention to the fact that he was then, like Auden,
a schoolmaster) describes life in terms of arrival at a seaside hotel,
barracks, school or sanitorium. By cunning ambiguity the extended
metaphor acquires characteristics of all four of these establishments,
the main point being that since this is life, 'These grounds are for
good, we shall grow no more.' It is a pessimistic poem, though to a
certain extent the neat alliteration and half-rhymes provide a note
of cheery acceptance even of the final atrophy:

> Grown used at last
> To having lost,
> Accepting dearth
> The shadow of death.

The third Ode (p. 85) is one of the most interesting performances in
the book and provides (particularly after the loss elsewhere of
fragments like 'Beethameer, Beethameer, bully of Britain') an
important added dimension of topical social comment and sheer
high spirits. It is addressed to John Warner, infant son of the novelist
Rex Warner, an Oxford friend, and treats him with friendly hyper-
bole as the expected spiritual leader. But though the ode is thus a

kind of parody of the central concern of the work, it is also full of a serious and valid energy of its own, doggerel for the most part (with strong echoes of Skelton and the Lawrence of *Nettles*[15]) but compelling and persuasive. Auden condemns both the proletariat ('Ugly and dirty') and the upper class ('Let's be frank a moment, fellows – they won't pass', p. 88), and he indiscriminately lumps together 'the Simonites, the Mosleyites and the ILP' (p. 92). For this he was criticized. Edgar Foxall wrote in *The Bookman,* March 1934, p. 475: 'When Auden indulges in his indiscriminate sneers at all classes he misses the point. The Labour Party may be weak and the ILP [the Independent Labour Party] insipid, but they represent the nearest point of contact with the masses. Those who worked in the Socialist movement before the first Labour Government know well that it was no mean achievement.'

Edgell Rickword (in *New Verse,* Nov. 1937) went further in seeing implications of Nazi 'degradation of women and regimentation of the Strength through Joy variety' in the following lines (p. 92):

> Living in one place with a satisfied face
> All of the women and most of the men
> Shall work with their hands and not think again.

This kind of prophecy, however, derives not from Nazism but from Lawrence (cf. *'The great mass of humanity should never learn to read and write – never'* and 'All schools will shortly be converted either into public workshops or into gymnasia', *Fantasia of the Unconscious,* pp. 83 and 77), and we have to remember the date at which it was written. Hitler was still a 'false-alarm' (he did not come to power until January 1933) and Mosley was only recently thought of as a future Socialist Prime Minister. Some of Auden's poems (e.g. *Poems,* 1930, No. xxii) are apprehensive about a proletarian revolution: the 'invalids' are to blame, and they had better do something about it. Mosley's answer (the Corporate State) did not seem immediately fascist. In June 1931 Harold Nicolson had dreams of gaining the Foreign Office through the New Party, and in December Christopher Isherwood was singing the praises of the New German Youth Movement in Mosley's *Action* ('They are sombre, a trifle ascetic and absolutely sincere. They will live to become brave and worthy citizens of their country'). To his credit, Auden is sceptical in the third Ode of the cult of youth (p. 89: 'They're most of them dummies who want their mummies') and refers slightingly to Toc H, and to Beaverbrook's Empire Crusaders (who had made a determined effort to capture the Hiking Movement). He has nothing to say for any of the political leaders of the time: England must be saved by the infant Warner, the miniature airman. All false prophets, jealous of Warner's powers, must be discredited and the real Lawrentian revolution ushered in, 'The official re-marriage of the whole and part'.

Some of the false prophets are not clearly identifiable. For Miss Belmairs and Moxon, see *Lions and Shadows* (pp. 104 and 111). I suspect that the 'bigger magician' was originally 'bugger magician', for when the poem appeared by itself in *Whips and Scorpions,* ed. Sherard Vines (1932), the word was replaced by asterisks. 'Pooty' is mid-Victorian slang for 'pretty', and 'piss-proud' means having false erections due to the desire to urinate (it was an eighteenth-century term, used especially of an old man who marries a young wife). Auden almost certainly found it in Eric Partridge's 1931 edition of Francis Grose's *A Classical Dictionary of the Vulgar Tongue,* a work which accounts for a good deal of obsolete slang in the ode. From it come, for instance, 'rufflers' ('notorious rogues pretending to be maimed soldiers or sailors'), 'member-mugs' (chamber-pots) and 'quarrons' (bodies). Grose has succeeding entries 'Piss Prophet' and 'Piss-proud'. See also 'Lord Lobcock' and 'like a tantony pig' in 'O for doors to be open' (CSP, p. 87).

Auden's images of the new life at the close of this ode are typical of his stylistic sureness of touch:

> Falcon is poised over fell in the cool,
> Salmon draws
> Its lovely quarrons through the pool.

The abbreviations intensify nature: without the article, these creatures cease to be mere species and impress their tangible qualities (we use the same process to talk of them as food). The Hopkinsian 'lovely' looks like a risk, but attached to 'quarrons' it comes off beautifully: the cliché and the obsolete thieves' slang justify each other, and the lines typify a perhaps not often remarked characteristic of *The Orators* in both its verse and its prose, that of its continual leaning towards the observed lyrical moment.

The fourth Ode (p. 94, dedicated to his pupils, and called 'Which Side am I Supposed to be On' in CP) extends the ambiguity of school and barracks to be found in the second Ode. His pupils are recruits on the side of repression, the schoolmasters merely veteran pupils perpetuating the legends and secrecy which maintain morale in their conflict against the 'They' who operate beyond the frontier. 'We' are the imperialists, the self-righteous ('When the bishop has blessed us'), but the imagery of class war is partly a metaphor, of course: what Auden is alluding to here is the divided psyche, the repressive Censor and the rebellious Id. It appears from stanzas 9ff that it is the Censor's fault that the Id is inspired by the Seven Deadly Sins to its heroic rebellion. The blinkered, defensive, 'frontier-conscious' routine of the Censor is contrasted with the suicidal determination of the Id to make itself felt, and Auden characteristically quotes some famous lines from the Old English poem *The Battle of Maldon* to make the point (ll. 312–13, 317–19):

> Hige sceal þe heardra, heorte þe cenre,
> mod sceal þe mare, þe ure maegen lytlað
>
> *   *   *
>
>   . . . fram ic ne wille,
> ac ic me be healfe minum hlaforde,
> be swa leofan men, licgan þence.

> 'Thought shall be the harder, heart the keener, courage the greater, as our strength grows less.' '. . . I will not leave, but by the side of my lord, so dearly loved, I intend to lie.'

But there is defection from one side to the other, efforts to unify the intellect and the senses by the few able to diagnose the illness, and these 'speak of things done on the frontier we were never told'. Though the war continues, this knowledge forces the speaker to predict defeat for his side: 'We shall lie out there.'

The final Ode (p. 100) similarly reflects the dawning self-awareness of the repressors, struggling against fate. In a parody of the contorted syntax of metrical versions of the Psalms, it provides a vulnerable confession of weakness, a prayer for illumination rather than death. It is left to the 'Epilogue' to take up for the last time the possible optimism of the Quest theme, an optimism denied in the 'Prologue' and the 'Journal', but implicit in the deepest insights of the book, particularly in the thematic development of the odes: in the way in which the internally felt loss and defeatism of Nos. I and II passes through the boisterous optimism of No. III to become the externally seen defeat of Nos. IV and V. Now, in a form similar to the folk ballad 'The Cutty Wren', Auden shows the Quest hero discarding the qualities that have hitherto hindered him – intellectualism, fear and neurosis ('reader', 'fearer' and 'horror') – and setting out with a fresh determination.

The Orators is not an easy work, but it is a stimulating one. Hayward's comparison with *The Waste Land* seems appropriate. Indeed, it is possible to feel that Auden involved himself in the imaginative world he had created with more ease, directness and energetic invention than Eliot did. Today, as his preface shows, he looks upon the work with amused toleration: actually, it preserves its power well, and is still surely the most significant and disturbing long poem of its era.

Part Two

THE MID-THIRTIES

4 The Plays

THE DANCE OF DEATH

As early as December 1926, Auden was deciding that 'the only remaining traces of theatrical art were to be found on the music-hall stage: the whole of modern realistic drama since Tchekhov had got to go; later, perhaps, something might be done with puppets' (*Lions and Shadows*, p. 215). His charade *Paid on Both Sides,* written in 1928, explored various kinds of dramatic symbolism and expressionism, and contained elements which he might have picked up from Berlin cabaret; but it is still very much a closet drama. It was not until 1932, when he founded the Group Theatre with Rupert Doone and Robert Medley, that the opportunity for writing plays for production actually arose, and his dramatic theories could be elaborated. Brecht may have been an influence here, but not an overriding one,[1] and it is clear from Auden's programme note for *The Dance of Death* that native dramatic forms (as in *Paid*) provided the most powerful stimulus for him: 'Drama is essentially an art of the body. The basis of acting is acrobatics, dancing, and all forms of physical skill. The music hall, the Christmas pantomime, and the country house charade are the most living drama of today.'[2]

Dance (1933) was patently written for Rupert Doone, who danced the main role, and the above programme note justifies the balletic nature of the piece. Actually, Auden disliked the ballet (*Lions and Shadows,* p. 215) and never wrote anything quite so experimentally terpsichorean again, though as a device for symbolizing the bourgeois death-wish and the protean roles it assumes, the part of the

Dancer is comparatively successful. The subject of the play, as is
clearly announced, is the decline of the capitalist class: the ramifica-
tions of this subject could really only be tackled in the space of thirty
pages with the use of a great deal of music-hall anecdote, potted
history and mime. On the whole, the play was not well received.
Leavis was polite but evasive (Auden was still writing for *Scrutiny*)
and concluded that the drama remained not much more than
schematic (June 1934). Kenneth Allott said in *New Verse*, Nov.
1937: 'I think it is the worst thing Auden has done.' It has been out
of print since 1953.

Actually it reads as an impressive attempt at popularizing the
Marxism in which Auden was currently interested. If it oversimplifies,
this is no greater fault than the obscurity of *The Orators*. The comic
Cockney characters planted in the audience have been attacked for
the obvious social reasons, but they are no more embarrassingly
out of Auden's range of experience and sympathy than, say, Eliot's
Cockneys in *The Rock*. The choruses have been criticized as doggerel,
but, again, this is what they are intended to be: parodies of musical
comedy (p. 8), tin-pan alley (p. 11), the popular ballad (p. 19, 33)
or the school song (p. 35).

The allegorical action is simple. The Chorus (the bourgeoisie) are
fun-loving until the Dancer (death-wish) steals their clothes (p. 11).
These are replaced with military uniforms (p. 14) by the Manager
(capitalism). Angry, and encouraged by the Audience (the proletariat), they threaten revolution, until the Announcer (nationalism)
persuades them instead to turn against 'the dictatorship of international capital' (p. 17). They agree, and beat up the Jewish Manager.
At this point they form themselves into a 'ship of England' (p. 19)
and mime a journey (reminiscent of a similar device in Brecht's
Mahagonny, Act II, scene xvi) whose progress is threatened by the
Audience, representing storm and rocks. The Dancer falls in an
epileptic fit (cf. *The Orators*) and is advised to take it easy (p. 23).
The Chorus then pursue various forms of the inner life (Lawrence's
view of the role of women is here satirized), but, as members of the
bourgeoisie, are incapable of mysticism: the climax of this part of
the play is the Dancer's attempted flight as a Pilot into 'the very
heart of Reality' (p. 28). He fails, as the Airman of *The Orators*

failed, and becomes paralysed from the feet up. The Manager feels it politic at this point (p. 31) to provide a panacea in the form of a night-club called the Alma Mater (a final nostalgic appeal to patriotism and social solidarity), and the Audience come up on to the stage. Their speech (to portray their bewilderment at this situation of being wooed by the bosses) is reflected in fragments of stream-of-consciousness prose, and literal translations, as from a phrase book, of idiomatic German phrases (e.g. 'self-understandingly' is *selbstverständlich,* 'of course'; 'I am so free' is *Ich bin so frei,* 'I don't mind if I do'; 'thou seest dreadful out' is *Du siehst schrecklich aus,* 'you look terrible'; and 'swindle not' is *schwindle nicht,* 'no kidding'). In a state of spiritedly expounded decadence and criminality (pp. 33–37) capitalism expires, and Karl Marx pronounces upon the Dancer's corpse: 'The instruments of production have been too much for him. He is liquidated.'

THE DOG BENEATH THE SKIN

Auden's next play (written in collaboration with Christopher Isherwood, but still largely his own) struck a happy balance between suggestive symbolism and myth, and direct caricature and propaganda; between doggerel, knockabout and pastiche, and some of Auden's finest lyrical and analytic poetry. *The Dog Beneath the Skin* is easily the most successful and original of the three plays written with Isherwood.[3] Curiously, it was not entirely well received at the time,[4] but it is the kind of work that improves with keeping: what may originally have seemed raw and youthful has now attained a fine period flavour.

The origins of the play are of some interest. Auden and Isherwood had already collaborated on an unpublished play called *The Enemies of a Bishop,*[5] which presented the victory of the Bishop over his enemies as a paradigm of Homer Lane's victory over false healers. Bloomfield reports Isherwood as saying that this play was based on Lampel's *Revolt in a Reformatory,* which he and Auden had seen together in Berlin, and Isherwood himself writes that they 'revised the best parts of it and used them again, five years later, in

The Dog Beneath the Skin'. Actually, Auden's earlier draft of *Dog,* called *The Chase* (a typescript of which exists in Exeter College Library, Oxford), is also largely about a revolt in a reformatory. Since it was this draft which Auden showed to Isherwood early in 1935, and upon which they collaborated, it becomes difficult to imagine what in *Dog* might have been cannibalized from *Enemies of a Bishop*. One suspects that there has been a confusion here between the two earlier plays.

The extent of the collaboration is also now uncertain. Isherwood has said: 'I always thought of myself as a librettist to some extent with a composer, his verse being the music; and I would say "Now we have to have a big speech here", you know, and he would write it' (*London Magazine,* June 1961, p. 51); but he holds that most of the play is by Auden. Bloomfield reports Auden as crediting Isherwood with 'Act I, scene ii, with the exception of the song, about half of Act II, scene i, and the Destructive Desmond episode.'[6] Since *The Chase* survives, it may be of interest to give a resumé of its action for purposes of comparison with *Dog*. The typescript presumably dates from after May 1934, when the Vicar's Sermon – which has not been typed out in the typescript and is merely referred to as 'the sermon from *Life and Letters'* – appeared in that magazine under the title of 'Sermon by an Armament Manufacturer'.

The Chase

ACT I

Chorus: Cf. *Dog,* p. 11. Mr Fordham is automating his mine, and a strike results.

Scene i: Introduces the Vicar, and three newspapermen whom he tells of the missing heir. The newspapermen describe the principal of the Reformatory, Augustus Bicknell (the name is made up of Auden's father's second name and his mother's maiden name). The texture is similar to that of *Dog,* including in this scene pantomime doggerel, parody of Kipling and a song-and-dance.

Scene ii: The Reformatory. George and Jimmy are new arrivals. The Vicar distributes moral largesse, but the boys are ready to revolt ('2nd Boy:

We demand der free air. Der zunlicht. 4th Boy: Good ole Fritz'). Introduces Bicknell and Sergeant Bunyan, who plays the O'Grady game. Bicknell is sanctimonious. George and Jimmy escape.

Scene iii: 'Curtains open at the top of the Cyclorama, disclosing the Witnesses, old men identical in nightshirts and night caps' (cf. *Dog*, p. 15).

Scene iv: The Vicarage. The Vicar's cook tells him he must have a cold supper because she is helping with the strike meeting. The Vicar indulges in a fantasy about the First World War, and stumbles on George and Jimmy who are hiding in the garden. Encouraged to help them by the Witnesses, the Vicar distracts Sergeant Bunyan's attention while they dress up in the toolshed as a dog and a woman. There is then an interlude in which the Prompter apologizes for the delay, and the Conductor consults him about names he can't read of those to appear in the heir-finding ceremony.

Scene v: Cf. *Dog*, p. 17. The Vicarage Garden. The Vicar introduces 'Miss James' (Jimmy) to Bicknell as his secretary-chauffeur. Alan Norman is chosen to find the missing heir, and is given the dog (George). The second newspaperman is drunk. Mildred Luce delivers her diatribe (cf. *Dog*, p. 31). Alan departs.

ACT II

Chorus: Cf. *Dog*, p. 117, the Act III chorus beginning 'A man and a dog are entering a city'.

Scene i: Cf. *Dog*, p. 120, Act III, sc. i. The Ninevah Hotel. Miss Vipond tells the hotel to let the dog stay. Alan goes to her room.

Chorus: 'Fordham has answered with a lock out.'

Scene iia: A picnic in a deserted mine. No news of Alan. Bicknell woos 'Miss James'. General Hotham and Hayboy (a research chemist) talk about the presumption of the lower classes. The Vicar answers them with the speech 'You too are patients' (printed in *New Verse*, Feb. 1935).

Scene iib: Iris waits for news, sings 'Seen when night was silent' (cf. *Dog*, p. 65). The Witnesses appear as explorers.

Scene iic: Bicknell protests love to 'Miss James'. Sergeant Bunyan says that there is trouble at the Reformatory: the boys are off to the strike meeting.

Scene iii: Cf. *Dog*, p. 138, Act III, sc. iv. The epithalamium at the Ninevah Hotel. The dog discovers a letter from Francis Crewe, the missing heir, to Miss Vipond saying that he's been shot during street fighting at the Power House. The Witnesses appear at a toll-gate ('The way be careful to remember is never lost/But to our tolls for upkeep you must pay the cost').

Chorus: The strike continues. Jimmy is with the strikers.

Scene iv: A concert at the Reformatory. 'Miss James' gives out prizes (and asks the winners if they are ready with keys, bombs, barbed wire, etc.). He is taken away by the police.

ACT III

Chorus: Cf. *Dog*, p. 155.

Scene i: The dog (in front of a drop representing a slum street) asks the audience who he is. 'Undergraduate: You're a s-s-symbol of M-M-M-Marx and Lenin? . . . Dreadfully clever little girl: You're the dog. George: Bravo.'

Scene ii: The Police Station. Alan is brought in. The Police are called out to a demonstration at the Power House. A policeman brings Alan workman's clothes. Dialogue between Alan's feet (cf. *Dog*, p. 112). George tells Alan about Francis's letter.

Scene iii: Outside the Infirmary. Alan says good-bye to George.

Scene iv: The operating theatre. Operation on Francis Crewe (cf. *Dog*, p. 104), who dies ('Francis: Be true, be true/To Pressan. She/Will teach you what to be'). The police charge the crowd offstage.

Chorus: Cf. *Dog*, p. 111.

Scene v: The Vicar says Jimmy has been shot while trying to escape, and expresses impartiality (cf. the Curate's speech in *Dog*, p. 175). The General wants reinforcements to attack traitors in the Reformatory, and asks the Vicar to preach a sermon to the audience 'to call 'em round'. The Vicar refuses and is arrested. The sermon (the General's 'special record') is played from a gramophone, while recruits pour on to the stage. The Reformatory is stormed; a machine-gun covers the audience, shooting down Alan as he runs through the auditorium. He dies in front of Iris. The Reformatory is fired, and Mildred Luce exults.

Chorus: 'If we end to-day with the apparent triumph of reaction or folly: there is an alternative ending/And the choice is your own' (cf. *Dog*, p. 179).

The Chase is evidently, with its involved interrelation of plots, a politically more ambitious play than *Dog,* but it has a far less interesting dramatic texture and range, even though it similarly bulges with theatrical devices. This is probably due to a sharp division of interest between the reformatory revolt and the search for the missing heir. Moreover, the relation of both these themes to the industrial unrest in the background is sketchy in the extreme, though it is intended to provide the point behind the violent and pessimistic climax to the play. The answer lay in telescoping the plots: thus, in *Dog,* George, Jimmy and Bicknell disappear, and Francis Crewe himself becomes the dog who accompanies Alan Norman. Although this telescoping means that the action of *Dog* is compelled to become much more episodic than that of *The Chase*, it also provokes the central message of the play in its new form: that only by an act of imaginative sympathy and self-abnegation (becoming the dog) can the hero come to understand his predicament and escape from it. Francis is the real Leader of the play. The new title (provided by Rupert Doone) emphasizes the centrality of this developed idea.

The dedicatory quatrain may be found in the BM Notebook, fol. 85, a page much influenced by Blake. It invokes the revolutionary as a healer or a poet, who, in his anatomy of a corrupt society, comes to understand the powerful role played by the bourgeoisie ('the genteel dragon'), just as Francis Crewe comes to see through the villagers of Pressan Ambo.

The opening chorus is in Auden's characteristic panoramic-descriptive mode, with imagery developed to a musical simplicity and accuracy that was to become more and more common in his middle period. Its initial idyllic appeal to a genuine love for England provides a perfect dramatic contrast to the agricultural desolation and chaotic proliferation of exurbia which is described in the second part. This is the landscape of decadent capitalism grinding slowly to a halt, the outward manifestation of an inner anxiety which is presented in the semi-choruses as the insomnia of the young men from among whom is about to be chosen a hero to undertake the Quest for the missing heir.

The Witnesses who play such a large role in *The Chase* as representatives of Necessity are reduced here (p. 15) to one embodiment only: they appear as the chorus leaders who conclude the chorus by singing eight of the ten stanzas of Part III of the long poem called 'The Witnesses', published in *The Listener* in July 1933. This poem elaborates and explains the function of the Witnesses 'to curse and bless'. It describes the despair of a hero who discovers that he is 'not the truly strong man': his exploits, therefore, though heroic, have

been in vain, for the Witnesses are displeased. Like the Watchers
(see CSP, p. 52), they represent for Auden a mysterious duality
which is a governing principle of human life (see also *The Orators,*
p. 34, with its overtones of Lawrence's cosmology as expounded in
Chapter 13 of *Fantasia of the Unconscious*). Although in their full
role in *The Chase* they attain a playful Cocteauesque humour (there
is much play with telephones and motor-bicycles), they plainly
allow Auden to pursue his developing interest in the numinous. As
Necessity and Time ('the clock'), therefore, they create for the
guilty Quest hero (the restless neurotic or radical bourgeois) an
atmosphere of indefinable menace which Auden evokes with
allusions to the plagues of Egypt, Birnam Wood coming to Dunsi-
nane and the Scissor Man from *Struwwelpeter*.

The action begins in 'a musical comedy or pantomime village
garden' (stage direction from *The Chase*), with the stereotyped
characters introducing themselves in verses reminiscent both of
Gilbert and Sullivan and of the doggerel of Lyceum pantomimes in
the 'thirties.[7] When Alan Norman is chosen to find Sir Francis
Crewe, the chorus invoke Love (p. 26: 'Enter with him', called
'I shall be Enchanted' in CP, and 'Legend' in CSP) to accompany
him on his quest. Love is seen as the archetypal bewitched fairy-
tale figure who accompanies the hero, helping him with his tasks,
and then demands to be sacrificed in order that he may return to his
real shape (cf. *The Frog Prince*). In this sense, therefore, the 'love'
of the chorus is (*a*) the quality that the successful hero needs in order
to pacify the Witnesses; and (*b*) the dog, Francis, the real hero who
assists Alan, and who is seen sniffing about, being kicked and patted,
throughout the chorus. On page 28, incidentally, it is still being
called George (see my synopsis of *The Chase,* above). Mildred
Luce's speech embodies the kind of vengeance that Auden was
writing about in *Paid on Both Sides:* her vain appeal to her watch
shows that the Witnesses ('we are the clock') are not responsive to
such vindictiveness.

Alan's journey has all the inconsequential logic of a dream. Indeed,
some of the scenes suggest the direct influence of Lewis Carroll:
compare the King of Ostnia with the King of Hearts (p. 46) or the
Poet with Humpty Dumpty (pp. 94ff). Alan's naïvety and obstinacy

are exactly suited to the kind of revue-sketch world he moves
through. The didactic point of these scenes is clear enough, so that
Auden is able to concentrate his more complex elaboration of their
relation to his theme into the choruses which punctuate them. The
scene is the Europe of the inter-war period, typified by Ostnia,
a corrupt East European monarchy, and Westland, a fascist dictatorship, countries which were to reappear in the later Auden and
Isherwood plays.

The scene on the boat where Alan meets the two Journalists was
written by Isherwood (except for the Cowardesque song 'They're
in the racket, too'). With its neat and very conventional characterization, its well-observed dialogue which isn't afraid to take
ironic short cuts across the pages of middle-brow fiction, and its
continual undercurrent of light farce, this scene sets the general tone
of the play. The description of Ostnia, for instance (p. 38), creates an
expectancy of something not far removed from the Fredonia of the
Marx Brothers film *Duck Soup*. Indeed, the whole scene in the
Palace at Ostnia (p. 46), with its parody of the Mass, and the King's
fussy, apologetic execution of the workers, has a violence and
offhand illogicality reminiscent of the Marx Brothers. And yet in the
introductory chorus (p. 43) Auden holds up Ostnia and Westland as
serious types of contemporary capitalist communities, whose follies
are similar to England's, and whose poverty, expanding 'like an
air-bubble under a microscope slide', will soon affect England's
'treasure and . . . gentlemanly behaviour'. The old man 'of the
sobriquet of Tiger senilely vain' is Clemenceau, whom, in a review in
Scrutiny (March 1933, p. 413), Auden had called a senile homicidal
maniac, and the 'naughty life-forcer in the Norfolk jacket' is
Bernard Shaw.

The King has directed Alan to Ostnia's Red Light district, and
the chorus on page 54 describes his journey through the city ('where
loyalties are not those of the family') to find it. The description here
of cruel poverty and deprivation has a force and pity which sets
the scene at the brothels (p. 57) at an ironical distance. Those who
visit the brothels are 'rebels who have freed nothing in the whole
universe from the tyranny of the mothers, except a tiny sensitive
area': the Chorus's accusation is suggestively and characteristically

phrased, and bears enough weight to allow the predicament of
Sorbo Lamb, former heir-finder turned dope-addict, to be presented
on the same cartoon level as the brothel proprietors' songs.

The following scene in the Westland lunatic asylum (about half of
which was written by Isherwood) is an evident satire on German
nationalism. Stephen Spender criticized the scene (*New Writing*,
Autumn 1938), saying that it was not frightening because the Nazis
were not really lunatics: perhaps the point is rather that the lunatics
of *Dog* are not frightening because they are not as mad as we now
know the Nazis to have been. The scene is high-spirited, not bitter,
and its prophecy of doom seems too genially dismissive. The First
Mad Lady's Song is adapted from an uncollected sonnet in *New
Verse*, October 1933.

On their way out of Westland, Alan and the Journalists encounter
the financier Grabstein, a figure probably based roughly on Sir
Alfred Mond, industrialist, politician and one of the architects of
ICI (compare 'President of the XYZ'). Auden had reviewed Hector
Bolitho's biography of Mond in *Scrutiny*, December 1933. Compare
Grabstein's 'I've founded hospitals and rest homes' (p. 88) with
Bolitho, p. 219, where a similar point is made about Mond; and
compare Grabstein's 'I've studied all the Italian Masters' with
Auden's point in his review that Mond was no artist and that his
taste for Italian painting was not relevant.

The chorus on page 91 (called 'The Cultural Presupposition' in
CP) is one of Auden's most famous poems, famous rightly for the
way it moves triumphantly from its point about man's self-consciousness and knowledge of death to its point about the dependence
of a flourishing highbrow culture upon a slaving and oppressed
proletariat. It does this not by any facile neatness or didacticism,
but by a simple rhetorical appeal to biblical authority. Auden may
have been influenced, as in other choruses in *Dog*, by Eliot's choruses
in *The Rock* (1934). More particularly, the echoes of the Beatitudes
here may have come via Owen's poem 'Insensibility', which Auden
included in *The Poet's Tongue*, published in the same year as *Dog*.

In his search for Sir Francis Crewe, Alan had been told by Grabstein to try Paradise Park.[8] The brutes that Alan meets here are all
self-deceivers. The Poet, Grabstein's son, is a Poundian egotist: he is

'the only real person in the whole world' and insists on speaking in several languages, quoting Aeschylus and Villon (a line already used by Pound in *Mauberley*). When Alan doesn't understand, the Poet is forced to speak English, and quotes Dryden. '*Cinders*' (p. 95) is the title of an early Auden poem (in *Oxford Poetry 1926*). The two lovers are similarly self-absorbed: their song is a loose variation on Lear's *The Owl and the Pussycat*, and manages to include an allusion to *Sweeney Agonistes* ('Two as one and one as two', p. 96). Neither they nor the invalids know anything about Sir Francis Crewe. The self-consciousness defined by the previous chorus, and demonstrated in Paradise Park, assumes the extreme form of absorption in disease, the Lane theory finally coming into the open in the chorus on page 102.

If disease has a psychological origin, as Lane's theory holds, it follows that conventional surgery is a waste of time. The belief 'in the physical causation of all phenomena', exposed by the parody of the Creed in the next scene, underlines the futility of the Surgeon's quasi-religious procedures (Isherwood compared an operation to a religious ceremony in *Lions and Shadows*, p. 294: perhaps this idea was his). It is hard to see how the bullet in Chimp Eagle's bowel could have a psychosomatic origin, especially as he got it during strike action at the docks (p. 100). However, in his Wagnerian duet with Alan (pp. 108–9), he knows that Francis is in England, and that he (Chimp) has forgotten his 'choice and lot' (it is Francis disguised as the dog disguised as the nurse, curiously enough, who hastens his death by giving him an injection of hydrochloric acid). Chimp thought that he could succeed by simple political action.

The night interlude which follows (pp. 111ff), though it contains two of the most striking choric passages in the play, is merely marking time on Alan's journey back to England. The dialogue between his two feet is taken from *The Chase*, now given a quasi-political point by the addition of Cockney dialect. It also attempts to maintain interest in the mystery of Francis's whereabouts, but the melodramatic confidence about the roller-skates has a limitingly Mortmere air. In the following chorus (p. 117) the hawk's eye moves in from 'Villas on vegetation like saxifrage on stone' down through the suburban 'sorrow' clinically catalogued, into the heart of the

city as Alan and the dog make their way to the Ninevah Hotel,
symbol of capitalist excess. In the vestibule he meets the two
Journalists, and the Second Journalist is given the opportunity to
sing his rhyming-slang song 'Alice is gone' (to the tune of 'Jesu, the
very thought of thee' according to *The Chase*). The restaurant scene
burlesques the sexual tyranny and (Isherwood's scene, this) the
militant philistinism of the rich: Destructive Desmond's appeal to
the cabaret audience as he is about to slash the Rembrandt is
borrowed from the presentation of Christ to the Jews, and the cry of
'Barabbas! Barabbas!'. Alan's involvement with this world is
represented by his affair with the film star, Lou Vipond. To the
accompaniment of an ironic epithalamium sung by the hotel staff,
he makes love to her as a shop-window dummy *('When the dummy
is to speak,* ALAN *runs behind it and speaks in falsetto'),* a device which
represents the isolated self-regard of conventional romance. Sex is
thus (as the speech by the dog's skin, p. 144, makes clear) merely an
'idea in the head'.

The skin represents the instinctive life, and it draws the contrast
between itself and the clock in the hall, which represents fate.
Francis's assumption of the skin (which is revealed to the audience
in this scene) is therefore essentially an attempt to break out of
duality. However, he later (p. 172) elaborates the social reasons for
it, and when he helps Alan to escape from the Ninevah Hotel in the
skin, and Alan is kicked by the Manager, says 'Ha ha! Now you
know how it feels!'

The chorus on p. 155 re-emphasizes the inevitable conditioning
and fate of the divided individual. Auden draws on Georg Groddeck's *Exploring the Unconscious* (1933) for some of the detail.
Compare 'his first voluptuous rectal sins' with 'The earliest sins . . .
are connected with the rectal tract' (Groddeck, p. 89), and 'the
greater part of the will devoted/To warding off pain from the
water-logged areas' with 'certain lower parts of the adult body
always contain an excess of fluid. . . . A great part, a very great part
of our unconscious mental energy is used up merely in warding off
pain from these water-logged places' (Groddeck, pp. 51–52). The
last notion is a particularly dotty one, since Groddeck proposed
that the water-logging was due to the effect of gravity. The chorus is

really attacking the escapism and optimism of the man who imagines
that 'five hundred a year and a room of one's own' are a sufficient
'change of heart'. In its allusion to the final sonnet in *Poems* (1930),
'Sir, no man's enemy', this probably shows a fresh awareness in
Auden of the difficulties in which the individual is involved: he
may easily be able to beware of others, whose illnesses he can
correctly ascribe to their various spiritual failings, but will he be able
to beware of himself, whose own heart whispers: 'I am the nicest
person in this room'? Two years later, in a broadcast, Auden was
still tackling solipsism in much the same terms.[9] The solution in
this chorus looks rather perfunctory: in a pastiche of the 'Give.
Sympathize. Control' passage from *The Waste Land,* Auden resorts
to an abbreviated didacticism.

Alan and Francis return to find Pressan Ambo in a fit of jingoism.
The Vicar, who with General Hotham has founded a rather Mosleyite
Boys' Brigade, delivers a sermon on the origins of sin, or more
particularly on the revolt of Satan against God, which he compares
to the growth of international Communism. His conviction that God
is on his side in this new battle develops into self-righteousness, and
the self-righteousness into hysteria. This splendid prose piece acts
as the climax of the play, evoking as it does the ironical fourth
Ode in *The Orators,* where the psycho-political struggle is suddenly seen from the side of reaction. Auden reprinted the sermon in
CP, and the view has arisen (probably due to Beach) that this means
that Auden now approves of the witch-hunting Vicar. On the contrary, a prefatory note in CP makes it plain that the subject of Auden's
satirical attack is still the same as it was when the piece appeared as
'Sermon by an Armament Manufacturer' in *Life and Letters,* or as
the General's gramophone record in *The Chase:* that is, the type of
the Super-Ego convinced that it is the Voice of God. Of course, out
of context it was bound to appear rather more of an in-group satire
than otherwise, but criticism of Auden for 'changing sides' here is
simply mistaken.

Francis reveals himself and denounces the village. He has
observed them 'from underneath', recording his observations in a
diary,[10] and did not like what he saw. With a handful of recruits
from the village he leaves to join 'the army of the other side', passing

out through the auditorium while the Journalists photograph the villagers, who have all turned into animals. Stephen Spender criticized *Dog* (*New Writing*, Autumn 1938) on the grounds that it presented 'a picture of a society defeated by an enemy whom the writers have not put into the picture because they do not know what he looks like although they thoroughly support him'. It is plain, however, just as it is plain in a work like Upward's *Journey to the Border*, that the hero joins the Communist Party. The vagueness (as in Upward) is part of the mysterious inevitability of it all, an inevitability supported by the final line of the 'Epilogue', the Marxist 'To each his need: from each his power', and by the whole drift of this deliberately grand and rhetorical chorus in which love is urged to wake from its dream and prove its vigours.[11] The play's extraordinarily lively and eclectic means to this serious end has deceived many into thinking less of it than they might. It deserves frequent revival.

THE ASCENT OF F6

The hero of *The Dog Beneath the Skin* was an innocent who led a charmed life. There was little dramatic conflict; the stage was free for incidental social satire. *The Ascent of F6*,[12] however, also written with Isherwood, is another matter: the plot (for which Isherwood was responsible) is more involved, the dramatic conflict is uppermost, and social satire is confined to the margins of the play – that is, to the boxes on either side of the stage where the main action takes place.

The hero is a man of action, and his problem is one of motivation: what lies behind Ransom's lifelong ambition to climb F6? Is he the Truly Strong Man or not? His character is based on T. E. Lawrence. his predicament owes something to Mallory's or Captain Scott's and his moods to Hamlet's, but at bottom Ransom is a character we have met before in Auden: in his attempt to deny and rationalize the powerful influence of his mother, he is merely John Nower or the airman in another guise. The influence of the mother takes a different form in *F6*: Mrs Ransom had deliberately withheld her love from

Ransom, and lavished it on his twin brother, James. Instead of this making Ransom strong and indepε dent as she had hoped, it left in him an unconscious desire to ιcplace James in his mother's affections, a desire which expressed itself in the aggressive mammary symbolism of climbing the mountain. The play was written 'very fast' (Isherwood in the *London Magazine,* June 1961, p. 51) and was dedicated, with peculiar appropriateness and without apparent irony, to Auden's brother, himself a geologist and mountaineer. The allusion to the 'stricken grove' is from Dante's *Inferno,* Canto XIII.

Ransom's first soliloquy establishes and explains his devotion to mountaineering ('the impassive embraces of this sullen rock', p. 14) as his rejection of the real world, which he finds irredeemably sordid and corrupt. Reflecting upon a passage from Dante (*Inferno,* Canto XXVI) where Ulysses is exhorting his men to undertake their last journey 'to follow virtue and knowledge', Ransom concludes that the world is not motivated by virtue and knowledge at all, but by power. Even Dante himself used his poetic gift for this purpose, 'power to exact for every snub, every headache, every unfallen beauty, an absolute revenge'. This is the Freudian view of the role of art, and it has a thematic importance at this point in the play: we cannot help reflecting throughout the action that Ransom's attempt on F6 and all it implies may in fact be an intentional symbol of the creative act of the poet.

The next few scenes sketch in the political situation that underlies the Government's desire to conquer F6 before the Ostnians. The reason is no more complex than it need be: according to native legend, the first white man to reach the summit will rule both British and Ostnian Sudoland, on whose common border the mountain lies. Power is therefore the ultimate motive: power which will satisfy a nation deprived of virtue and knowledge, symbolized by the petit-bourgeois Mr and Mrs A who act as chorus, bored and unhappy; power which will satisfy the vested interests of the politicians and generals, represented by Ransom's brother James, Lord Stagmantle, General Dellaby-Couch and Lady Isabel.

The jingoistic colonialism behind all this is perhaps too obvious, and the dialogue of the expository scene (pp. 19ff) is based largely on the clichés of the middlebrow novel ('Aha, so that's their little game', 'Look here, Ransom', and so on); but this is quite deliberate. It makes these exemplars of naked power appear clearly as stereotyped bogeys. They are only marginally more realistic than the villagers of Pressan Ambo, and only marginally less mad and threatening. They fail to persuade Ransom to undertake the expedition, even though F6 is his 'fate'. It is only when Mrs Ransom reveals how she has concealed her love for him in order to make him 'truly strong' that Ransom consents (p. 38). The rest of the first act shows how the expedition provides vicarious excitement for Mr and Mrs A (they continue to react throughout the play), and it also shows, in a passage added after the first edition, how Mrs Ransom is mysteriously influencing her son. Her song (p. 43), cannibalized from Bicknell's song to 'Miss James' in *The Chase,* Act II, scene iv, perfectly expresses her deadly possessiveness. Before she can reassert her power over Ransom, he must conquer the Demon reputed to live at the top of the mountain. Since, as we have seen, his ascent of the mountain is, as Auden later put it, 'a symbol of the *geste* . . . a symbol of the act of aggression',[13] the Demon must represent the ultimate source of responsibility for his aggressiveness: i.e., the mother who conditioned the rivalry of the brothers for her love. Ransom is therefore climbing F6 to face the past, or to obtain, like Dante, not virtue or knowledge, but revenge.

It has been presumed that the ascent was based on the Everest expedition of 1924.[14] This is probably correct, but the action also reflects aspects of Scott's expedition to the South Pole: the rivalry with the Ostnian Blavek, for instance, and the choice of companion for the final assault on the summit (compare the disappointment of Wright at not going on to the Plateau with Shawcross's jealousy of Gunn). Gunn and Shawcross are both weak characters, who conceal their weaknesses in boyish bravado and head-prefect priggishness respectively. Gunn is a compulsive stealer, too (cf. *The Orators*), and Shawcross idolizes Ransom to compensate for his own inadequacies. Lamp and the Doctor are less interesting characters, but their presence is necessary.

I believe that these four companions of Ransom's symbolize his four faculties: Intuition, Feeling, Sensation and Thought. Auden had attempted such symbolism before, and was to do so again with immense elaboration.[15] He may originally have had in mind Lawrence's four great ganglia, but in later poems the symbolism was probably suggested by Jung's *The Integration of the Personality* (1940).

In *F6*, Intuition is represented by the Doctor, vegetative and worried about his fatness; Feeling is represented by Shawcross, who is entirely motivated by his hero-worship of Ransom and his jealous hatred of Gunn; Sensation is represented by Gunn, who lives for thrills, sex and fast cars; and Thought is represented by the botanist Lamp, in single-minded pursuit of his Polus Naufrangia. By treating these faculties in isolation in this way, Auden emphasizes the expedition's representation of the imprisoned will (as the four faculties are made to say in *For the Time Being:* 'We who are four were/Once but one,/Before his act of/Rebellion;/We were himself when/His will was free,/His error became our/Chance to be'). Naturally, this symbolism is hardly one of which an audience would be aware, but it is evidently one of those classifying principles upon which Auden likes to build the development of his themes.

The allegorical pattern is reflected in the scene where they each look into the monk's prophetic crystal: the faculties desire their limited satisfactions, but Ransom himself feels called to the spiritual leadership of the multitudes of the weak and deprived (p. 54). In his following interview with the Abbot, this wish is elaborated and exposed for the self-deception that it is. If Ransom is to conquer the Demon and save mankind, he can only do so by the exercise of power ('government requires the exercise of the human will: and the human will is from the Demon', p. 58). This dilemma, according to the Abbot, admits of only one solution, and that is to renounce the world and become a monk. Ransom, however, has gone too far already merely to 'return to England and become a farm labourer or a factory hand' (alluding to T. E. Lawrence). Ransom provokes the Abbot to admit that he himself, as ruler of the monastery, has not succeeded in making a complete abnegation of the will, and is in fact subject to visitations of the Demon. Jung's *Commentary on the Tibetan Book of the Dead* (1935) is the probable source of the Tibetan funeral ritual and its meanings.

Ransom is in a quandary: he wants to climb F6, but recognizes that in doing so he will be playing a corrupt and spurious role. On the other hand, how can he be certain that renunciation of the will is not in itself an act of the will, a subservience to the Demon? Ransom's appeal to 'the history and the creator of all these forms in which we are condemned to suffer' (p. 60) reveals at this point what is an essentially religious despair. In the end, his 'faculties' decide for him. News comes through that Blavek and his party have reached F6 and are 'hammering the whole south face full of pitons and hauling each other up like sacks!' (p. 61), an unethical procedure which was adopted by the Germans in the 'thirties out of their intensely nationalistic competitiveness. Gunn, Lamp, Shawcross and the Doctor (the faculties) are outraged and excited. They now want to beat Blavek. Ransom (the will) wearily concludes: 'Very well then, since you wish it. I obey you. The summit will be reached, the Ostnians defeated, the Empire saved. And I have failed' (p. 62). This whole scene (II.i) was one of the most heavily revised: the revisions effectively turn a number of verse passages into prose, elaborate the Abbot's offer and clarify Ransom's predicament.

The action is now comparatively straightforward until the *dénouement*. Ransom plays Hamlet to a discovered skull (p. 67), which provides opportunities for dramatic irony ('those to whom a mountain is a mother') and a potted history of mountaineering. Horace de Saussure (1740–99) was the creator of scientific mountaineering; for 'Balmont' read 'Balmat', the Swiss guide who accompanied Dr Michael Paccard on his conquest of Mont Blanc (Marc Bourrit jealously exaggerated Balmat's part in the climb); W. F. Donkin and Henry Fox were lost in 1888 attempting Mount Dychtau in the Caucasus; Edward Whymper conquered the Matterhorn in 1865 after many attempts (Hadow slipped on the way down, and four of the climbers were killed); and the 'pair . . . whom Odell saw' were George Leigh-Mallory and Andrew Irvine, last seen on 6 June 1924 attempting Everest (N. E. Odell was a day behind them, collecting geological specimens).

After this, an avalanche kills Lamp (Thought); Shawcross (Feeling) commits suicide; the Doctor (Intuition) is left behind; and Gunn (Sensation) finally gives up, collapsing through exposure. Though it is not a close allegory, this seems to be the right order for the loss of the faculties, and it leaves Ransom alone for another Shakespearean soliloquy (p. 83, cf. *King Lear*, III.ii. 1–9). Such a sober and dramatic moment is uneasily served by pastiche of this kind, and the uncertainty of tone is maintained in the following passage of voices from the stage boxes (compare 'Snow on the pass. Alas' with Gertrude Stein's 'Pigeons in the grass – alas' in *Four Saints in Three Acts*). Ransom himself collapses at this point (p. 86), and the remainder of the play is an expressionistic enactment of his psychological predicament, with which one might compare the central scenes of *Paid on Both Sides*. Rupert Doone once complained that all Auden's plays were resolved 'in dream' (Bloomfield, p. 17).

This fantasy presents James as a Dragon and Ransom as a Quest Hero. Ransom is imagining (p. 89) how his expedition is being exploited by his brother as a panacea for the unhappy lives of the oppressed. They play chess, and though James wins, Ransom, by an appeal to the mysteriously veiled figure on the summit, challenges the victory. James collapses, saying: 'It was not Virtue – it was not Knowledge – it was Power!' (p. 91). Ransom in his delirium is evidently wishing that his brother might die instead of him, but he blames this guilty fantasy on the veiled figure: 'It wasn't my fault! The Demon gave the sign.' That is to say, he is not responsible for the conditioning in infancy which made him jealous of his brother.

The Abbot then proceeded to judge the case, calling as witnesses the victims of the Demon: Shawcross, Gunn, Lamp and the Doctor. These do not wish to accuse (it was only the subconscious that recognized his guilty desires), and Ransom is now sorry that he has blamed the Demon. He rushes to the Demon's defence. This recognition that the Demon is of his own making (and represents his reasons for climbing the mountain) dismisses the other figures in his fantasy, and leaves him alone at last in peace with the Demon, now unveiled as his mother. He had climbed the mountain to please her, and to displace James in her affections. The final scene (with its reminiscences of *Peer Gynt*) gives him an illusory triumph at the moment of his death.

ON THE FRONTIER

The Ascent of F6 was called a tragedy, but *On the Frontier*[16] is humbly described as a melodrama. Isherwood said that 'there's more of Auden's work in *On the Frontier* than any of the plays, because he not only wrote all the poetry but also a big share of the prose' (*London Magazine,* June 1961, p. 51). Since writing *The Ascent of F6,* Auden had been to the Spanish Civil War, and much of *On the Frontier* was written while the authors were on their way to the Sino-Japanese conflict (see Isherwood, *Exhumations,* p. 141). As a bold and simple dramatization of the European situation of the time, it is undeniably their most topical play, and some critics (e.g. Francis Scarfe in *W. H. Auden,* 1949, p. 24) think it the best. But its very political awareness (its direct exposure of leader-worship, senseless preparation for war and the impotence of the man in the street) makes it less suggestive than their previous work. It is urgent, dramaturgically neat and quite sincere: but it lacks a myth. It is a play that leaves no clear images in the mind. With it, the collaboration between Auden and Isherwood (one of the most promising in theatrical history) came to an end. They later had thoughts of doing a musical based on Isherwood's *Goodbye to Berlin,* but nothing has come of the project. Auden himself, except for translations of Brecht and Cocteau, and a half-hour radio play called *The Dark Valley* (based on his earlier cabaret sketch, *Alfred*), seems to have written no other plays.

On the Frontier focuses sharply on the two imaginary countries that appear in all the Auden and Isherwood plays: Ostnia, the decadent monarchy, and Westland, the fascist dictatorship. The action takes place in the 'Ostnia–Westland room', a symbolically divided setting where the Vrodnys and Thorvalds live, the members of each family (except Anna Vrodny and Eric Thorvald) remaining unaware of those of the other; and in the house of Valerian, a cultured Westland industrialist, *éminence grise* behind the mad Leader.

The first scene establishes this Krupp-like figure as superbly authoritative and perceptive. He is a talkative Shavian character, who casually exposes his secretary as an Ostnian spy (p. 114) and goes on in a long monologue to justify the present régime and his position in it. This speech (pp. 116ff) is a good example of Auden's aphoristic expository prose:

If I had been born in the thirteenth century, I suppose I should have wanted to be a bishop.

*   *   *

The world has never been governed by the People or by the merely Rich, and it never will be. It is governed by men like myself – though, in practice, we are usually rich and often come from the People.

*   *   *

Today, a creative man becomes an engineer or a scientist, not an artist. He leaves that career to neurotics and humbugs who can't succeed at anything else.

This kind of thing may be an impediment to the dramatic develop-ment of the story, but it does establish Valerian as someone in whom one is interested, and this can be said of hardly any other character in the play, not even Eric and Anna (who are much more conven-tional than their prototypes John and Anne in *Paid on Both Sides,* and seem merely functional).

Indeed, the roles of Eric and Anna, by approaching the symbolic, stand out uneasily in the context of the scrupulously naturalistic and antiphonal Vrodny-Thorvald scenes. Eric's pacifism provides no occasion for a predicament, so that his love for Anna emerges as a grateful objective correlative for a solution which has no real political meaning: 'We found our peace/Only in dreams' (p. 190). Similarly, the psychological motivation behind the puppet leader (a peasant tamed by Rameau), or behind the storm-trooper Grimm who is finally goaded to the point of killing Valerian, has a simplicity and obviousness which does not attain conviction. Only Valerian, magnificently calm and cynical in a disintegrating world, is con-ceived with a genuine imaginative control of both his political function and his personal values, his public and his private face. And even so, the character remains largely on the level of caricature, perhaps so witty and ironical only because the play would otherwise have no real intellectual or choric centre.

The actual choruses are more brief and more detached from the main action than in the earlier plays, though they provide a skilfully varied comment from an important social class not otherwise represented in the play, the dissident proletariat. The first chorus, of workers (p. 111), uses the same rhythmical formula for its refrain as the later 'Refugee Blues' (CSP, p. 157); but, in accordance with its function as a text for music, it is much less expressive, and its very flatness mirrors the weary desperation of industrial regimentation. The next chorus, of prisoners (p. 128), echoes the repressed defiance of the first in terms which are prophetic without being particularly convincing or inspiring. The rather tired allusion to Shelley's *Mask of Anarchy* in the third chorus, of dancers (p. 153), similarly suggests that working-class resistance is based on slogans rather than on intelligence or energy. It seems to take the outbreak of war to stir them to action. The fourth chorus, of soldiers (p. 171), is much the most sympathetic, and much the most satisfying poetically. The fifth chorus, of newspaper readers (p. 186), is merely another variation on the rival radios of the scenes in the Ostnia-Westland room.

The final impression of the play is that the millions who suffer are not in control of their destiny, and that despite the broadly Marxist terms of the political analysis, the 'full flower and dignity of man' will not be attained without the 'will of love' (p. 191). As agents of that will, Eric and Anna dwell uneasily within the brisk realism of their dramatic context, and the tone of their final *Liebestod* points forward – in its stylistic gestures towards emotion, as distinct from a stylistic embodiment of emotion – to the medium of opera.

5 Poems 1933–1938

During this period, Auden taught in a school in Gloucestershire, worked in the theatre and in films, and began to travel extensively, particularly in Belgium, Spain, Iceland and China. A developing interest in an historical, rather than a psychological, view of man facilitated his slow return to Christianity. Many of the poems are lyrical, biographical or topographical, concerned with popularizing ideas met with before in his work, such as the Freudian theory of art as compensation, or the Lane theory of psychosomatic illness. And most important of all, there seems to be a deliberate attempt to broaden the appeal of his poetry by experimenting with a variety of traditional and popular forms.

'A Summer Night' [*Listener,* 7 March 1934; LS; CP, p. 96: 'A Summer Night 1933'; CSP50; CSP, p. 69], in its consideration of the continued opposition of the private and the public worlds, is a key poem. In his introduction to Anne Fremantle's book *The Protestant Mystics* (1964), p. 26, Auden refers, as an example of the Vision of Agape, to 'an unpublished account for the authenticity of which I can vouch.' The quoted account begins: 'One fine summer night in June 1933 I was sitting on a lawn after dinner with three colleagues, two women and a man . . .', and tells of a mystical sense of a communal awareness shared by them on the occasion. It then goes on to say: '. . . and among the various factors which several years later brought me back to the Christian faith in which I had been brought up, the memory of this experience and asking myself what it could mean was one of the most crucial.' The account in several points would thus seem to fit Auden's own circumstances, and may well be his own. This poem relishes such a magical moment with a full consciousness that it is the privilege of those 'whom hunger does not move', and weighs present harmony against future change, that 'crumpling flood' soon to 'force a rent . . . through dykes of our content'. Auden is still thinking of social revolution: the poem proposes that the (largely erotic) delights it describes will always be the objective of men, as natural as heredity (stanza 11) and powerful to assuage the violence which will necessarily come to an unjust world.

'Paysage Moralisé' [*Criterion,* July 1933; LS; CP, p. 47; CSP 50; CSP, p. 71] is Auden's second published sestina. William Empson had complained that the capacity to conceive such a large form as the sestina as a unit of sustained feeling had been lost since the age of Sidney, whose double sestina in the *Arcadia* he was discussing (*Seven Types of Ambiguity,* 1930, Chap. 1). This poem of Auden's (sharing two of its six key words with Sidney's) looks like a conscious effort to rebuff Empson. However, as with the earlier sestina in *The Orators* (p. 46), the complex exploration of the concepts embodied in the key words is allegorical rather than emotional: the poem is an ingenious exercise in the suggestiveness of multiply defined symbols. One could say that the *valleys* and *mountains* are the female and male principles (like Lawrence's moon and sun) which govern human behaviour: the *valleys* representing the protection, maternal or erotic, of the womb; the *mountains* the phallic motif of the Quest. *Water* represents those creations of man which satisfy his sense of purpose, particularly art. *Islands* represent the individual's possibility of escape from society (which is itself represented by the *cities*). *Sorrow* represents the condition of man, his motivating passion.

'O What is that Sound' [*New Verse,* Dec. 1934; LS; CP, p. 222; CSP 50; CSP, p. 72] is a much anthologized and compelling ballad whose point lies in one's presumption that the eighteenth-century soldiery were as likely as not to be the instruments of repression, and that therefore the second speaker of the poem is an honest rebel, for whom the cause of continued resistance is more important even than the girl he loves (the situation might be imagined as taking place at any time between the first Jacobite uprising and the American War of Independence). The rebel's scale of values is not approved by Auden, however, and the poem is thus an important political comment appropriate to his developing emphasis on love and individual values. The contemporary application is obvious, and the poem's success is built upon the way this application lurks teasingly within the simple musicality and accumulating menace of the pastiche.[1]

'Our Hunting Fathers' [*Listener*, 30 May 1934; LS; CP, p. 95: 'In Father's Footsteps'; CSP50; CSP, p. 74] consists of two stanzas, each of which is made up of a single sentence: the total effect is of an immensely involved couplet. It is an intellectual statement of some complexity, and the effect is somewhat deceptively formalized by the elaborate prosody and orotund Yeatsian diction (the poem acted as the epilogue to Britten's eponymous symphonic cycle of 1936, though its obscurity makes it an odd choice as a text for music). The poem contrasts two views of love. The first stanza shows how in the eighteenth and nineteenth centuries it was felt to be the driving power which, tempered by reason, provided the individual with his basic motivation. It is like Pope's Ruling Passion, or Shaw's Life Force. The animals are to be pitied because in them the quality is innocent and undirected: only man can consciously put it to a purpose. The second stanza develops the modern view that love is, on the contrary, not a noble force at all, but one to be denied because it inevitably leads to the guilt of individualism and self-regard. 'His southern gestures modify' means to sublimate love's genital impulses into not a selfish love, but a universal, social love.[2] Thus the stanzas contrast reason's collaboration with reason's modification, individualism with collectivism, Victorian *laissez-faire* with the Communist revolution.

'Through the Looking Glass' [*New Verse*, Feb. 1934; LS; CP, p. 113; CSP50; CSP, p. 74], which is about the conflict between the two conventional pitfalls of love, demonstrates Auden's developing clarity and abundance of invention. The poet finds himself at Christmas forced to a radical assessment of his emotional commitment. The person he loves has issued some kind of ultimatum (stanza 1), and the poet reflects that he must respond by discovering what kind of love he really wants. Is it the self-demanding, egotistical love of dreams, in which the lover becomes only a mirror-image ('the heaven of failures', stanza 2) and acts as an eccentric piece of furniture in a basically womb-like family ambience (stanza 3)? Or is it a loyal and devoted love, in which the family are forced to take a back seat (stanzas 4 and 5)? The latter is asserted ('which I say you rule'), but in its pretended denial of a sexual motive is revealingly totalitarian. Between these two possibilities, selfish indulgence and total commitment, the poet is lost in his dreams. He is a 'would-be lover who has never come/In a great bed at midnight to your arms', and who can perpetually delude himself through his pride that his self-love is a satisfactory substitute for this, even the occasion for congratulation (stanza 6).

The final stanzas, with their beautiful images of life as a journey by sea in which all landmarks have been lost, break away from this dilemma. It is the poet's very self-consciousness which is likely to be his ruin: if you try to steer in a storm, you will break your rudder. Better to let the storm blow itself out, and you may still reach your destination, 'The birth of natural order and true love', with the two worlds of lover and family peaceably united.

'Two Climbs' [*New Oxford Outlook*, Nov. 1933; LS; CP, p. 41: 'The Climbers'; CSP50; CSP, p. 76] similarly contrasts the claims of lover and family. Clearly, the 'climbs' in this allegorical sonnet represent both an escape from the drab bourgeois world of petty authority and spiritual malaise, and an attempt to discover and face a greater reality. On his own, the poet fails: the mountains of his quest represent his own angst, and they torment him. He comforts himself by indulging in a form of living of the very kind he was trying to escape from. In love, however, the escape was easy, except that it was a deceptive escape: together the lovers felt themselves self-sufficient, and refused to face the real implications and possibilities of life. The suggestion is that their love was still a form of self-regard. They saw each other's eyes (reflecting themselves) and thus, as in a mirror, appeared 'left-handed' (compare the previous poem, 'Through the Looking-Glass'). The symbolism of the mountains is, as in 'Paysage Moralisé', partially erotic.

'Meiosis' [*New Verse*, Oct. 1933; LS; CP, p. 79; CSP50; CSP,

p. 77] was originally the last in a sequence of five love sonnets. It elaborates, with a full biological symbolism, the theory lurking in so many poems of this period that love can be essentially a selfish and predatory force, working to obstruct the free and natural development of society. The lover is ensnared by his struggle 'to possess Another' because he imagines that his goal *is* possession, whereas the final purpose ('the snare') is forgotten in the pleasure of orgasm ('their little death', cf. *la petite mort*).

This purpose is the evolutionary development of the species, advanced by the cycles of reproduction which 'love' controls. Auden addresses the spermatozoon which has been set free by the love that it has never heard of, and which can now 'set up building', i.e. impregnate the ovum. Behind this act of the spermatozoon lies the whole of human history, which has, in a biological sense, only been a preparation for it ('Cities and years constricted to your scope'). At this moment the condition of man ('sorrow', cf. 'Paysage Moralisé', CSP, p. 71) is reduced to a single impulse of fertilization: it is in this act that the future of the human race resides. And yet, when the fertilized egg is born and grows up, human history and human desire will once again seem as complex as before ('Shall be as subtle when you are as tall'), since the son will share all the delusions about love that the father was seen to have had at the beginning of the poem. But not quite all, the poem concludes, since evolution works continually to improve the race: the life force ('The flood on which all move and wish to move') cannot be impeded by individual selfish demands of love ('Hopeful falsehood').

The title 'Meiosis' (first given in CP) has occasioned some confusion. John Bayley (in *The Romantic Survival,* p. 165) takes it to mean rhetorical understatement; Robert Bloom (in *Shenandoah,* Winter 1967, p. 31) takes it in its rarer genetic sense as the process of chromosome reduction in gametes which are undergoing maturation. It is evident that both meanings may be fairly applied, though the genetic sense provides a reason for believing that the son may be superior to the father, since as Bloom points out, the spermatozoon only carries half the male chromosomes, and may therefore very well carry the better half. That Auden had the genetic sense in mind is borne out by the BM Notebook, fol. 11, which contains a diagram contrasting meiosis with mitosis in their psychological implications. The diagram is followed by the conclusion: 'The course of every natural desire is that of the orgasm. Being satisfied they desire their own death.' This comment provides a very good gloss on the sonnet.

'A Misunderstanding' [*Bryanston Saga,* Summer 1934; LS; CP, p. 72: 'Nobody Understands Me'; CSP50; CSP, p. 77], like the previous two sonnets, clearly contains allusions to a love situation whose possibilities of spiritual enrichment seem thwarted by the compulsive psychological demands of its own machinery. And yet, unlike the other two, it is not self-evidently a 'love' poem. It describes the elusive sense of *déja vu* of dreams: the garage-boy, the botanist and the deaf girl symbolize that power of the external world to conspire with the individual's intuition of the ordained, which itself is a metaphor for the experience of falling in love. This meaning is made evident in the sestet, where the lovers' roles are not clearly understood: which is the strong partner? Each looks to the other, and (it is suggested) is disappointed.

By contrast, the last line quite strongly suggests a context of the psycho-political (compare 'physician, bridegroom and incendiary' with the 'lancet, speech or gun' of the dedicatory poem to *The Dog Beneath the Skin,* a roughly contemporary piece which is quite clearly about the individual's possible resources against a dangerous and corrupt society). But the characteristic triad is also suggestive of Father, Son and Holy Ghost, which could be interpreted to mean that the central figure is suffering from a form of religious mania. If this is indeed the poem's basic metaphor, the 'green chateau' could be a mental home, and the girl would appear to be deaf because she is a nurse trained to ignore the ravings of the patients. The sestet would then refer to his therapeutic sessions at the mental home. Such an interpretation would explain the ambiguity and obscurity of a verbally simple and striking poem. In a sense, any interpretation of the poem's vehicle that made a story out of its mood of mystery and anxiety would support the ultimate tenor which so strongly seems to involve a personal relationship.

'Who's Who' [*Rep,* April 1934; LS; CP, p. 17; CSP50; CSP, p. 78] was perhaps prompted by Auden's contemporary review of

Basil Liddell Hart's biography of T. E. Lawrence (*Now and Then,* No. 47, Spring 1934). This sonnet examines the real nature and desires of the popular hero, desires which, like Lawrence's, are seen finally to be for the ordinary and the mundane. The idea that the hero is a perfectly average man (the innocent youngest son, in fact) is very common in Auden. Sonnet XVI of 'The Quest' is a development of the idea.

'Schoolchildren' [*Listener,* 21 July 1937: 'Hegel and the School-children'; AT; CP, p. 52; CSP50; CSP, p. 78] is rather later in date than its context here suggests. After Auden's visit to Spain early in 1937, he returned for the summer term to Downs School, Colwall, where he had previously taught. This perhaps explains the idea of the two kinds of captivity developed in the first stanza: the world of the second Ode in *The Orators* is being reassessed; the schoolmaster has seen a real war. The poem's urgency and simplicity of style underlines the direct emotional nature of its statement.

The poem's original title explains many of the ideas in the poem about the merely potential freedom of the child: 'the bars of love are so strong' and 'the tyranny is so easy' because, according to Hegel's *Philosophy of Right,* it is through love and obedience that the groundwork of the ethical character is laid in childhood. The aim of education is to enable the child to stand by itself, and to become a free personality. The purpose of authority is to cancel itself. The pathos of this process is very delicately delineated by Auden. Relevant, too, is the Freudian notion of infantile sexuality: 'the professor's dream is not true' (originally 'the dream of the don . . .') perhaps refers to Lewis Carroll's obsession with the child's innocence. The dream is not true, because 'the sex is there'. Auden is question-ing the validity of Hegelian education in the light of a real 'rebellion': how can the child become a free personality, as Hegel professed, when the educators are themselves 'condemned' and unable to become free? How can the child's touching trust and fidelity ever of itself germinate 'the new life', when adults themselves are unable to break loose from the easy tyranny?

'May' [*Listener,* 15 May 1935; LS; CP, p. 214; CSP50; CSP, p. 79] shows much of Auden's skill with the precisely suggestive epithet and bold image; Auden's genius for parading dense meaning in the pictorial lyric reached a high point in the mid-thirties. Spring is conventionally regenerating, and here seems to symbolize a dawning of maturity ('The real world lies before us'), both personal and historical. On the personal level, the awakening is sexual. The ambiguous grammar of 'light' in line 1, and the double meaning of 'vessel' (implying both yachts in the sun, and tumescence), give to the 'careless picnics' a particularly erotic flavour. Stanza 2 shows that the idyll is predicated by the historical landscape, by the escape from the medieval forests and by the *felix culpa* of the enlightenment ('The dangerous apple taken'), and therefore is an illusory one: this is because the 'real world' is now one in which the subconscious motive is understood, and love no longer compellingly self-sufficient. The neuroses laid bare in the third stanza lurk behind the natural impulses in the fourth stanza to bring home the insufficiency of those natural urges: these cannot account for the lost world of traditional morality represented earlier by the fairy-tale 'angel vampires'. The freedom gained is seen as debilitating: the psychologically ill are only 'willing' to recover, the picnics are 'careless', because sex has become a recurrent panacea, an indulgence.

'A Bride in the 30's' [*Listener,* 20 Feb. 1935; LS; CP, p. 36; CSP50; CSP, p. 80] elaborates in a wider personal and public context the preceding poem's conclusion: 'Before the evil and the good/How insufficient is/Touch, endearment, look.' The poem explores this insufficiency by showing that love both retreats from the world of public morality and is yet, half-aware, the creator of it. It is easy to feel that love has no responsibility to its environment (stanzas 2 and 3) and exists for itself alone. Even so, love brings an alertness, an enlarged sensibility (stanza 4) that cannot avoid contemplating the real world (stanzas 5 and 6), from which images like newspaper photographs press in upon the rapt lover. Stanza 7 asserts that society is conditioned by the will of the individual, that Hitler and Mussolini and the rest are somehow the product of the inadequate and stunted private love, and that the child's conditioning narrows his choice and puts limits to his natural desires (stanzas 8 and 9). In such a situation it is imperative that the individual should be aware of the deep division between his private desires and the public good which should result from them. Erotic love is insufficient because it does not care (and Auden wishes it did) if its object is Lubbe or Hitler, scapegoat or tyrant, and it is afraid to recognize that man as a superior animal with a moral sense ('to whom the gods awarded/The language of learning, the language of love') has this power to choose, through love, the kind of society he wishes to have.

'On This Island' [*Listener,* 18 Dec. 1935: 'Seaside'; LS; CP, p. 214; CSP50; CSP, p. 82] is rightly famous, not only for its superb imitative and descriptive language, but for the delicately prophetic suggestions in the final stanza. The ships are engaged in 'voluntary' errands, as though coercion were soon to come, and they are like 'floating seeds' in another sense; they may themselves germinate into quite different instruments. The poem bears the same sort of relationship to Arnold's 'Dover Beach' as a postcard does to a letter. The vague echoes of Shakespeare in the first stanza reinforce the poem's sense of rediscovered Englishness (a feeling very much present in the contemporary *Dog Beneath the Skin*). The 'stranger' of the opening line may be ultimately the same as the 'stranger' of 'The Watershed' (CSP, p. 22); but he is a stranger who has a simpler, more instinctive feeling that he belongs somewhere, and may therefore respond more responsibly to the veiled warning of the last stanza.

'Night Mail' [*TPO: Centenary of the Travelling Post Office,* 1938; CSP, p. 83] was previously uncollected. In 1935 Auden worked for six months with the General Post Office Film Unit. He produced a song for the film *Coal Face* (see CSP, p. 88), this verse commentary for *Night Mail,* and played the part of Father Christmas in *Calendar of the Year.* He also wrote part of the script for *The Way to the Sea,* a film made by the Strand Film Company, which does not appear to have survived. In *Coal Face* and *Night Mail* he collaborated with Benjamin Britten, whom he first met on 4 July 1935, and with whom he also planned an abortive film project about the Negro in Western civilization.[3]

Night Mail was originally to be entitled *Scottish Mail-bag,* and was a dramatic account of the nightly journey of the postal special from Euston to Glasgow. The commentary is a striking performance, full of perceptive detail and evocative rhythms. It has probably not been realized, however, what a feat it represents, for

Auden's images did not, as in a scenario, prescribe the images on the screen: he fitted the verse to an edited version as a composer does. In 'Poetry and Film' (*Janus*, No. 2, May 1936) he was reported as saying that he 'even found it necessary to time his spoken verse with a stop-watch in order to fit it exactly to the shot on which it commented – although the pan shot does offer a means of getting the visual rhythm to follow the rhythm of the poetic line'.

'As I walked out one Evening' [*New Statesman*, 15 Jan. 1938; AT; CP, p. 197; CSP50; CSP, p. 85] has been described by Auden himself as a 'pastiche of folksong' (Spears, p. 110). This is evidently what it is, though the later sophistications of the ballad stanza (as found in, say, Burns or Housman) are clearly acknowledged, and the illusions of love are as subtly qualified as they are in other poems of Auden's in this period. The imagery in the first two stanzas, for instance, while indicating fullness and fruition (crowds as harvest wheat, the river brimming), suggests at the same time the levelling in store (the harvest to be cut down, 'brimming' not only like a cup, but as in 'brimming with tears'). The lover's vow is magnificent, but the railway arch may be intended to signify a comparatively sordid rendezvous, and anyway Time's winged chariot is hurrying near, as it must in a poem of this kind.

The imagery in this central section is typically striking, and complex without being obscure. A phrase like 'appalling snow', for instance, is literal (the snow makes the valleys pale) and yet reinvigorates a common cliché about bad weather: the careful doubleness of the epithet manages to recapture its most useful sense of 'dismaying'. The following lines, too, create a complex movement of thought: Time destroys youthful joy in two ways; it destroys actual manifestations of it in physical exuberance and prowess (in the 'dances' and in the action of the diver), and it also destroys it in the metaphor of a girl's party dress, breaking her necklace and her 'brilliant bow'. The fusion of these different images is very casually done, and in fact the phrase 'the diver's brilliant bow' is taken from *Poems* (1928) No. III. The clocks continue with their message of doom and impotence in stanza 11, introducing a world where nursery-rhyme morality has been thrown to the wind. The nursery-rhyme formula is continued in stanza 14: 'You shall love your crooked neighbour/With your crooked heart', a prescription which echoes the 'Be Lubbe, be Hitler, but be my good,/Daily, nightly' of 'A Bride in the 30's'. The conflict between the lover's ironical idealism and life's unhappy perversion from its possible ends is not resolved in the poem: the poet, hidden listener of the dialogue, is left alone, aware only of the continued flow of the river, the eternal progress of human life towards its future.

'Twelve Songs' are from Auden's best period as a writer of lyrics. No. I: ' "O for doors to be open and an invite with gilded edges" ' [*Spectator,* 31 May 1935: 'In the Square'; LS; CP, p. 219; CSP50; CSP, p. 87] is about art as wish-fulfilment. In a sense, we are all beggared cripples, and their fantasies are our fantasies. But ultimately art cannot make these fantasies real: the statue is silent. Though the poem is largely an exercise in an inventively sensual exuberance, the Yeatsian refrain and its symbolism reinforce the serious meaning of the poem. Some of the phrases come from Grose's *Classical Dictionary of the Vulgar Tongue* (see p. 72): 'lobcock' occurs there, as does 'To follow like a tantony [St Antony] pig', i.e. to follow close at one's heels.

No. II: 'O lurcher-loving collier, black as night' [*New Verse,* Summer 1938; AT: 'Madrigal'; CP, p. 220; CSP50; CSP, p. 88] is a charming poem in the Elizabethan manner, written for the film *Coal Face* and set by Benjamin Britten (see p. 107). A lurcher is a poacher's dog, used for catching rabbits and hares: the metaphor in line 4 is from hare-coursing. A version of the sixth line may be found in the last line of Act I of *The Ascent of F6*.

No. III: 'Let a florid music praise' [LS; CP, p. 213; CSP50; CSP, p. 88] demonstrates Auden's power – at its height in the mid-thirties – to expose, within the space of a brief lyric, the dreadful dichotomy between the outward and the inward impulses of love, between the positive aesthetic sense of the lover and his negative needs. It depends upon the poised diction ('florid', for instance, suggests not only the decoration of baroque music, but the healthy radiance of the loved-one's face) and upon the sense of grand public statement which the contrasted stanzas imply; but it also depends upon an uninsisted yet consistent use of metaphor which, in the Augustan manner, barely conveys its vehicle at all. Thus, Beauty's conquest of the citadel of the loved-one in the first stanza creates the terms whereby in the second stanza Death may be seen as able to reassert his power easily through the allegiance of the unloved, who have no encouragement to pay homage to beauty: 'Their secretive children walk/Through your vigilance of breath/To unpardonable Death'. The submerged metaphor is of a secret betrayal to a greater power which, in the last line of the poem, is even acknowledged by the poet. This is not merely Death in the temporal sense, but Death as a psychological state of the selfish will ('The weeping and striking') which the absence of love encourages.

No. IV: 'Dear, though the night is gone' [*New Verse,* Apr./May 1936: 'The Dream'; LS; CP, p. 200; CSP50; CSP, p. 88] presents a dream capable of the Freudian interpretation that the loved-one confessing another love must mean the unconscious desire of the lover to break off the affair himself. The pressures inherent in the situation are symbolized in the poem by the presence of the other couples, inert and hostile: though the room is timeless ('Our whisper woke no clocks'), it is crowded with beds and 'lofty as/A railway terminus', cunningly suggesting that it is here that partners are changed like trains.

No. V: 'Fish in the unruffled lakes' [*Listener,* 15 Apr. 1936; LS; CP, p. 201; CSP50; CSP, p. 89] celebrates an act of love in terms of a union of human attributes with animal ones: the beautiful animal merely acts and is gone, despite its beauty; man is self-conscious, aware of time and of the obligations of morality, envious of the animal. But the third stanza shows that man does have animal beauty, and that his conscious surrender to its powers ('voluntary love') can have a beauty of its own.

No. VI: 'Now the leaves are falling fast' [*New Statesman,* 14 Mar. 1936; LS; CP, p. 217; CSP50; CSP, p. 90] illustrates the combination, in Auden's lyric work, of musicality and pictorialism with an essentially angular and symbolical imagination. The result, as critics have remarked, reminds us of Blake. And the theme is a Blakean one, too, of the daunting and reproving bonds of environment, and of the ideal world of the imagination, 'From whose cold cascading streams/None may drink except in dreams.'

No. VII: 'Underneath an abject willow' [LS; CP, p. 232; CSP50;

CSP, p. 91], together with No. v, was set to music by Britten in
1937. It is a simple *carpe diem* injunction which reflects the predominantly tranquil and passionate mood of Auden's love lyrics
in this period. The first line is taken from *Poems* (1928), No. ii,
where in a rather less convincing mood of prophetic gloom Auden
had reflected 'how everyman/Shall strain and be undone,/Sit,
querulous and sallow/Under the abject willow'. Though it ignores
arguments about the gulf between the human and the instinctive
life which so frequently figure in Auden's poetry, this later lyric is a
pleasant attack on the lover's 'unique and moping station'.

No. viii: 'At last the secret is out, as it always must come in the
end' [*The Ascent of F6,* II.v; CP, p. 199; CSP50; CSP, p. 91] loses
a great deal out of context. As the chorus immediately preceding the
anagnorisis of *F6,* it contributed a delaying and modifying comment
on the rather melodramatic unveiling of Ransom's Demon as his
own mother. Such a Freudian secret presented chorically as a
matter of bourgeois gossip is just the kind of tonal playfulness that
lends Auden's drama its very individual kind of sophistication. The
chorus as a separate item becomes a very different kind of thing:
the 'clear voice suddenly singing', far from becoming a telling
Eliotelian symbol, seems irrevocably weighed down by all the rest of
the Agatha Christie paraphernalia.

No. ix: 'Stop all the clocks, cut off the telephone' [AT: 'Funeral
Blues'; CP, p. 228; CSP50; CSP, p. 92] is a good pastiche of the
stoical lament and flamboyant imagery of the traditional blues
lyric. Its first two stanzas (followed by different third and fourth
stanzas) may be found in *The Ascent of F6,* II. v, where Stagmantle
and Isabel lament the phantasmogoric 'death' of James Ransom.
In *Another Time* it was refurbished as one of 'Four Cabaret Songs
for Miss Hedli Anderson', along with Nos. x and xii of this group,
and 'Calypso' (CSP, p. 158).

No. x: 'O the valley in the summer where I and my John' [AT:
'Johnny'; CP, p. 220; CSP50; CSP, p. 92] is much closer to popular
song, with its predictable epithets and cliché images, and represents
perhaps one extreme of Auden's chameleon-like excursions into a
popular idiom in the 'thirties.

No. xi: 'Over the heather the wet wind blows' [AT: 'Roman

Wall Blues'; CP, p. 221; CSP50; CSP, p. 93] appeared first in
Auden's script for *Hadrian's Wall*, a radio programme broadcast
on 25 November 1937. The opening line is similar to a line in the
opening chorus to Act II, sc. v, of *The Ascent of F6* ('Over our empty
playgrounds the wet winds sough'). Piso worships a fish, because
ichthus, the Greek word for fish, was a rebus for Christ.

No. XII: 'Some say that love's a little boy' [AT: 'O Tell Me The
Truth About Love'; CSP, p. 94] is one of Auden's Cowardesque
pieces, and extends the range and variety of the 'Four Cabaret
Songs', in which form it later appeared. It is good that it is now
included in Auden's collected volume, for this is a vein (one thinks of
Gunn's songs in *The Ascent of F6*) which he tapped with great
success.

'His Excellency' [LS; CP, p. 17; CSP50; CSP, p. 96], with its
return to the short line and half-rhyme for an account of the failed
idealism and doubtful material success of the managerial capitalist,
suggests a recasting of typical material from *Poems* (1930), and
breaks little new ground. It is clearer and more incantatory than the
earlier Ridingesque poems, but less allusive and suggestive. It was
given a satirical edge by Benjamin Britten in the song cycle *On This
Island* (op. 11).

'Casino' [LS; CP, p. 91; CSP50; CSP, p. 97] uses the metaphor
of gamblers to represent a lost generation: fortune to them is an
oasis in a waste land, to which they are attracted as to a religion
(stanza 3). The poem proposes that they have resigned their will,
and retained only their appetite (which remains unsatisfied, stanza
2). The casino is sterile: no Minotaur, no clue; not even the consolation of art (the fountain, the laurel). The gods have departed, 'and
what was god-like in this generation/was never to be born'. Auden
uses the metrical form of 'Schoolchildren', the loosely stressed and
modulated quatrain which seems at times so near to syllabic verse,
and which allows the great flexibility of argument and authoritative
flow that characterizes so many poems of the 'thirties onwards.

'Oxford' [*Listener*, 9 Feb. 1938; AT; CP, p. 80; CSP50; CSP,
p. 98] is a poem of this kind of flexibility, though it has been much
pruned. This present poem of four stanzas originally had ten, and it
is hard not to feel that the point of the restless 'knowledge of death'

being refused by 'the natural heart' (stanza 4) is lost without the missing stanzas' elaboration of the role of Wisdom and Knowledge in relation to Success and Violence, and the desire of Eros Paida-gogos (*paidagogos,* a teacher of boys) for the instinctive natural world which is still so near in Oxford.

Auden once wrote: 'I cannot believe . . . that any artist can be good who is not more than a bit of a reporting journalist' (*New Verse,* Apr./May 1936, p. 24), a view which has lent ammunition to detrac-tors, but which is faithful to some of his ambitions at this time, and which is sensibly elaborated in its particular context. 'Dover' [*New Verse,* Nov. 1937; AT; CP, p. 111; CSP50; CSP, p. 98] is one of the poems which depends, in this way, upon its accumulated socio-logical analysis of the ethos of the frontier town. Its function as a frontier enables Auden to turn it into a symbol of how man exists in time, as a traveller, facing the future and the past, a victim of forces outside his control. Auden brilliantly expands the significance of man's predicament from the local to the cosmic ('tides warn bronz-ing bathers of a cooling star/With half its history done') without straining the vivid descriptive links in the chain of argument. Like so much of Auden, its appeal lies very much in the understated air of laconic understanding, somewhere between tenderness and im-partiality ('Nothing is made in this town', 'Not all of us are unhappy' and so on).

'Journey to Iceland' [*Listener,* 7 Oct. 1936: 'A Letter to Chris-topher Isherwood, Esq'; LI; CP, p. 7; CSP50; CSP, p. 100] sets the thematic tone of *Letters from Iceland* (1937), the travel book written in collaboration with Louis MacNeice.[4] The poem is an investigation of this statement, taken from the prose letter which follows it: 'We are all too deeply involved with Europe to be able, or even to wish to escape.' Iceland represents the traveller's 'limited hope' that there is somewhere 'where the affections of its dead can be bought/by those whose dreams accuse them of being/spitefully alive'. It is the North which means 'Reject', providing an ascetic refuge for 'the pale' who 'from too much passion of kissing feel pure in its deserts.'[5] It is also Auden's ethnic homeland (his family is of Icelandic descent), his favourite saga world and a place of 'natural marvels'. The 'horse-shoe ravine' is Ásbyrgi, a rock island shaped

like a hoofmark of Sleipnir, Odin's horse; the bishop who 'was put
in a bag' was Jón Gerreksson, who was drowned in a sack in the
river Brúará near Skálholt in 1433; the 'great historian' is Snorri
Sturluson (d. 1241), whose bath may be seen at Snorralaug. But
behind the tourist front is eternal human nature (stanzas 8–10).
The poem concludes with some cannibalized lines from an uncollected sonnet ('The fruit in which your parents hid you, boy', *New
Verse,* July 1933) and offers no actual location for the romantic wish
for a 'fabulous country'; this is the illusion of the escapists, the mad
driver ('airman' originally, as Hoggart points out, p. 227) and the
writer who 'runs howling to his art'. The poem 'Hammerfest' in
About the House provides an interesting comparison with the conclusions of this poem.

'Detective Story' [LI; CSP, p. 102] is introduced in *Letters From
Iceland* as being about 'why people read detective stories'. Really,
of course, it is about guilt, for in Auden's parable the murderer and
his victim are ultimately the same: 'Someone must pay for/Our loss
of happiness, our happiness itself.' As usual in this period, Auden's
casual relish in making the allegory work prevents the poem from
becoming too soberly moralizing. It is interesting to compare it
with his later essay 'The Guilty Vicarage': 'I suspect that the typical
reader of detective stories is, like myself, a person who suffers from a
sense of sin' (*The Dyer's Hand,* p. 157). See also 'To T. S. Eliot on his
Sixtieth Birthday (1948)' (CSP, p. 275).

'Death's Echo' [*New Statesman,* 16 Jan. 1937: 'Song'; LI; CP,
p. 224; CSP50; CSP, p. 103] concludes Auden's 'Letter to William
Coldstream, Esq' in *Letters From Iceland,* and summarizes his
feelings during a fortnight in which little of importance happened
(and which is wittily described in the letter, 'a little donnish experiment in objective narrative'). Its immediate context is the final
mention of:

> The news from Europe interwoven with our behaving
> The pleasant voice of the wireless announcer, like a consultant surgeon
> 'Your case is hopeless. I give you six months.'

Thus Death's mysterious and insistent injunction in the refrain to
'dance while you can' acquires a sinister overtone of evasion as well

as being in a Yeatsian sense a call to order. The farmer and the fisherman, the travellers, the lover, the dreamer and the drunkard have all embraced life with enthusiasm, but Death's answer under-lines the ultimate emptiness of their various objectives: 'Not to be born is the best for man.' This, we feel, is *not* Auden's conclusion, but he is showing how the pastoral, social, erotic or spiritual utopias are all irrevocably bonded to their negative motivations or conditions: the despair of lean years, loneliness, post-coital sadness or the morning-after hastens man's awareness of his mortality.

'The Price' [*Poetry,* Jan. 1937; LI; CP, p. 226; CSP50; CSP, p. 105] is introduced by Auden in *Letters From Iceland* as follows:

Went for a short walk in the afternoon to the bridge over the half-lake, half-river which fills this valley. I was thinking about a picture of the seven ages of man I saw in some book or other. A girl playing a flute to a young man, two infants wrestling in a meadow, and an old man staggering to a grave, you know the kind of thing. After tea the thoughts developed into a poem.

The poem evidently contrasts in its two stanzas the cherished order of life created by the imagination, and the price paid by the individual organism which houses that imagination. Some critics (Beach, p. 141; Bloom, *Shenandoah,* pp. 40–41) take the second stanza to indicate the penalty of 'experience', as though the first stanza represented only a childhood world. It seems to me, however, that the second stanza is about gestation and birth (nine nights represent-ing nine months, in a slight parody of the Creation), and that to be 'Bride and victim to a ghost' is not so much a Gothic symbol as a riddle for the body being invested by the soul. This, in other words, is the reality behind the 'phantasy' of the seven ages view of life. It opposes to the comforting landscape the essential solitariness of the human condition.

Letter to Lord Byron [LI; CLP], a cultural and autobiographical exercise in a rhyme-royal reminiscent of the uncollected Part I of 'A Happy New Year' (*New Country,* 1933), is lighter in tone than the Iceland poems in CSP, but more important. Its range of subject and civilized, ironic tone make it a masterly innovation in its period. This was the right moment for Auden to be informative about his life and ideas in a mode that allowed him to be extremely funny as well, but the poem takes in more than the merely personal or literary, showing a sharp nose for cultural pretentiousness and socio-political lies, and above all a suspicion of technology and the antiseptic habitat of Economic Man.

'Danse Macabre' [*Listener*, 17 Feb. 1937: 'Song for the New Year'; AT; CP, p. 59; CSP50; CSP, p. 105] is an ironical oration whose probable context, in view of the time of writing, is the Spanish Civil War, where 'matters are settled with gas and with bomb'. The fanatical speaker (deliberately an *alter ego* of the poet, himself a 'spoilt Third Son') represents that puritanical intolerance of human nature which finds fascism so attractive. The parole-breaking Devil is a red-herring: like the Vicar of Pressan Ambo, the speaker uses the myth of the Fall of the Angels to account for human sin, and to excuse his need to conquer and to punish. He is, like the Vicar, a type of the Super-Ego convinced that he is the voice of God.

'Lullaby' [*New Writing*, Spring 1937; AT; CP, p. 208; CSP50; CSP, p. 107], perhaps the most well-known of Auden's lyrics, achieves the beauty of its effect by the way in which the moment of happiness is weighed gravely and consciously against an awareness of all that can threaten it. The delicately hinted rhymes, the harmony between the musical line and the extended statement, and the careful epithets: all these reinforce the poem's gravity. The second stanza proposes that on the one hand Eros can lead to Agape, and on the other that 'abstract insight' can induce Eros: the lover and the desert saint are closer than they might appear. The parallelism reappears in the final stanza, where the two extreme states are guarded by the types of love they can induce ('involuntary powers' are powers not of the human will, i.e. providence). One may object that the object of the love is not convincingly present in the poem, and certainly the 'dreaming head' of the final stanza moves nearer to being a stage property than its appearance in the first stanza, but the poem is rightly considered one of Auden's greatest achievements in the genre.

'Orpheus' [*London Mercury*, June 1937; AT; CP, p. 158; CSP50; CSP, p. 109] explores the nature of art, avoiding any conclusions: indeed the poem is brief enough for its questions wholly to pre-

dominate. The influence of Rilke seems likely. Is art a celebration of
life, or a desire to control it? Why celebrate life, when those who
live it have no need of art ('content with the sharp notes of the air')?
The final question opposes to the power of natural circumstances
('the weak snowflake') the greater power of human desire for
knowledge ('the wish') and human creativity ('the dance'). The
human will is, therefore, superior; its powers, like those of Orpheus,
may metaphorically charm trees and stones. And yet it may, like
the snowflake, 'oppose': its power may be power to do us harm, to
make us unshy, unhappy.

'Miss Gee' [*New Writing*, Autumn 1937; AT; CP, p. 209;
CSP50; CSP, p. 109], a poem written in ballad form, has come in
for an unusual amount of unfair criticism.[6] The idea that if you
refuse to make use of your creative powers, you produce a cancer
instead, was one of those implicit in the psychosomatic theories of
Homer Lane (see *Lions and Shadows*, p. 303). Auden would have
found it also in Groddeck, who makes much of the idea that even
male cancer can be a compensation for the inability to become preg-
nant (see *Exploring the Unconscious*, p. 80). Miss Gee represses her
sexuality into guilty dreams about the Vicar, and thus develops an
incurable tumour. The ballad is not intended to be a psychologically
subtle or sympathetic character study, but a direct piece of polemic,
rather Brechtian in tone. Our natural desires (Auden still believes)
may defeat us if we deny them. The point about the Oxford Groupers
dissecting her knee is that such a pious and sanctimonious movement
as Moral Rearmament has a totally irrelevant notion of where the
cause of moral distress and unhappiness lies.

'Victor' [*New Writing*, Autumn 1937; AT; CP, p. 233; CSP50;
CSP, p. 112], another ballad and a companion piece to 'Miss Gee',
shows how a repressed personality can break out into religious
mania when faced with a sexual situation it is unable to control.
Victor's impulse to murder his faithless wife arises both from a
hinted sexual inadequacy (he is presented as a typically anal-erotic
personality) and from what Auden later called 'the constant tendency of the spiritual life to degenerate into an aesthetic performance'.[7] His spiritual dialogues with nature confirm only the projection of his own neuroses into the real world, the Super-Ego

acting as the supposed agent of the divine. The violence of the story is possibly more suited to the genre of popular ballad than are the more commonplace, and therefore more distressing, circumstances of Miss Gee: but it should be remembered that the tone of these poems is deliberately exaggerated and distancing.

'As He Is' [AT; CP, p. 179; CSP50; CSP, p. 117] concerns the anomalies of man's position in the animal universe, a subject which was as fascinating to Auden in this period as it once had been to Pope. The distinction of 'gun and lens and Bible' (perhaps only an imperialist version of the earlier dissident 'lancet, speech and gun') gives man his particularly paradoxical status: he is a 'militant enquirer' and also 'Able at times to cry'. He is 'The Brothered-One, the Not-Alone', whose highly developed social organization and historical awareness ('His money and his time' which his 'family have taught him/To set against the large and dumb,/The timeless and the rooted') yield violence and unease within the species as well as love.

His psychological conditioning is expounded in stanzas 4 and 5. He has no access to his real nature (the locked tower) because of the repressive hidden presence of family (Auden is returning to the ideas of *Paid on Both Sides* here), and so he is divided between his actual mania and his vision of what might be, his vision of love. The sixth stanza postulates a Blakean duality in heraldic terms: man is a victim of the contraries which govern his life, even though he vainly hopes that they may be reconciled. His arms, therefore, remain the lamb and the tigress to which he is obliged to be faithful. The deserters to his cause in the final stanza are therefore the revolutionaries, the spiritual avant-garde, whose treason and ambush may eventually, through 'further griefs and greater', bring about the real 'defeat of grief'. In other words, the lamb and tigress must be reconciled. (Compare 'Sonnets from China', No. I, line 11, in CSP, p. 128. The whole poem may be compared with 'The Riddle', CSP, p. 149.)

'A Voyage' [CSP, p. 119[8]] is a sequence of six poems which Auden wrote after he and Isherwood had visited China, in 1938, to cover the Sino-Japanese war. It describes the voyage from Marseilles to Hong Kong, and some of its material is duplicated in a piece called 'Escales' by Auden and Isherwood (*Harper's Bazaar,* Oct. 1938, pp. 78–79, reprinted in *Exhumations*), which was not, therefore,

included in *Journey to a War*, the travel book that was the outcome
of the visit.

No. I, 'Whither', reiterates the point made in 'Journey to Iceland',
and to a certain extent in 'Dover', that truth and falsehood go everywhere and that travelling discovers nothing. For the medical
metaphor, compare 'Escales' (*Exhumations*, p. 144):

This voyage is our illness: as the long days pass, we grow peevish, apathetic,
sullen; we no longer expect, or even wish, to recover. Only at moments, when
a dolphin leaps or the big real birds from sunken Africa veer round our squat
white funnels, we sigh and wince, our bodies gripped by the exquisitely painful
pangs of hope. Maybe, after all, we are going to get well.

In No. II, 'The Ship', what appears at first to be an equally obvious
metaphor (the ship as European society) gathers its momentum with
some power: the conflict between East and West will have a violent
outcome about which the sonnet (and this is typical of Auden's
sonnets) is vague, discreet and yet finally unnerving. It does this by
being laconic, and neat. We are certainly prepared for an Augustan
neatness (e.g. 'One doubts the virtue, one the beauty of his wife'),
and yet the sentiments at the end strike deeper than this: 'no one
guesses/Who will be most ashamed, who richer, and who dead'.
The added room allowed by the six-foot line that Auden has chosen
here contributes to the slightly menacing and obtrusive rhythm of
the poem.

The element of understatement in No. II contrasts dramatically
with the macabre directness of the following sonnet, 'The Sphinx'.
The sphinx represents an earlier, lost civilization which has nothing
to do with the brash optimism of the latest one ('shrill America'),
and is, in its own admonitory presence, a numinous reminder of the
eternal possibility of suffering. It is interesting to compare the prose
account in 'Escales' (*Exhumations*, p. 145), which has more resource-
ful descriptive detail, and thereby becomes a far less persuasive
statement (this is not really a question of verse *v.* prose, for Auden
has camouflaged the verse shape of the sonnet as far as he can):

There it lies, in the utter stillness of its mortal injuries; the flat cruel face of a
scarred and blinded baboon, face of a circus monstrosity, no longer a statue
but a living, changing creature of stone. A camera, if cameras had been

invented, could have shown how that face has changed through the centuries, growing old and blind and terrible in the blaze of the sun, under the lash of the wind and the desert sand. Once, no doubt, it was beautiful. Long ago, it could see. Now it lies there mutilated and sightless, its paws clumsily bandaged with bricks, its mane like an old actor's wig, asking no riddle, turning its back upon America – injured baboon with a lion's cruel mouth, in the middle of invaded Egypt.

In Nos. IV and V, 'Hong Kong' and 'Macao', Auden sees the imperialist origins of these Eastern ports as essentially comic: the Hong Kong financiers have created a sophisticated world where all violence is forced to take place off-stage; in Macao the paternalism of the Roman Catholic Church similarly ensures that evil will be reduced and localized to manageable and pardonable proportions: 'nothing serious can happen here.'

In the final sonnet, 'A Major Port', there is something more like a political forecast. The kind of self-aggrandisement that Western civilization has brought (the banks crowding out the 'low recessive houses of the poor') is only an unnatural phase of life which it is possible to change: 'We learn to pity and rebel.'

'The Capital' [*New Writing*, Spring 1939; AT; CP, p. 100; CSP50; CSP, p. 122] contains one of Auden's most obsessive subjects, the alienation of the big city, but here it is turned into a fairy tale. The wicked uncle hints at forbidden pleasures, and the farmer's children are lured to the flattering city, where each selfish illusion is shattered and the pieces are swept out of sight.

'Brussels in Winter' [*New Writing*, Spring 1939; AT; CP, p. 151; CSP50; CSP, p. 123], as a morality is rather more persuasive than the preceding poem. Here the whole meaning of the capital is more sharply felt, even though 'it has lost/The certainty that constitutes a thing'. Its cold, isolating presence is seen paradoxically as a gigantic illusion, so that the old, the hungry and the humbled are absorbed in the hardships of life as they might be at the opera; and it is seen as concentrating life into manageable moments for the lonely rich whose 'windows glow like farms': here only money can bestow the freedom of the city.

'Musée des Beaux Arts' [*New Writing*, Spring 1939: 'Palais des Beaux Arts'; AT; CP, p. 3; CSP50, CSP, p. 123] is another

Brussels poem, for, as Arthur Kinney has pointed out,[9] it was when Auden spent the winter of 1938 there that he saw the special Brueghel alcove in the Musées Royaux des Beaux-Arts. Besides the explicit mention of *Icarus,* the poem contains imagery that refers to two other Brueghels: *The Numbering at Bethlehem* (11. 5–7) and *The Massacre of the Innocents* (1. 12, though, as Kinney points out, the horse isn't actually scratching its behind on a tree). This is one of Auden's most celebrated short poems. Its long irregular lines create a very casual-sounding argument, which the rhymes subtly enforce: Auden's statement about suffering is elaborated to the point at which the poem's centre of interest has become art-criticism. Maurice Charney thinks (*Philological Quarterly,* Jan. 1960) that the observation may have come from Lewis Namier (though it is not one to have escaped admirers of Brueghel's painting). Namier used it as an example of ironic humour, what he called 'historical comedy': 'at close quarters, the actions of men are in no way correlated in weight and value to the results they produce' (*England in the Age of the American Revolution,* 1930, p. 148).

'Gare du Midi' [*New Writing,* Spring 1939; AT; CP, p. 9; CSP50; CSP, p. 124] may also date from the Brussels visit. At any rate, the suggestion in this economical little drama is that the 'infection' of the city from the south is somehow connected with time-saving Nazi diplomacy in Western Europe in the post-Munich period; that the man is not a spy but a bureaucrat. His anonymity has a kind of sinisterly shabby respectability. Perhaps the point is simply that, as with many of the best Auden poems of this scale, one can imagine a variety of backgrounds which would give life to the symbol. He might even be literally employed in germ warfare (cf. the sinister, tall-hatted botanist in 'Certainly our city . . .', *Look, Stranger!,* No. XXI).

'The Novelist' [*New Writing,* Spring 1939; AT; CP, p. 39; CSP50; CSP, p. 124] shows how at this time Auden professed a belief in the superior powers of the novelist, who by a process of sympathy and self-abnegation can understand, interpret and create human character in all its variety, whereas a poet merely generalizes. The idea is found, for instance, in *Letter to Lord Byron:* '. . . novel writing is/A higher art than poetry altogether/In my opinion, and success implies/Both finer character and faculties' (CLP, p. 40). This view of the novelist is clearly influenced by his admiration for Isherwood.

'The Composer' [*New Writing,* Spring 1939; AT; CP, p. 5; CSP50; CSP, p. 125] celebrates the purest of the arts, music. However, Auden reinforces this notion, curiously, by imagery which, in contrast to the practical clumsiness of the poet ('rummaging', 'painstaking'), presents the composer's skills as being like the skills of the seducer (the 'gift', the sensual liquid caresses, the pouring out of wine). Indeed, the composer seems to be credited with very little: the cliché overtones of 'absolute gift' suggest that he would be a fool not to take his chances; his techniques come naturally to him. It is clear that music is here intended to be seen as instinctive, generous, even sanctifying, but one cannot help feeling that there is something unconsciously lowering in that last line, despite its evidently intended sacramental allusion.

The critico-biographical sonnet provided Auden with a convenient outlet for his response to books sent to him for review. In many cases the result is more impressive critically than the review itself, for, as Auden later recognized (see *The Dyer's Hand,* p. xii), his critical talent is for the indirect and the aphoristic. In 1939, he reviewed Enid Starkie's biography of Rimbaud for the *New Republic;* in 1938 he reviewed Laurence Housman's memoir of his brother A.E. for *New Verse.* The two poems that follow are reactions which condense critical discoveries and at the same time attempt to make them accessible to a wider public.

'Rimbaud' [*New Writing,* Spring 1939; AT; CP, p. 121; CSP50; CSP, p. 126] contains imagery that inevitably suggests Blake's 'The cistern contains; the fountain overflows' – a thought that Auden takes up again in 'New Year Letter' (1. 199), where he describes Rimbaud as having 'strangled an old rhetoric'. Not only did Rimbaud help to break the tyranny of the alexandrine; he helped to free truth from its confinement in art, to bring the experience of poetry into real life as a *'dérèglement de tous les sens'* (the 'weak and lyric friend' being, of course, Verlaine). But finally 'integrity was not enough'. The new life as merchant and explorer is seen as the failed visionary's second attempt at wholeness (Dr Starkie's work on Rimbaud began with her monograph on the African period).

'A. E. Housman' [*New Writing,* Spring 1939; AT; CSP, p. 126] similarly rather flatters the literary myth. Laurence Housman's *A.E.H.* (1937) made clear, with diplomatic indirectness, some of the reasons for the split between the scholar and the poet, what Auden in his review (*New Verse,* Jan. 1938) called 'Jehovah Housman and Satan Housman'. His love for Moses Jackson does not appear to have been declared; and his life exhibits various kinds of compensation for a repressed homosexuality. 'Food was his public love' may have been suggested by Laurence Housman's remarks on his brother's atheism, remarks which elaborate A.E.'s observation that there was no word for 'God' in a certain South African tribe: 'I have myself heard a similar story of the trouble missionaries have had to find the word for love, 'appetite for food' being the nearest equivalent' (*A.E.H.,* p. 115). Housman considered himself something of a gastronome (see Grant Richards, *Housman 1897–1936* [1941], especially Chapters 5, 11 and 26).

Auden himself has provided a comment on lines 9 and 10 of his sonnet: 'The inner life of the neurotic is always projecting itself into external symptoms which are symbolic but decipherable confessions. The savagery of Housman's scholarly polemics, which included the composition of annihilating rebukes before he had found the occasion and victim to deserve them, his obsession with punctuation beyond the call of duty, are as revealing as if he had written pornographic verse' (*New Statesman,* 18 May 1957, p. 643). The sonnet concludes with an explanation of Housman's obsession with death, with which one might compare Auden's *New Verse* review, where he linked Jehovah Housman and Satan Housman: 'But they had one common ground upon which they could meet; the grave. Dead texts; dead soldiers; Death the Reconciler, beyond sex and beyond thought. There, and there only, could the two worlds meet.'

'Edward Lear' [*Times Literary Supplement,* 25 Mar. 1939; AT; CP, p. 76; CSP50; CSP, p. 127] owes much to Angus Davidson's *Edward Lear* (1938) for details of Lear's life. Indeed, to read Davidson's biography and to read Auden's interpretation of it is to see something of the poet's skill in posing and lighting his significant detail like a photographer. Sometimes this skill leads to distortion. Fear of dogs and dislike of Germans, for instance (Davidson, pp. 79 and 224), suggest greater vulnerability and contemporaneity than the facts warrant. The anecdote (Davidson, p. 47) of the two young Englishmen overheard in Calabria ('Why, he's nothing but a d——d dirty landscape painter': a title gleefully adopted by Lear himself) is combined with Lear's sensitivity about his ugliness (Davidson, p. 15) to produce the celebrated thumbnail line: 'A dirty landscape-painter who hated his nose.' Here something of Lear's intelligence and humour is lost for those who do not know the source: he becomes instead a lachrymose melancholic afflicted by epilepsy (this is his 'Terrible Demon', Davidson, p. 93), an almost theatrical presence, a pantomime Romantic. Auden builds his caricature around Davidson's commonplace observation that 'whimsical humour is closely allied with tears' (p. 197), and that Lear's comic verse was, like Housman's scholarship, a compensation. The 'cruel inquisitive They' of the limericks are seen as the adults that Lear himself cannot bear to face. Davidson had made the point thus (p. 196): 'What a world of implication there is in Lear's "they"! "They" are the force of public opinion, the dreary voice of human mediocrity: "they" are perpetually interfering with the liberty of the individual: "they" gossip, "they" condemn, "they" are inquisitive and conventional and almost always uncharitable.' Like Housman and like Rimbaud, Lear was a victim of society: but as Auden was to write in 'New Year Letter', ll. 111–12, '. . . the live quarry all the same/Were changed to huntsmen in the game.' Compare this with Ransom's view of Dante's art as a form of revenge (*The Ascent of F6*, p. 14).

'Epitaph on a Tyrant' [*New Statesman*, 31 Jan. 1939; AT; CP, p. 99; CSP 50; CSP, p. 127] portrays a simple dictator, flattered, manipulated and ultimately innocent, very reminiscent indeed of the Leader in *On the Frontier* (published three months previously). Real understanding or real exposure of motivation is perhaps sacrificed to the rhetorical device of the last line: the inversion of cried/died is very striking, but it fails to carry the weight of opposition to the portrait built up in the previous lines in quite the way one imagines it was intended to. It is as though Hitler were seen as a puppet not really responsible for the outcome of his moods.

'Sonnets from China' [JW: 'In Time of War'; CP, p. 319; CSP50; CSP, p. 128, which omits the sonnets originally numbered IX, X, XIV, XV, XX, XXV and XXVI and the 'Commentary', and adds 'To E. M. Forster' from JW] represent a new scope of historical understanding and new powers of generalization and condensation in Auden's work. The discarded 'Commentary' made it clear that this sonnet sequence is an attempt to evaluate man's predicament in 'the epoch of the Third Great Disappointment' (the first two being the collapse of the Roman Empire and of medieval Christendom). The Sino-Japanese war thus becomes the main exemplum of a far more ambitious account of the vagaries of human destiny in the machine age than any kind of verse journalism would have allowed. It is this that gives *Journey to a War* its real distinction as a travel book: in its discussion of evil, of human nature and society, 'Sonnets from China' is Auden's *Essay on Man*. It never loses sight of the ultimate problem of how human happiness and justice are to be achieved, even when it is dazzling the reader with its mercurial insights into dramatized history and boldly symbolized cultural phenomena.

No. I begins with the Creation, where the material world is seen to achieve its nature effortlessly, merely by existing in time ('from the years their gifts were showered'). In contrast with the vegetable and animal worlds, man is an unformed creature, capable of creating vastly different civilizations ('On whom the years could model any feature') and not easily classifiable as gregarious or predatory (compare 'a leopard or a dove' with 'As He Is', CSP, p. 117). Despite his error and mistrust, however, man is still (and this forms the *leitmotif* of the sequence) capable of shaping his own future: he 'chose his love'.

In No. II the lost Eden is interpreted as the impossible utopia of 'the poet and the legislator': it is impossible because it is the way back and not the way ahead, which is described as a 'maturity' which 'as he ascended/Retired like a horizon from the child'. Man is thus in a state, not of Being, but of Becoming, and his world is fraught with danger. One of the dangers is language (No. III), which, though it gives man power, exercises its own tyranny ('They' of 1. 9 are words) by obsessing man with ideas removed from reality.

Auden then contrasts the unprogressive life of the Noble Savage (No. IV) with the epic life of the *comitatus* (No. V), when the migrating tribes settled in Europe: the hero's decline into a stagnant authoritarianism represents the period of political growth and consolidation in the early Middle Ages. No. VI presents the monastic tradition's pursuit of truth in solitude, from astrological prophecy to the first glimmerings of humanism. No. VII is a history of poetry in any culture, whereby the intuitive and prophetic becomes the rational and satirical; Homer to Juvenal, say. No. VIII is a brief description of the Enlightenment in terms of capitalism, democracy, science and paper credit: here is Auden's account of the 'Third Great Disappointment' in the sestet of the sonnet, where industrial urbanization is the price paid for the advances described in the octave ('He gathered into crowds but was alone'), a theme which is to become an important element in Auden's work of the 'forties. No. IX uses the myth of Jove and Ganymede to account for man's misuse of his powers, perhaps in the context of church history, and No. X [*New Verse,* June/July 1936: 'The Economic Man'] looks in a different way at the similar theme of how we account for evil in an age of disbelief.

At this point the historical preamble is really over. Man is now at a stage of civilization at which consciousness of his failure to create a just society is equally mixed with his hope that he may eventually do so (No. XI). This opposition of admonitory 'history' to the 'buoyant song' of art or love becomes the underlying theme of the remaining sonnets, which now turn to the actual situation in China. The war is happening (No. XII) and is terrible, but Auden retains a sense of the justice of a cause: 'Yet ideas can be true, although men die' (cf. *Spain 1937*). The ideas which are not true (i.e. Japanese imperialism) are therefore those which create the evil, and Auden links East with West at this juncture: 'And maps can really point to places/Where life is evil now./Nanking. Dachau.' This abbreviated close is, technically speaking, admirably pungent. No. XIII [*New Statesman,* 2 July 1938: 'Chinese Soldier'] pays rather obvious respects to the fate of the common man in war: 'He added meaning like a comma when/He joined the dust of China, that our daughters/ Might keep their upright carriage' smacks a little of questions about rape at a tribunal for conscientious objectors.

Less journalistic is No. xiv, the account of the hospital, where the isolation of suffering cannot be imagined by the uninjured, or No. xv, where the conferring leaders are perhaps rather melodramatically seen as out of touch with the armies waiting for their orders. No. xvi [*New Writing,* Autumn 1938: 'Exiles'] is about the alienation of the imperialist class, and No. xvii contrasts the essentially national self-regard of appeasement or isolationism (last three lines) with the primitive enthusiasm of the 'dancers' (cf. *The Dance of Death*), who appeal to 'the elementary rhythms of the heart' and 'speak to our muscles of a need for joy', and are pleased at the events in Austria, China and Spain: the fascist in all of us. No. xviii [*Listener,* 3 Nov. 1938] was originally the final sonnet of the sequence, and as such gave greater importance as a whole to its theme of man's choice of life. The 'warm nude age of instinctive poise' is the Eden which man has turned his back on: 'We live in freedom by necessity,/A mountain people dwelling among mountains.' The optimistic Nos. xix and xx, and the admonitory No. xxi, take on a greater importance in this new arrangement.

The 'one/Who for ten years of drought and silence waited' in No. xix is Rilke. Muzot was the little château in Switzerland where in February 1922 Rilke completed the *Duino Elegies:* 'I have gone out and stroked my little Muzot for having guarded all this for me and at last granted it to me, stroked it like a great shaggy beast' (*Selected Letters of Rainer Maria Rilke 1902–1926,* trans. R. F. C. Hull, 1946, p. 354). Rilke thus becomes a symbol of possible fulfilment even at a time of apparently total evil and violence, and is an evident influence upon the style of the sonnet sequence itself. No. xx contrasts two kinds of forbears, those 'who wanted to persist in stone for ever' because they were unloved, and those whose only memorial is their posterity, content to remain unknown, and therefore still likely to be a living force in life through their transmission in the blood.

To end with the Forster sonnet (No. xxi), which formerly stood as the dedication to *Journey to a War,* is to provide something in the nature of a Forsterian anti-climax: Auden has been writing about man, and he ends by locating the 'international evil' in the genteel prejudices of the English middle-class that Forster exposed in his novels: the prejudices of Lucy (*A Room with a View*), Turton (*A Passage to India*) and Philip (*Where Angels Fear to Tread*). The sword (sadly now given an indefinite article like much else in revised standard Auden) is *the* sword with which Charles Wilcox felled and accidentally killed Leonard Bast in *Howard's End*. Miss Avery's silent accusation is turned into a general symbol, relevant, appropriately enough, to the angels guarding Eden against any human access.

Part Three

THE LONG POEMS

6 New Year Letter

The real appeal of *New Year Letter*[1] lies not so much in the fineness of the points made (and Auden's intellect is very nimble) as in the particular tone of the discourse in the 'Letter' and its odd relationship with the 'Notes' which follow. The octosyllabic couplet is perhaps just too narrow for discursive verse (as the heroic couplet is just too broad: tailoring of resources gives these forms their distinctive features), and thus appears to be continually pushing further and further away the decisive statement. Auden's natural critical categorizing and qualifying accentuates this effect, and so do the 'Notes', hung elusively on to the poem like invisible Christmas-tree decorations. The reader turns to the back, as if to find the answer, but finds merely an extension to the problem. This applies even in cases where the meaning is transparent: are the 'Notes' authorities or examples, analogues or applications of the ideas which the poem is throwing out? It is not certain. The familiar accusation that the 'Notes' are merely undigested material which the precipitous prosody of the 'Letter' could find no room for is only a half-truth, for without the resources of the 'Notes' the 'Letter' would be overburdened, not only with material, but with the necessity to furnish at every point its awareness of the dialectic: the reader's mental energy is better deployed (he is doing more creative work) in interpreting the 'sources' for himself.

The 'Notes' have been compared with Eliot's in *The Waste Land*, but these, we know, were a distinct afterthought. One may better compare them with Pope's notes to *The Dunciad*, which are similarly

deployed contributive material. Auden is, I think, almost light-
heartedly aware that he is having it both ways, that the work is
something between Blake's *Marriage of Heaven and Hell* and a
metaphysical treatise, with nutshell political theory and the prag-
matic philosophical discoveries of a great talker thrown in for good
measure. We should not forget that the principle section of the work
is an informal neo-Augustan epistle, because this safeguards the
aphoristic tone of the whole. This is why it is so difficult for an
English reader to remember that the title of the work which he
knows is not the original title, or the one which Auden himself
prefers.

Auden's permanent settlement in the United States at this time
(he became a naturalized citizen in 1946) is clearly connected with
New Year Letter, if only because his choice of New York, the
world's most notoriously alienating metropolis, the city of Lorca,
Mayakovsky, Hart Crane, seemed a deliberate act of self-discovery,
an environmental act of good faith in respect of his personal quest
for truth, a decisive acknowledgment that 'Aloneness is man's real
condition' (l. 1542). Thus the 'Letter' ('addressed to a Whitehall'
but 'under Flying Seal to all', ll. 315–16) is a public explanation of
what to many in wartime England seemed a kind of defection.
Auden is here struggling for a system of belief more coherent than
the 'pink liberalism' (see the original text of *Letter to Lord Byron*)
which had shown itself powerless to avert the war. He is concerned
to elaborate with greater rationality the human situation as outlined
in the potted history of 'Sonnets from China', particularly in the
context of metaphysics. America seemed the most typical human
environment in the epoch of the Third Great Disappointment, and
the 'Letter' makes this clear (ll. 1519–24):

> More even than in Europe, here
> The choice of patterns is made clear
> Which the machine imposes, what
> Is possible and what is not,
> To what conditions we must bow
> In building the Just City now.

Auden no doubt felt he had seen enough of two wars against the fascists profitably to face a third: what seemed necessary was to explore a state of affairs in which there were no effective sanctions that civilization could use against the Nazis. If this involved him in a study of metaphysics, particularly of existential philosophers like Kierkegaard and theologians like Niebuhr, well and good: the conditions for building the Just City had to involve a new, unified sense of man's purpose and man's needs, something of greater authority than the monistic systems of Marx and Freud.

The goal is Christianity, but one of the agreeable strengths of *New Year Letter* is that its religious conclusions are less diplomatically argued than honestly sought. Indeed, the seeking is an important thematic element in the whole work, not only in the sonnet sequence 'The Quest', where it is dramatically embodied, but incidentally even in the relaxed 'Letter' itself. When MacNeice reported: 'Auden, for example, working eight hours a day in New York, is getting somewhere',[2] he was doing more than justifying a regretted absence; he was respecting the single-mindedness of spiritual purpose in Auden's retreat. Today we can understand that Auden's quest for 'true happiness or authenticity of being'[3] had a greater value as art at this point of time than any of the heroics that he might have been expected to produce in Europe. A comparison of his sonnet on the dead Chinese soldier (CSP, p. 134) with, say, Keith Douglas's 'Vergissmeinnicht' shows the weakness of the non-combatant: Auden had already perhaps exhausted in his imagination the subtlest of mythologies based on hostility. The actual conflict was largely to elude as subject-matter even the enlisted poets of the war (Auden was actually unfit for active service). Auden's poetry had been fully concerned with the European situation for a decade. The war itself barely modified his experience of this situation. 'To go in quest means to look for something of which one has, as yet, no experience,' he later wrote, apropos of the Quest Hero,[4] and much of his later poetry is involved in this search for the Just City, a search which is not private, but shared.

'Prologue' is an early use of syllabics. Spears (p. 248) is wrong about the earliest use of syllabics being in *The Sea and the Mirror*. Indeed, *pace* Blair, pages 150–1, 'Prologue' would seem to be

134   W. H. AUDEN

antedated by 'In Memory of Sigmund Freud', which has the same
syllabic stanza pattern, 11/11/9/10, and probably also by 'Heavy
Date', both from *Another Time*. 'Prologue' was first printed in the
Allied Relief Ball Souvenir Programme, 10 May 1940, and was
called 'Spring in Wartime'. As a poem of war, it argues that although
war is so antisocial that it betrays even the simplest forms of organization, and brings the kind of chaos that even a beehive has pro-
gressed from (stanza 7), it is not man's greatest fear. As a poem of
spring ('O season of repetition and return'), it summarizes one
aspect of the position reached in the 'Letter', where in the last lines a
skilfully periphrased God is enjoined to make himself manifest. As
the final stanzas of the 'Prologue' put it, 'neither a Spring nor a
War can ever/So condition his ears as to keep the Song/That is not a
sorrow from the invisible twin'. This Song (and the knowledge that
invests the reassembled bones of the previous lines, in allusion to
Ezekiel xxxvi. 7) is man's involuntary awareness of a transcendental
reality which makes him weep by reminding him that his imperfections are not essential qualities (double meaning of 'accident') but
an aberration from his true nature, his 'substance'. It is this double
nature of man (expressed in the book's epigraph from Montaigne)
that is his central alienation.

The 'Letter' falls into three parts, which Edward Callan aligns
with Kierkegaard's three categories of the aesthetic, the ethical and
the religious.[5] I do not think, however, that too much should be
made of this correspondence. Part I is little more than a poetic
apologia, and Part II, though a concentrated exposure of the dualism
which Kierkegaard opposed, is none the less only a very tentative
espousal of the existentialist position: its focal point is the apology to
Marx. Part III corresponds even less obviously to Kierkegaard's
category of the religious. It is longer than Parts I and II together,
and more varied, including a good deal of generalized history and
political theory, some spiritual autobiography and a description
of America. Its conclusion is, admittedly, an appeal to God,
but it is to God seen first of all as a unicorn: the quest imagery
reminds us that Auden's ideal here is still 'Our faith well
balanced by our doubt' (l. 962), a line pleasantly glossed in the
'Notes':

> With what conviction the young man spoke
> When he thought his nonsense rather a joke:
> Now, when he doesn't doubt any more,
> No one believes the booming old bore.

Kierkegaard's categories should be taken, not as a hidden key to the work, but as a parallel expression of ideas that have already deeply influenced the argument.

The 'Letter' is dense, but a commentary of sorts may be helpful. Auden begins Part I by presuming a shared anxiety and a shared interest in finding life's true direction. The poem at line $13n$* (called 'We're Late' in CP) shows how this sought direction needs to be continually reviewed. 'The sleepless guests of Europe' cannot see what may be done, and 'the dead say only how'. That is to say, history will describe what has been chosen in the past, but is not concerned with current choices. This is exactly the main point of the earlier *Spain 1937* (see p. 258).

Lines 30–35: Personal order is possible, especially through the medium of art (the same sun shines on the Nazi invasion of Poland as on Auden playing Buxtehude in a cottage on Long Island).

Lines 56–98: Order is the aim of both Art and Life, but it is something which cannot be willed (man's condition, in other words, is of Becoming not Being) because the state of Being is a whole which must comprehend all contraries. The account of Choice at line $63n$ reinforces this view, because our 'free-will' is really only our subjective view of the complex influence of Causal and Logical necessity. Moreover, the order of art is concerned with 'autonomous completed states' (l. 86), which Auden ingeniously glosses by reference to Hans Spemann's account of embryonic induction and to Henry James's account of the 'casual hint' which produced *The Spoils of Poynton:* in other words, the 'hint' for the poem corresponds to the frog ectoderm which is transplanted into its field of induction (the *Triton* head = feeling) and produces the words of the poem (i.e. the 'presumptive primordia', the first rudiments of the organ being induced, whose pattern of growth is the meaning of the poem). What I think Auden means to imply by this devious analogy is that poetry is as factitious as *Triton* with a tadpole's horny jaws

* Note material is indicated throughout by n after the line number.

instead of teeth. His gloss (l. 78n) about the political inadequacy of artists is more straightforward, but less convincing; and his side-track about the Spanish War (l. 87n) merely amusing. Why should writers 'be/Of some use to the military'? Auden's own parable about the duck-shooters and tree-fellers (*New Verse,* Autumn 1938) is the best refutation of that. Auden's general position is sound enough, and his expression of it much-quoted: 'Art is not life, and cannot be/A midwife to society.' Not a midwife, but a nurse, perhaps?

Lines 99–126: Writing can be a compensation for life's oppressions or inadequacies, a Freudian theory familiar in Auden (e.g. in the biographical sonnets of *Another Time,* CSP, pp. 126–7). This digression is an opportunity for an important account (l. 109n) of Kierkegaard's categories of the aesthetic and the ethical, and a brilliant set of definitions of the different kinds of artist.

Lines 127–232: This is a personal passage in which Auden acknowledges as judges sitting in perpetual session those poetic mentors whose achievement he most wishes to be measured by. The first judge is Dante (the account of Amor Rationalis may be found in *Purgatorio,* XVII; 'Malebolge's fissure' is the eighth circle in Hell), and the other two are Blake and Rimbaud. It is clear that the other poets mentioned, Dryden, Catullus, Tennyson, Baudelaire, Hardy and Rilke, are merely present in the court and are not judges, of whom, according to mythology, there should be only three. The confession involved here is not undefiant, especially in the notes.

Lines 233–318: The time's malaise is here seen in terms of a detective mystery, a particular form of the quest. The mystery cannot be solved, because the democracies are inefficient, and the dictatorships ('one inspector dressed in brown') capricious. The malaise is essentially a personal guilt: these are 'vast spiritual disorders' (l. 266). Auden manages to suggest this within the context of the decade's violence (ll. 267–78) through his gloss on Nazi persecution of the Jews at line 275n. This is the sonnet entitled 'The Diaspora' in CP. The diaspora is the dispersion of the Jewish tribes (see John vii. 35), and Auden's fusion here of Christ with the Jewish victim has a Rilkean obliqueness: what the oppressors are denying is their human nature, their common citizenship. Our recognition of the guilt which we, as human beings, hold in common with the oppressors tempts us to perform useless sacrifices (compare ll. 280–4 with 'the minotaur of authority' in *The Sea and the Mirror*, CLP, p. 243) or to indulge in dreams of revenge (ll. 289–94). The unrhymed sonnet about Nietzsche at line 280*n* praises him for debunking 'our liberal fallacies', but doubts that Hitler ('This tenement gangster with a sub-machine gun in one hand') is the kind of Superman that he intended. In fact, as Part I concludes, 'No words men write can stop the war' (l. 296), and yet the 'candid psychopompos' (Hermes, as conveyor of souls to the place of the dead, as god of dreams) can satisfy with oracular riddles, even where a direct solution is impossible – a defence of the poem itself.

Part II. Lines 319–82: Auden begins Part II with a landscape of self-discovery which can ossify those obsessed with the past (ll. 337–40: the image is of Lot's wife). We fear the future because we desire stability of one sort or another, and do not wish to change.

Lines 383–426: Embodying this fear of having to make choices is the Devil, but the Devil is unwittingly the agent of God. He represents 'fear and faithlessness and hate' (l. 416). The injunction *retro me* is that spoken by Jesus to Peter, who tried to argue (Matthew xvi. 23) that Jesus would not have to be killed. Thus the Devil is the voice that, by luring us from our real choice, shows us what our real choice is. Auden says *credo ut intelligam,* that he believes in order to understand: the phrase is Anselm's, quoted by Charles Williams in *The Descent of the Dove* (1939), p. 109: *'Credo ut intelligam,* said Anselm, and defined the wiser method. *Intelligo ut credam,* Abelard almost said, and might have added *dubito ut credam.'* Williams was a great influence on Auden in the 'forties.

Lines 427–66: This passage examines the subjective world of the individual, which, Auden says, lives 'in eternity' because it has no real contact with events beyond its own continuum, nor even much control over its own physical habitat, as the poem at line 453*n* elaborates (the genteel 'sex' is replaced by 'prick' in CSP, p. 189).

Lines 467–527: The Devil's cunning enables him to agree with us when 'we contradict a lie of his': thus he develops a flatteringly co-operative argument from the valid premise that the intellect 'parts the Cause from the Effect' (i.e. is guilty of the dualism of empirical science), and ends by urging men to throw away intelligence altogether and rely upon 'the *Beischlaf* [sexual intercourse] of the blood' (l. 524). In other words, the Devil becomes D. H. Lawrence.

Lines 528–56: The Devil also quotes one's favourite authors against one. He is ironical, prodding, reactionary, and to Auden in particular, in Rilke's lines about the gnat, he offers the instinctive life as an escape from responsibility.

Lines 557–630: Auden now examines the paradox of dualism and monism. In our retreat from the necessity of having to make our choice, we try to create a world in which we can account for our sin. The Devil does this for us in two ways: by dualism, by denying any relationship between the universal and the particular; and by monism, by turning the particular into the universal. Auden's allegory here is playful and difficult: he presents the Devil as defeating his own ends, because he cannot be both God and dualist. 'Pure evil would be pure passivity, a denial by an existence of any relation with any other existence; this is impossible because it would also mean a denial of its own existence' (l. 563n). The Devil has to keep us doubting in order to keep us sinning (and not merely doing evil, as deterministic monist systems might allow).

Lines 631–64: One of his methods is to associate the truth with a lie, make us recognize the lie and so 'treat babe and bath-water the same'. Auden gives two examples of disappointed millennialists, the early Christians and Wordsworth ('Parousia', the Second Coming, is a term borrowed from Williams).

Lines 665–750: Such a one is also Marx, because although he destroyed the Rousseauistic political philosophy which had come to justify totalitarian regimes, his was merely another half-truth, merely another way of expressing man's 'universal, mutual need', and he now represents the end of an era, together with Galileo, Newton and Darwin.

Lines 751–86: The reason for this is that human law will always be imperfect, and the law of God elusive. The rondeau at line 761n glosses this serene impersonality of the *lex abscondita* (cf. 'Law Like Love', CSP, p. 154). Here Auden returns to the failure of hopeful political systems.

Lines 787–833: Disappointed political idealism gives the worst hangovers. The gloss at line 803n points the contrast between the political realist and the political idealist (see *Hudson Review,* Winter 1951, p. 590, for Auden's reference to Fouché as the originator of the police state and to Napoleon as someone who merely 'wanted to astonish his mother'), and at line 818n he notes how a society's expectations can be turned inside out ('Hans-in-Kelder' may have come from Grose, who glosses it as 'Jack in the Cellar', i.e. the child in the womb). Perhaps this is the lesson to be learnt from opposing Hitler or Economic Man with 'the vorpal sword' of Agrarianism: but the Jabberwocky *was* killed in Carroll's poem (from which the phrase was taken). Out of the Devil's juggling with ideas and possibilities ('his hocus-pocus') comes, however, a possible dialectic for the 'either/ors', the 'impatient romantics' who can see only one side of the paradox. The Devil is even, in a sense, the father of poetry (l. 829n), for poetry can 'be defined as the clear expression of mixed feelings'. Thus the diabolic gift of hocus-pocus might be identified with art, a magic lamp which if used properly might be 'a sesame to light'.

Part III. Lines 834–59: The introductory passage restates the subjective value of the experience in art and friendship of 'the privileged community'.

Lines 860–913: But, he continues, these moments of harmony and love may come to anyone, even though they do not mean that the state of Being is thereby permanently possible for man. If man imagines that they do mean this, then he creates the hell of denying his own nature: man *is* imperfect. The sinister events that symbolize this hell are reminiscent of the apocalyptic climax of the first chorus of *The Dog Beneath the Skin,* p. 16. Line 898n, however, suggests that this hell is not really binding: the paradox is that man knows it is not, but is unwilling to admit that his existence might be different.

Lines 914–74: Being is beyond our will; therefore we are thrown back into the Purgatory of trying to come to terms with our lives (ll. 924–5: 'We . . . need their stratagems to win/Truth out of Time'). Auden uses the metaphor of climbing a hill to suggest once more that life is a quest and a renunciation.

Lines 975–1000: Auden pauses to describe himself in the act of writing, 'A tiny object in the night', and states his determination to act for himself alone, wary of the claims of political causes. Line 990n refers to Hitler in the ruins of Warsaw, who is reported to have said 'Why do they try to resist my destiny?' (cf. Auden's article 'Mimesis and Allegory' in the *English Institute Annual,* 1940, the source of many ideas in the 'Notes' to Part III). Hitler is thus, as a determinist, a 'particle who claims the field': Auden's responsibility can be only to his friends.

Lines 1001–33: This passage takes up the idea of Hitler as a denial of more than twenty centuries of Europe: this decadence is not comparable even with the fall of Rome, because at least the barbarians expressed 'the pure instinctive joy/Of animals', whereas the present destruction is 'the refined/Creation of machines and mind'. The 'metaphysics of the Crowd' is the result of 'Industry's Quicunque Vult' (literally, 'whosoever wishes'): that is to say, its power, like the Athanasian Creed, gives an automatic hope of salvation to the individual.

Lines 1034–86: Auden contrasts the private and the public life: each demands allegiance from us, and neither is escapable.

Lines 1087–1152: Auden elaborates his own past environment into a *paysage moralisé,* whereby the geological history of the Pennines comes to represent man's impulse towards civilization, and their once-mined interiors a sign of 'the deep Urmutterfurcht [primeval anxiety] that drives/Us into knowledge all our lives' (ll. 1141–2).

Lines 1153–77: Having acknowledged such a power, Auden concludes that it does not have to be obeyed. We must become 'patriots of the Now' (l. 1169).

Lines 1178–1230: This passage rather fatalistically describes the aimlessness and inevitability of violence. Auden is now concerned with the development of 'Economic Man', who has arisen since the Renaissance, since the time of 'Luther's Faith and Montaigne's doubt'. The sonnets at line 1213n encapsulate in the manner of the biographical sonnets in *Another Time* the philosophies of these individualists. The first sonnet, 'Luther' [*Christian Century,* 2 Oct. 1940], makes the point which is reinforced in the note at line 1220 – a quotation from Kierkegaard, ' "The Just shall live by

Faith" ' (quoted by Williams, p. 165) – that there may arise a situation in which 'worldliness is honoured and highly valued as piety'. Montaigne gave 'The Flesh its weapons to defeat the Book' by a retreat from authority into intelligence. Many of the ideas for the second sonnet come from Williams, e.g. p. 194: 'though Letters are not and never can be Religion, yet style has had an immense influence on Religion', and p. 192: 'He found two sources of the world's distresses: "Most of the grounds of the world's troubles are matters of grammar" and "The conviction of wisdom is the plague of man".'

Lines 1231–52: Economic Man, therefore, reached the stage of being able to examine ideas for their utility: their justificatory purposes could no longer disguise their falsehood (l. 123n). Line 1243n explores the limited value of science from an ethical point of view by reference to Kierkegaard's distinction between tribulations and temptations (cf. line 63n with its distinction between Fortune and Virtue, between causal and logical necessity). Psychology, for instance, is dangerous because it tempts man to think that since the suffering of his tribulation can be removed, he will not have to suffer at all (see 'Mimesis and Allegory', pp. 13ff). Protestantism, as line 1245n goes on to expound, 'remains in nature as the sphere of decision', fighting the tendency of reason to turn 'useful concepts' into 'universals', 'the kitsch'. This idea is ironically brought out at line 1245n in the poem about the Council of Trent (called 'For the Last Time' in CP), at which, though invited to attend, the Protestants were not able to vote, and where – far from the relaxation of formalism that one might have expected – many of the dogmas under examination were defined more rigidly than they had ever been defined before. The poem describes how, just at the moment of this 'success', four heralds gallop up with their news. They represent the world of nature in which decisions have to be made, in which, in Tillich's words, 'the Kairos determines the Logos', Time governs the Word. The words that compose the last line of the poem (*Postremum Sanctus Spiritus effudit:* 'Here the Holy Spirit spoke for the last time') are those that were written up on the wall of S. Maria Maggiore at Trent, when the Council's sittings had finished, and are quoted by Williams, page 187.

Lines 1253–1331: Auden charts the opposition of the intellectuals to Economic Man, now in the guise of the nineteenth-century bourgeois, and concludes that the *Verbürgerlichung* (say, suburbanizing) of 'joy and suffering and love' cannot be counteracted by so simple a means as the impulse towards chaos of the Romantics: 'The bourgeois were not real devils but false angels' (l. 1277*n*). In any event, the warnings of Blake, Rousseau, Kierkegaard and Baudelaire were ignored, and Economic Man has become ruled by his environment (ll. 1285–1301). There follows a briskly satirical passage exposing man's lack of freedom in all its variety.

Lines 1332–75: This lack of freedom is blamed on society and on politicians, but these are only projections of the individual will (ll. 1366–7: 'The average of the average man/Becomes the dread Leviathan'). Thus the current war is a result both of individual English hypocrisy and of individual German apathy.

Lines 1376–1443: The idea of an intellectual élite and the idea of an indiscriminate identity of individuals both lead to tyranny. The individual should be not 'dissociated', not 'integrated', but 'differentiated' (l. 1388*n*). It is the Ego which is responsible for this double 'social lie'. If the Ego denies *amor naturale* (l. 1402*n*), there comes a time when realization of selfish isolation produces a reaction in favour of a belief in fate, as typified in Wagner (compare l. 1432*n* with 'Mimesis and Allegory', p. 7), who carried the Romantic heresy of exalting causal necessity over logical necessity further than anyone else.

Lines 1444–1524: Auden breaks off again here to remind the reader of the setting of the poem: New York in the small hours of New Year's Day. This gives him the opportunity to characterize America, which does not have Europe's history, but shares the same heresies, and makes even clearer 'The choice of patterns . . . Which the machine imposes' (ll. 1520–1).

Lines 1525–72: It is the machine which compels us to admit that 'Aloneness is man's real condition'. Auden justifies this in terms of both American life and American literature.

Lines 1573–1650: As dawn breaks, the Good Life seems, as ever, so desirable as to be possible, but 'wishes are not horses' and the facts of war and the humiliation of civilization are undeniable. Man cannot escape from his predicament. The labyrinth of line 1629n is of his own making: if he were a bird he would know what to do, but he is not ('apteros', wingless, a Daedalian predicament). All he can say is that every individual is different, and that real unity begins there (ll. 1641–2, 'That all have wants to satisfy/And each a power to supply', strangely echo the famous dictum of Marx).

Lines 1651–1707: The final invocation avoids addressing God directly, though the images of unicorn, dove, fish, and so on, are traditionally Christian. Line 1668 (*Quando non fuerit, non est:* 'There is not when he was not') is quoted by Williams, page 39, and explicitly refers to Origen's belief in the co-eternity of the Son with the Father. *O da quod jubes, Domine* at line 1684 ('Give what thou commandest') is also quoted by Williams, page 66. The success of the ending lies in the way in which Auden has been able to merge this affirmation (vague as it is) with the reiterated need for a quest for the New Life. The poem at line 1708n [*Harper's Bazaar,* Dec. 1939: 'Nativity'] takes the Christian family out of the context of man's fallen nature, shows it as contriving 'to fumble/About in the Truth for the straight successful Way/Which will always appear to end in some dreadful defeat', and leads directly into 'The Quest', the Rilkean sonnet-sequence which follows.

'The Quest' first appeared in the *New Republic,* 25 November 1940, with the following prefatory note:

The theme of the Quest occurs in fairy tales, legends like the Golden Fleece and The Holy Grail, boys' adventure stories and detective novels. These poems are reflections upon certain features common to them all. The 'He' and 'They' referred to should be regarded as both objective and subjective.

I think what Auden means by this is indicated when, after listing the essential elements in the typical Quest story he asks: 'Does not each of these elements correspond to an aspect of our subjective experience of life?'[6] In other words, the sequence is intended as a heavily conceptualized account of a personal quest for 'true happiness or authenticity of being'. The 'Letter' has already established modern man as an existential hero (ll. 1543–4: 'each must travel forth alone/ In search of the Essential Stone'), and it remains for his predicament to be analysed with the particular kind of dynamic obliqueness and

metaphysical symbolism which the Rilkean sonnet provides, to be
embodied in a moral landscape which owes as much to the fairy-tale
and to Kafka as to theology. I do not wish to suggest that the
sequence is merely a heavily evasive spiritual autobiography; on the
other hand, it is clear that the 'he' and 'they', though needing
reappraisal in each context, do represent the world of the self and
the not-self. If the 'they' is sometimes a close cousin of Lear's 'they'
(see p. 124), this is quite suitable to the bold colours of the sequence,
and to Auden's essentially wry treatment of autobiography elsewhere.

The framing sonnets (Nos. I and XX) present the object of the
quest (the unknown) in terms of the garden in *Alice in Wonderland*.
Spears suggested that the 'it' of No. I ('The Door')[7] was the threshold
between the conscious and unconscious mind, but this seems to
involve an irrelevant Freudianism. It is true that Auden believes
that 'to go in quest means to look for something of which one has,
as yet, no experience', and the unconscious may play its part in the
unknown. Auden possibly had read William Empson's essentially
Freudian treatment of *Alice* in *Some Versions of Pastoral* (1935).
But sonnet No. XX makes it clear that the rose garden is not, in fact,
an individual subconscious, but a state of authenticity of being that
is achieved largely through love: it is not unrelated, in fact, to the
garden in the *Roman de la Rose* or in Eliot's *Burnt Norton,* a poem
which as Eliot himself confessed, also makes use of *Alice*. In No. I
it is unattainable, and to fallen man appears merely as an inscrutable
authority lurking in time; as a key to the past or the purging flood
of memory; or as the guiding principle of the future, its authority
(the Queen of Hearts, based on *Richard III*) or its questioning of
authority (Lear's Fool), with the possible suggestion in the political
metaphor of a contrast between the Gods of the Old and the New
Testaments.

Man's distance from the unknown is reflected in No. II ('The
Preparations'), which deals with his mistaken sense of self-sufficiency – the Pelagian heresy, in fact, as the sonnet's evident source in
Williams's *The Descent of the Dove* makes clear. Williams (p. 66)
wrote of St Augustine's reaction to Pelagianism and the question of
sin: 'Man precisely was not *in* a situation – not even in a difficult

situation. He was, himself, the situation.' Augustine felt that only the grace of God could alter the situation, but Pelagius thought virtue was easily attainable through reason. Auden concludes: 'One should not give a poisoner medicine,/A conjurer fine apparatus, nor/A rifle to a melancholic bore.' Nor, by implication, is it valid for fallen man to take up a means to salvation which is itself similarly related to his disease, this means being his own will.

No. III ('The Crossroads') uses the fairy-tale formula of the year and the day as the time allotted to complete a task, pointing out that everyone thinks this long enough but still needs the extra day to complete 'the journey that should take no time at all'. No. IV ('The Pilgrim') describes the landscape of sin which makes the hero homeless. The point is that his 'Greater Hallows' (relics of saints, therefore any sacred object) has not been stolen by evil powers, but has been lost by sin (see 'K's Quest', p. 48) and is only waiting to be reclaimed by innocence. No. V ('The City') shows the effect of the fragmentation of the community of seekers, in preparation for the more personal sonnets on the three temptations.

These temptations seem not unrelated to the three temptations of Christ as recounted in Mark iv. No. VI ('The First Temptation') is about the artist, whose 'gift for magic' tempts him to turn 'his hungers into Roman food', i.e. to relish and re-relish aesthetically what should have been a spiritual discipline. This corresponds to the biblical temptation to perform miracles, to turn the stones into bread (cf. Shadow's machine in *The Rake's Progress*). No. VII ('The Second Temptation') is about a nihilistic disgust with the material world and the flesh, the temptation of suicide ('And plunged into the college quad, and broke'). This corresponds to the biblical temptation of Christ to prove his godhead when placed on the pinnacle of the temple: the temptation involves spiritual pride in both cases. No. VIII ('The Third Temptation', first published as 'Ganymede' in *Common Sense,* April 1939) is the temptation to selfish isolation, which appears to provide the discipline that gives power ('soon he was king of all the creatures') but which is merely an obsession with self. This corresponds to the biblical offer of the kingdoms of the earth, the temptation to worship Satan in return for power.

No. IX ('The Tower') shows how the artist tries to have it both ways. Like Plato's watch-tower of the soul, or like Acrisius's tower where Danae was imprisoned, the tower of the artist provides at once a challenge to the divine and a retreat from it. It is a retreat because it is a retreat from life ('For those who dread to drown of thirst may die'; for life as the sea, cf. *The Sea and the Mirror* and *The Enchafèd Flood*) which is none the less as compulsive as a magic spell. No. X ('The Presumptuous') and No. XI ('The Average') describe the abortive quests of those who are not really heroes. No. XII ('Vocation') shows the cynicism of the cowardly: the official is 'amused', not because the request to suffer is presumptuous, but because the refusal of it is believed. The metaphor is of an Army Draft Board, where the reason for rejection (e.g. flat feet) may seem absurd but is welcome all the same. Thus he becomes a tempter instead of a martyr, a Falstaff instead of a Hal. No. XIII ('The Useful') elaborates on this idea of failed heroes proving useful to others who are still trying, and No. XIV ('The Way') points out the dangers in it as a negative not a positive encouragement: 'how reliable can any truth be that is got/By observing oneself and then just inserting a Not?' The chapel in the rock is from the Grail legend, the Astral Clock is the fourth dimension of theosophists like Ouspensky, and for the Triple Rainbow see C. M. Doughty, *Arabia Deserta* (1888), II, 305: 'These were the celestial arches of the sun's building, the peace in heaven after the battle of the elements in a desert-land of Arabia.'[8]

In No. XV ('The Lucky') the traditional luck of the third son in fairy-tales is equated with Grace: in other words, the Lucky are the Elect, and the failed are those who fail in No. II, the Pelagians. The nature of the real hero is described in No. XVI ('The Hero'). He will not seem like a hero, because 'only God can tell the saintly from the suburban' ('Letter', l. 1277n). The hero has a Kierkegaardian patience and humility, and, like T. E. Lawrence, does not feel that he 'owes a duty to his fame' (this sonnet may be compared with the earlier one, probably based on Lawrence's life, 'Who's Who', CSP, p. 78). No. XVII ('Adventure') shows further how the crowd plays for safety, and No. XVIII ('The Adventurers') takes up the contrast in Williams, pages 57–59, between the Affirmative Way and the Negative Way. The Negative Way is the way of the ascetic desert fathers, whose fruition is seen only in art and superstition, and leads only to the Dry. In No. xix ('The Waters') the conditions of modern life ('With time in tempest everywhere') treat the saintly (active 'sufferers') and the insincere (passive 'suffering') alike, because the right question has not been put (cf. the Grail legend). This sonnet ends, like Humpty Dumpty's recitation about the fish, on a 'but'.[9] The final sonnet, No. xx ('The Garden'), describes the world of innocence which must be recaptured if the quest is to be successful. Sins are not deadly, but merely the 'earnest' (i.e. not deadly earnest) subject of children's play; the body ('dogs') is free of the interfering superego ('their tall conditions', i.e. their masters); and love casts aside all duality ('flesh forgives division as it makes/Another's moment of consent its own').

The 'Epilogue' [*Nation*, 7 Dec. 1940; CP: 'Autumn 1940'] reiterates with melancholy riddling the need for humility and striving in the face of certain violence and probable death ('the narrow gate where/Events are traded with time'). It is dignified and elegiac, and behind it is real feeling (for instance, 'this year the towns of our childhood/Are changing complexion along with the woods' probably means that Birmingham is being bombed), even though the final injunction can do little more than grandly invoke the attitude to time and spirit of Eliot's *Burnt Norton* (e.g. stanza 16).

7   For the Time Being

For the Time Being,[1] subtitled 'A Christmas Oratorio', was written between 1941 and 1942 (see Spears, p. 205) and carries the argument of *New Year Letter* one important stage further, into the Christian faith. It might be said that argument is therefore left behind, and it is patently true that there is a world of difference implicit merely in the form of the Christmas oratorio, as distinct from that of the digressive verse epistle or the mythological sonnet sequence. But even so, the sense of exploratory didacticism, of justified and expository faith, is continually lurking in the later work; and the fact that its meta-phorical terms happen to be the Christian story of the Incarnation does not hinder Auden's compulsive urge to use these terms as parable, that is, as a description of the continual demands of the Eternal upon an individual living in Time. There is nothing merely functional or celebratory about the oratorio: it uses the traditional formulae to present a spiritual predicament, and it is therefore the same *kind* of formal discovery as its companion piece, *The Sea and the Mirror,* even though as an objective correlative the Bible or the Corpus Christi play is more closely relevant than *The Tempest.*

It is precisely because the Christian story is itself already, after centuries of theological comment, so heavily endowed with symbolic significance that *For the Time Being* sometimes falls comfortably (in a way that *The Sea and the Mirror* does not) into its received terminology. Auden would probably be the first to admit that subject-matter of this kind offers no particular head-start to poetry concerned with the problems of faith, and may even, in a sense, be too easy a way out. As Auden himself has written: 'There can no more be a "Christian" art than there can be a Christian science or a Christian diet. There can only be a Christian spirit in which an artist, a scientist, works or does not work. A painting of the Crucifixion is not necessarily more Christian in spirit than a still life, and may very well be less' (*The Dyer's Hand*, p. 458).

Thus Auden is concerned throughout the oratorio to make it clear that he is writing about his contemporary civilization. Simeon's meditation elaborates the basic belief that man must reach a certain spiritual impasse before he can be saved. Auden is influenced here by Reinhold Niebuhr's view of Protestantism as the continuous process of voluntary assent. The predicaments of the characters in the oratorio therefore provide a dramatized analysis of the predicament of modern man, who is continually faced with the choice of accepting or rejecting the Word made Flesh. What this really means must remain a theological mystery to the non-Christian, but it is apparent from Auden's treatment of it in this and other works (even some early ones) that it represents in the vaguest sense *a point of view* from which the social and psychological malaise of the world is susceptible of being transcended. It is not a rational point of view, because reason has failed: 'The liberal humanism of the past had failed to produce the universal peace and prosperity it promised, failed even to prevent a World War.'[2] The presentation in the oratorio of Herod as such a liberal humanist may be flattering to Herod (and the joke is a good one), but it is unflattering to liberal humanism.

The oratorio falls into nine parts, most of which correspond to the traditional division of the nativity story in the Church festivals and the medieval drama. The first part, 'Advent', is an essentially choric dialogue on man's condition. The first chorus (Yeatsian trimeter in a rondeauesque stanza) describes the emptiness and apathy of a society in the grip of winter and of war. Auden's talent for evoking doom is employed in his description of the impotence of progressive political power, a Hercules who is 'utterly lost', aware like Childe Roland 'of/Being watched from the horrid mountains/ By fanatical eyes' but of seeing no one, 'only hearing/The silence softly broken/By the poisonous rustle/Of famishing Arachne' (p. 134). All belief has been undermined. 'The watchman's tower' and 'the cedar grove' suggest Greek philosophy and the Greek gods, the terms in which Auden expounded the first two Kierkegaardian categories of the aesthetic and the ethical.[3] 'The civil garden' is thus left vulnerable to 'a wild passion' which is both objective and subjective, i.e. is both Hitler and the individual's tendency to nihilism and self-destruction.

This power is glumly delineated by the Narrator (p. 135) in a familiar context of bourgeois life. He is a kind of flat Eliotelian version of Auden's earlier dramatic anatomizers of doom, out of the Witnesses by the choruses from *The Rock:* the grisly embodied threat has been replaced by a problem of identity.

In the following chorus (p. 137) this state of despair is seen as self-induced: it arises from the unwillingness to believe ('Dreading to find its Father lest it find/The Goodness it has dreaded is not good') and the demand for the absolute conviction of a miracle. The following recitative makes clear Auden's attitude to such a rational search for God (e.g. of Joseph in the third section) by stating that 'The Real is what will strike you as really absurd'. The garden, which is described in *The Enchafèd Flood,* p. 29, as the innocent earthly paradise where there is no conflict between natural desire and moral duty, can only be reached through the desert ('the place of purgation for those who reject the evil city because they desire to become good', *The Enchafèd Flood,* p. 24). Although these symbols seem very Eliotelian (the waste land, and the rose-garden from *Burnt Norton*), it is clear from their discussion in *The Enchafèd Flood* that they are intellectual, even rather bookish, symbols, unlike the numinous counters of Eliot. The elegiacs of the chorus on p. 139 contrast man, in familiar Auden fashion, with other forms of life, and hope for the 'magic secret of how to extemporize life'.

The second section, 'The Annunciation' (p. 141), introduces a device from the morality plays in its personification of the four faculties. If man is to 'extemporize' life (and the word suggests not only the recapturing of an unselfconscious natural innocence of action, but also the existence of such an action 'out of time', i.e. ex-temporizing, redeeming the Time Being), he must attain that

wholeness of personality which was fragmented by the Fall. Thus
Intuition, Feeling, Sensation and Thought are the means by which
he may get glimpses of that redeemed life which his fallen nature
denies him ('We alone may look over/The wall of that hidden/
Garden whose entrance/To him is forbidden'), though of course he
can be misled by the information which these faculties separately
give him (cf. C. G. Jung, *The Integration of the Personality*, 1940).
Their speeches describe the exclusive limitations of their separate
points of view, and in style and import (the fantastic and symbolic
landscapes, the heresies of the divided personality) may be compared with the third part of Caliban's speech in *The Sea and the
Mirror*.

Gabriel then tells Mary that she has been chosen to do 'the will
of Love', and therefore may repair the sin of Eve (p. 146). This
moment of the supernatural cannot be said to be very convincingly
done. Auden is plainly more interested in the *idea* of the encounter of
the Eternal and the Temporal: as a mysterious marriage and a
divine gestation, it predictably calls forth the familiar sensuality,
paradox or homely detail of the seventeenth-century baroque, and
this not even the musical gusto (and quasi-Revivalist refrain) of the
final solo and chorus can do much to enliven (p. 147).

It is as if aware of this that Auden insistently modernizes the third
section, 'The Temptation of St Joseph' (p. 149). What was familiar
to medieval drama as 'Joseph's trouble about Mary' is inevitably
(at all events to an audience that would take such an attitude to
cuckoldry) seen as comic (*'Mary may be pure,/But, Joseph, are you
sure?'*). Auden, however, takes the opportunity of using Joseph as
an example of someone who needs to have a demonstrable reason
for believing (compare the second chorus, p. 137), someone who is
unwilling to take the leap of faith. He is not to be satisfied, but must
behave as if nothing unusual had happened. He must atone for all
man's habitual domination and patronizing of women (this speech
of the Narrator's is doubly amusing in that the examples of man's
aggressive masculinity are on the whole so absurdly and vulnerably
Thurberesque): 'you must be/The Weaker Sex whose passion is
passivity' (p. 152). Joseph and Mary then become types of the ideal
couple prayed to by 'common ungifted/Natures': by the romantics,

'enchanted with/The green Bohemia of that myth/Where knowledge of the flesh can take/The guilt of being born away'; by the bourgeoisie, 'whose married loves/Acquire so readily/The indolent fidelity/Of unaired beds'; even by unborn children, for 'in/The germ-cell's primary division/Innocence is lost'.

In the fourth section, 'The Summons' (p. 157), the star of the nativity, the sign of the Incarnation, serves also as a symbol of man's discarding of worldly wisdom ('orthodox sophrosyne') and his beginning in the way of faith, which must take him into a state of dread (cf. Kierkegaard's 'dizziness of freedom', the state of fear and trembling in which the choice is made).

The three wise men are types of the various intellectual heresies of denying the 'extemporized' life. The experimental scientist proves that objective reality can provide no clear answers about the truth; the philosopher discovers that the present does not exist; and the sociologist tries to make Eros ('the Venus of the Soma', i.e. the body) instead of Agape the basis of the just society by a simple smokescreen of utilitarian political theory. All three have reached a stultifying impasse in their knowledge and use of nature, time and love: the star provides them with a totally new possibility, the chance of discovering 'how to be human now'. Auden has underlined the bewilderment of Eliot's magus to the point at which the three wise men seem merely puerile ('At least we know for certain that we are three old sinners,/That this journey is much too long, that we want our dinners'), but this is evidently a deliberate ploy, for the following speech of the Star takes up the idea of the Quester as a bewildered child taking 'the cold hand of Terror for a guide'.

The Fugal-Chorus, and its ironical praise of Caesar which follows (p. 160), enlarges upon that world of material progress which the wise men have created, and which can no longer satisfy. Caesar's seven kingdoms – Philosophy, Physics, Mathematics, Economics, Technology, Medicine and Psychology – have all developed incredibly in modern times (e.g. 'Last night it was Tom, Dick and Harry; to-night it is S's with P's' alludes to the development of philosophical language: the everyday human examples which were used by the eighteenth-century philosophers have largely been superseded by the mathematical symbols used in symbolic logic).

But we cannot for this reason presume that the material word is a vehicle of the Truth because these ideals lie behind any 'Perfect State', even the Third Reich, as the Narrator observes in his exposure of the delusion (p. 163).

He introduces the Chorale, which prays 'that Thy Primal Love/ May weave in us the freedom of/The actually deficient on/The justly actual' (i.e. 'actual' in the double sense of 'at the moment' and 'active'). This Chorale was set to music by Britten for a BBC programme called 'Poet's Christmas' in 1944.

The fifth section, 'The Vision of the Shepherds' (p. 165), completes the picture of a generalized humanity awaiting the Good News. Unlike the wise men, the shepherds know nothing except how to keep the 'mechanism' going, and yet they, too (perhaps they especially), 'know that something will happen'. To a certain extent they are symbolical: in a contemporary review Auden wrote of the civilized world at the moment of the Incarnation, 'Its philosophical dualism divided both society and the individual personality, the wise from the ignorant, the Logos from the Flesh.'[4] Thus the words of the angelic chorus on p. 168 have a particular relevance to the poor and oppressed of society (as shepherds in the Corpus Christi play traditionally were, e.g. in the two Wakefield Shepherds' Plays of the Towneley Cycle), in that 'the old/Authoritarian/Constraint is replaced/By His Covenant,/And a city based/On love and consent/ Suggested to men'.

The sixth section, 'At the Manger' (p. 171), begins with Mary's lullaby [*Commonweal*, 25 Dec. 1942] predicting that the human element in Christ's nativity which she has contributed will bring him anxiety and death. This is followed by a duet of wise men and shepherds, contrasting the paths by which they have been brought to the threshold of the truth: the 'impatience' of the intellect and the 'laziness' of the flesh (Auden cheerfully uses the tomb/womb rhyme he had exposed in 'New Year Letter', l. 552). They conclude (p. 175) with an address to the Child in the person of that Love which 'is more serious than Philosophy'.

Even so, 'The Meditation of Simeon' which follows (p. 178) shows that the philosophical meaning of the Incarnation is considered very much of importance. Auden's Simeon is not a weary old man like Eliot's Simeon (whose peace was granted through his intuition of the incarnation) but an earnest theologian whose conversion must be insistently and rationally explained, so that his meditation becomes much more like a sermon, punctuated by alliterative summary exclamations from the chorus. Simeon traces different attitudes to the Fall, and shows that only when man's sense of sin is complete can the Word be made Flesh (the double sense of the Incarnation as a historical event and as a continual discovery of the individual is clearly intended). At this moment the unknown is no longer to be feared, and necessity is seen only as the freedom to be tempted, something which occurs to every man, so showing the traditional truth about fairy tales where heroism and success are not the prerogative of the exceptional. Dualism and monism are confounded, the universe is revealed as being real and various at the same time as being a divine totality, and art and science are justified. The 'Meditation' is a condensed and exhaustive statement of Auden's religious position at the time, a time when he was deeply influenced by Niebuhr. As such, it is probably more valuable for its ability to illuminate other writings of Auden's than as art in itself; for it is a prime example of that weakening tendency to cold abstraction, only occasionally revived by *ad hoc* metaphor, that demythologizing of the Christian kerygma, which almost seems to make the nativity drama an excuse and not an end in itself.

Much more imaginatively telling is the eighth section, 'The Massacre of the Innocents' (p. 185). It begins with a complaint from Herod [*Harper's Magazine,* Dec. 1943] that the rumour of the Incarnation is a threat to the orderly rational world which he has so patiently constructed and wishes to continue to govern. He has tried to stamp out superstition, but without much success, and now he predicts that belief in the Incarnation will mean that 'Reason will be replaced by Revelation ... Idealism will be replaced by Materialism ... Justice will be replaced by Pity' (p. 158). The elaboration of this state of affairs in a fantasia of specific examples gives the speech its particular flavour of wit and hidden irony that links it with earlier prose set-pieces of Auden's. Herod is not far from the truth,[5] and his child-like dismay and petulance make him a momentarily sympathetic figure ('Why can't people be sensible? I don't want to be horrid').

However, in supposing that the rumour might be true, he is forced to face his terrible predicament: God has given him the opportunity to kill God. The alternative would be the (to him) impossible demands of belief: 'once having shown them how, God would expect every man, whatever his fortune, to lead a sinless life in the flesh and on earth. Then indeed would the human race be plunged into madness and despair' (p. 189). Herod is rational, liberal and humane: he cannot bring himself to believe without proof, and so unhappily is forced to order the Massacre of the Innocents that his reasoning demands. What one admires about this part of the oratorio is that Auden has rejected the temptation to make Herod into the traditional raging tyrant. Herod is more effective for Auden's purposes, not as a Hitler, but as a representative of those attitudes which have no ultimate sanction against a Hitler. It is at this point (perhaps a little late) that the interest of the non-Christian is guaranteed.

The following soldier's song (p. 190) maintains the humour and intensifies the colloquial. A comic soldier was traditional in this part of the Corpus Christi play (e.g. Watkyn in the York cycle) and George is the archetypal amoral adventurer who finds a cheerful refuge in the army. It is left to Rachel (see Matthew ii and Jeremiah xxxi) to weep for the massacred infants (the dogs and sheep are once more symbols of the self-absorption of flesh and intellect).

The final section, 'The Flight into Egypt' (p. 192), takes up Rachel's description of 'these unending wastes of delirium', and treats the desert through which the holy family must pass as a symbol of the lifeless decadence of the modern world (the geysers and volcanoes turn up again in Caliban's speech in *The Sea and the Mirror*). The voices of the desert tempt with a surrealist fantasia punctuated by quasi-limericks like jingles in a travel brochure. Once they are safe, the Narrator breaks in with a speech [*Harper's Magazine*, Jan. 1944] describing the end of the modern Christmas, when all the decorative paraphernalia is put away: 'Once again/As in previous years we have seen the actual Vision and failed/To do more than entertain it as an agreeable/Possibility' (p. 195). We are back in 'the modern Aristotelian city', with the Atonement still to come (Auden evidently, like Milton before him, finds the Incarnation a more intellectually entertaining proposition than the Atonement), with 'bills to be paid, machines to keep in repair,/Irregular verbs to learn, the Time Being to redeem/From insignificance'.

This time-scale applies at once to the life of Christ, to the history of man and to the life of the individual; and Auden ends the speech with an aphorism from Kafka ('One must cheat no one, not even the world of its triumph') which reinforces the necessity for endurance, endurance of the mundane rather than endurance of the suffering one might be tempted to pray for. The final chorus celebrates this transformation of the mundane by the Incarnation as 'the Land of Unlikeness . . . the Kingdom of Anxiety . . the World of the Flesh' where the quester will achieve his fairy-tale wish.

8 The Sea and the Mirror

This 'Commentary on Shakespeare's *The Tempest*'[1] is a semi-dramatized discussion of the relationship between life and art in the context of spiritual possibility. Its starting point is Prospero's Epilogue:

> Now I want
> Spirits to enforce, Art to enchant;
> And my ending is despair,
> Unless I be reliev'd by prayer,
> Which pierces so, that it assaults
> Mercy itself, and frees all faults.

Prospero's words are, of course, a kind of pun, an actor's appeal for applause, but for Auden their suggestion that the artist as a maker of illusions is in need of supernatural grace when his belief in these illusions has been shattered, is a powerful one. It is one that is heavily reinforced by the allegorical interpretations of *The Tempest* which circulated in the nineteenth century, that Prospero is the artist, Ariel his imagination, Caliban his animal nature, and so on. Although these interpretations seem to have lost their critical following in this century (certainly since the work of Wilson Knight) they are present in D. G. James's *Scepticism and Poetry* (1937), a book which, in its attempt to show Shakespeare tending towards a Christian symbolism, may have stimulated Auden at this date. If we accept a crude identification of Prospero with Shakespeare, then it is possible to see the familiar Kierkegaardian categories lurking in

Auden's interpretation of Prospero's course of action: his enchantment belongs to the aesthetic, his forgiveness to the ethical, and his abdication to the religious sphere, and the whole action of the poem (taking place immediately after the end of Shakespeare's play) symbolizes a similar process of self-awareness, in a vocational context, going on in Auden's own consciousness.

The poem falls into three main parts: (a) Prospero gives Ariel his freedom; i.e., Auden feels that his spiritual quest takes him beyond a reliance on art. (b) The other characters soliloquize in celebration of their regeneration, though they are negated by the unrepentant Antonio; i.e., man's pride is beyond the reach of either the aesthetic or ethical appeal. (c) Caliban addresses the audience about his own role, and that of Ariel; i.e., he discusses what is expected from art in its treatment of reality, and of the rival worlds of the flesh and the spirit.

The 'Preface' of the Stage Manager to the Critics (p. 201) suggests that art, by presenting its audience with the surprising fulfilment of their secret wishes (stanza 1), reveals the human motive behind it. With reality it is a different matter: 'O what authority gives/Existence its surprise?' (stanza 2). Rational explanations do not ultimately help, and art, because it is essentially human, can only evoke emotions from its presentation of the human predicament; it cannot arouse the will or account for our sense of being victims of life (stanza 3). In the end, the religious sense has no need for art ('the smiling/Secret he cannot quote'), for it is the Unknown which has supreme importance (Shakespeare allusions are blended here with Eliot).

'Prospero to Ariel' (p. 203) begins by establishing the basic terms on which the Unknown must be approached: the creative imagination is responsible for the denial of a reality that has to be faced ('I am glad I have freed you/For under your influence death is inconceivable'), and is ultimately a poor exchange for life itself ('giving a city,/Common warmth and touching substance, for a gift/In dealing with shadows'). Art is basically a compensation for life, 'the power to enchant that comes from disillusion' (cf. 'New Year Letter', Part I), and it has great power to reveal and explain life's disorder.

Prospero's first song is based on this idea (p. 205). Art's function as truth is so powerful, he says, that we cannot bear too much of it. He turns to the other characters of the play, admitting his own responsibility for Antonio's treason. Here, I think, is a suggestion of the failure of liberal humanism to avert Hitler. This is not the particular responsibility of the artist, though in the second part of the poem Antonio, in his arrogant self-sufficiency, stands outside Prospero's power, and, while he denies it, will continue to call it forth. Prospero's 'impervious disgrace' is, however, not the defiant tempted Ego of Antonio, but the recalcitrant Id of Caliban, whose 'absolute devotion' Prospero has himself desired. All the other characters have 'been soundly hunted/By their own devils into their human selves'. Thinking of Miranda and Ferdinand leads him into his second song (p. 207), about the erotic ideals of youth, middle age and old age: as an old man, Prospero will find it hard to embark on his spiritual quest without being able to speak about it ('shall I ever be able/To stop myself from telling them what I am doing,/ – Sailing alone, out over seventy thousand fathoms – ?'). The Kierkegaardian leap demands suffering 'without saying something ironic or funny/ On suffering' (cf. 'The Quest', No. XII). Prospero's final song (p. 209) shows him, even as 'trembling he takes/The silent passage/ Into discomfort', still wishing for Ariel's song, as though at the moment of rejection art had attained a fresh poignancy and power.

'The Supporting Cast, Sotto Voce' (p. 211) is something of a virtuoso performance as, 'dotted about the deck', the changed characters deliver, each in an appropriate verse-form, an account of how the magic has changed them and how they mean to pursue their destinies.[2] Antonio, whose speech comes first, and whose refrain ironically dominates the whole section in its expression of his unregenerate will, represents man's freedom to create the disorder which exists for art to make sense of. *The Tempest* is about the purgation of evil, but Antonio's virtual silence in Act V could indicate that he has not, as the personal agent of this evil, repented. In his stanza about Hitler in 'September 1, 1939', Auden wrote: 'I and the public know/What all schoolchildren learn,/Those to whom evil is done/Do evil in return' (*Another Time*, p. 112). Prospero is responsible for his brother, because he put the temptation to usurp in his way: in other words, it is the irresponsibility of art in the real

world which guarantees art's continuing importance as a means of
healing the errors which its isolation has created. As long as Antonio
exists, Prospero will not be able to give up his role. As Antonio
says, 'while I stand outside/Your circle, the will to charm is still
there' (cf. 'New Year Letter', ll. 64–75). Prospero's 'all' is 'partial'
because it is not a 'true gestalt', and Antonio is half-justified in his
sarcastic view of it as a familiar Circean charm ('As all the pigs have
turned back into men') which can easily be resisted by the unaccom-
modating will.

Ferdinand's sonnet (p. 212) takes a hint from the involved syntax
of his speech in *The Tempest* (e.g. at III. i) to create a tone of innocent
obscurity which pleasantly borders on pastiche, though in its awareness of 'another tenderness', a Light which enables the lovers to
possess 'the Right Required Time' of the Kairos, it is seriously
Christian.

Stephano's ballade (p. 213) involves his search for identity. His
belly, representative of his body and heavy with drink, exchanges
cravings with his mind, not only in the sense that it wishes to get rid
of the alcohol as fast as Stephano wishes to consume it ('Between
the bottle and the "loo" '), but because it is the belly which has learnt
to need the alcohol through the mind's desire to escape from its
'disappointments' and 'ghosts'. The search for identity is assisted by
drink, because it dispels melancholy ('The high play better than the
blue') and imparts the illusion of a unity of mind and body, even
though 'The will of one by being two/At every moment is denied'.

Gonzalo (p. 214) is representative of the interpretative reason 'in
whose booming eloquence/Honesty became untrue'. His prediction
(of the ideal Commonwealth) did come true in a sense, but he is
guilty of making the song of the Absurd sound 'ridiculous and wrong'
because of his compulsive and pedantic rationalization (the reference
is to his vision of the political threat, represented by Ariel's song at
II. i. 295).

Adrian and Francisco (p. 216) express, in a rather camp couplet,
their realization that their superficial life must come to an end: their
appalled resignation is largely a theatrical gesture, a reaction of the
corrupt court.

Alonso's letter (p. 216) is to be opened by Ferdinand after his death. It was first published in the *Partisan Review,* October 1943. Its central image is of the 'Way of Justice' as 'a tightrope/Where no prince is safe for one instant'. On one side is the sea, on the other the desert, each lying in wait to tempt the prince from his path, or to purge him of his error if he does stray. The sea represents the life of the senses, the desert the life of the spirit, each of which should ideally balance the other. Auden elaborated the sea-desert symbolism in *The Enchafèd Flood* (1951), e.g.: 'The sea, then, is the symbol of primitive potential power as contrasted with the desert of actualized triviality, of living barbarism versus lifeless decadence' (p. 28). The statue in the last stanza is borrowed from *The Winter's Tale*.

The Master and Boatswain (p. 220) sing of the prostitutes of Stephano's song in *The Tempest,* II.ii.47. They take a hard, practical, even Freudian, view of the consolations of sex. They see it fatalistically as a kind of chain reaction stemming ultimately from a hopeless search for a lost maternal love ('nightingales' is slang for prostitutes; cf. Eliot's 'Sweeney among the Nightingales': 'The nightingales are singing near/The Convent of the Sacred Heart').

Sebastian's sestina (p. 220) shows him glad to have been found out before he was able actually to murder Alonso ('my proof/Of mercy that I wake without a crown'). His guilt has only been a dream, his error in a sense exposed by the sword which he took up against his brother: now he has woken from the dream, and ceased to be a negative personality even though his nature has been revealed in its full weakness. He is 'glad today/To be ashamed, not anxious, not a dream', and 'It is defeat gives proof we are alive'.

Trinculo (p. 222), as a clown, is a type of the artist, whose loneliness is symbolized by his tallness. His humour is seen as a nervous reaction to his alienation from life: 'A terror shakes my tree,/A flock of words fly out,/Whereat a laughter shakes/The busy and devout.'

Miranda's villanelle (p. 223) expresses her certainty of love in terms of fairy-tales, as Ferdinand had done in terms of striving for a vision of the Logos. Ferdinand is hers 'as mirrors are lonely' in the sense that Ferdinand's eyes are more attractive mirrors for her, so that her looking-glass will no longer reflect her image, and was even lonely when she used it, for it could not see itself in her eyes as Ferdinand can. The conceit is a familiar one in Elizabethan poetry, and its use as a refrain enforces what the other images also propose, that her love is largely an aesthetic pleasure ('O brave new world') and is expressive of a magical harmony ('children in a circle dancing').

The third, and longest section, 'Caliban to the Audience' (p. 225), is an insistent, amusing and exhausting prose disquisition on the role of art, written in the style of Henry James. Auden is concerned to examine art's particular place in society (as he must be concerned to defend the aesthetic character of the individual creative consciousness), but the admonitory and ventriloqual voice of Caliban, for ever confiding, cajoling, comforting and castigating, forces a recognition of the unbridgeable gulf between what men wish to be like and what they really are. The speech concludes that for the artist or for any human agent the opposed contraries of life (Caliban, Ariel) are almost impossible to reconcile: only the Supreme Artist is able to create 'the perfected Work which is not ours', of which art itself is only a 'feebly figurative sign'.

The argument, as in earlier prose pieces such as the 'Address for a Prize-Day' in *The Orators* or the Vicar's Sermon in *The Dog Beneath the Skin,* is imaginatively detached from the normal functions of the kind of rhetorical prose it resembles: the Caliban persona ensures that what is said derives from the point of view (however imaginatively varied) of man's fallen sensual nature, his 'impervious disgrace', which still imagines that its attempted transformation by the imaginative order of art is something whose failure is a suitable subject for a sermon. Behind Caliban, as it were, is Auden himself, attempting in this way to show that he can assimilate the unassimilatable, and find a role in front of the theatre curtain for the one character who may be neither left on the island nor taken on board ship for the new life. Even if one takes this only as a literary joke, it is a very good one, and sustains the theme admirably. Caliban's style partakes of the smiling drone of the unnerving bore.

The speech falls into three parts. First of all he takes the audience's part in enquiring of Shakespeare why he should have introduced Caliban into *The Tempest* at all. 'Our native Muse' is presented as a hostess faced by an unwelcome guest. Although she doesn't, for instance, have any suburban worries about 'what the strait-laced Unities might possibly think', she does draw the line at Caliban, and so do the audience, because to them Art is a wholly other world of which they feel privileged to have glimpses, and in which opposites are reconciled and time is in control (p. 229: 'what delights us about her world is just that it neither is nor possibly could become one in which we could breathe or behave'). Caliban in such a world appears as a distorted parody of what he is in real life, 'a savage and deformed slave' instead of the 'nude august elated archer of our heaven', i.e. Eros. In the mirror of art, Caliban appears 'incorrigibly right-handed'. The address to Shakespeare ends lightly with the parallel possibility (pp. 233–4):

Is it possible that, not content with inveigling Caliban into Ariel's kingdom, you have also let loose Ariel into Caliban's? We note with alarm that when the other members of the final tableau were dismissed, He was not returned to His arboreal confinement as He should have been.

If there is a veiled Christian joke in this, the joke must be Caliban's.

The second part of his speech is addressed, on Shakespeare's behalf, to young poets for whom Ariel, the creative imagination, is a faithful servant at first (p. 236: 'the eyes, the ears, the nose, the putting two and two together are, of course, all His, and yours only the primitive wish to know'). In time, the partnership goes sour, but Ariel refuses to be set free (p. 237):

Striding up to Him in fury, you glare into his unblinking eyes and stop dead, transfixed with horror at seeing reflected there, not what you had always expected to see, a conqueror smiling at a conqueror, both promising mountains and marvels, but a gibbering fist-clenched creature with which you are all too unfamiliar.

The artist, in other words, may too easily ignore his Caliban nature. To have chastised the flesh, or to have given it complete freedom, might have been ways of reaching the truth, but these would have distracted the artist *qua* artist. When his 'charms . . . have cracked' and his 'spirits have ceased to obey', then he is left alone with 'the dark thing' he 'could never abide to be with' (p. 239).

The third part of Caliban's speech is *in propria persona* as he addresses the audience on the subject of himself and Ariel. The first two parts of his speech have shown that he can upset both the work of art and the artists by his eventually unignorable presence: now it is the audience's turn to be brought face to face with the choices they must make in real life (p. 240):

... you have now all come together in the larger colder emptier room on this side of the mirror which *does* force your eyes to recognize and reckon with the two of us, your ears to detect the irreconcilable difference between my re-iterated affirmation of what your furnished circumstances categorically are, and His successive propositions as to everything else which they conditionally might be.

Caliban then describes life as a journey in which the moments of actual travel are few; even when the right step is taken, this only brings the traveller so 'far outside this land of habit' that he immediately becomes vulnerable to the twin heresies of desiring either a retreat into the immediate (via Caliban) or an escape into the possible (via Ariel).

The first of these courses gives Auden an opportunity to indulge in a version of his own Eden (cf. *The Dyer's Hand,* p. 6), in a sur-realistic dream landscape which represents the childhood nostalgia of those who 'have never felt really well in this climate of distinct ideas' (p. 243). Caliban responds to their plea by conducting them instead to what is really 'the ultimately liberal condition', an arid solipsistic universe, 'where Liberty stands with her hands behind her back, not caring, not minding *anything'*. The result is the despair of having nothing to choose, because you are the only subject in the world.

The second course is taken by those who wish to escape from the chaos of life to 'that Heaven of the Really General Case', a Platonic universe of transcendental reality, to which they imagine Ariel is able to lead them. Instead they arrive in a world without causal necessity, without objectivity, in which events may have any inter-pretation because all sense of *haecceitas,* or Thisness, has been lost. This is the Quest's Negative Way, and, like the first course, leads to an annihilating despair.

Caliban presents these alternative routes ('the facile glad-handed highway or the virtuous averted track') as the horns of a dilemma

which faces the artist, too, for he cannot successfully portray both
the truth and man's condition of estrangement from it; and worse,
where he is successful in doing this, 'the more he must strengthen
your delusion that an awareness of the gap is in itself a bridge, your
interest in your imprisonment a release' (p. 248).

So art in a sense can be self-defeating, for an awareness of life's
inadequacies can itself become an interesting game. And in life itself
the irreconcilable categories, Ariel and Caliban, act out in *ad hoc*
fashion (the metaphor being of 'the greatest grandest opera rendered
by a very provincial touring company indeed', p. 248) fallen man's
version of the perfect life, Becoming not Being. At the moment of
realization that this is such a shoddy performance, we are aware
(Auden asserts) of 'that Wholly Other Life': 'it is just here, among
the ruins and the bones, that we may rejoice in the perfected Work
which is not ours' (p. 250).

The reader has a slight sense of the *deus ex machina* at this point.
Auden has subtly and brilliantly exposed the contradictions that
govern both art and life, but he has not (despite Caliban's confident
and persuasive rationality) been able to show how they may be
resolved, except by this gesture towards deity. However, in the
'Postscript' (p. 251) the totality of the individual is lyrically and
mysteriously expressed by Ariel's love for Caliban, and reinforced
by the Prompter's echo '. . . *I*'. The song puts man firmly at the centre
again, his body and spirit precariously but tenderly united:

> Both of us know why,
> Can, alas, foretell,
> When our falsehoods are divided,
> What we shall become,
> One evaporating sigh
>
>   . . . *I*

9 Poems 1939–1947

The earliest poems from this New York period appeared in *Another Time* (1940) and the latest in *Nones* (1951). Auden's attention was evidently devoted to the important longer poems of this period, but even so his shorter pieces reveal developing strengths, particularly in the lighter modes. His mental energy was beautifully channelled by the relaxed conversationalism which seems to have been the chief stylistic influence that America provided, while his inventiveness and variety appear as great as ever.

'In Memory of W. B. Yeats' [*New Republic,* 8 Mar. 1939; AT; CP, p. 48; CSP50; CSP, p. 141] contains two basic, related points: that a poet's work ultimately becomes independent of him, because he has no control over the interpretation which posterity will give it; and that therefore it is conditioned by society, and its role in society can be no more than a passive one. The rather sinister dramatization of Yeats's death in the first section is thus an essential part of the mystery of a poet's destiny, and the numb elegiacs reinforce the sense that the external world, in the grip of winter, is quite irrelevant to the internal world of poetry: the external 'instruments' measure the fact of the weather and the fact of Yeats's death, but the internal 'guts' receive and modify his life's work.

Similarly, the metaphor of revolution represents the purely material fate of the poet's body: the city is in revolt, but the country-side (the poetry) goes on as usual. The poems, by being still read, continue to live ('By mourning tongues/The death of the poet was kept from his poems') and the poet, in ceasing to be a physical being,

takes on the affective value of his *oeuvre* ('he became his admirers').
An interesting parallel, in this connection, is provided by Mittenhofer
in Auden's opera libretto *Elegy for Young Lovers:* as a character, he
was derived in many ways from Yeats.

In an article entitled 'The Public *v*. the late Mr William Butler
Yeats',[1] which was written at about the same time as the poem,
Auden elaborated some of the arguments about Yeats's talent and
beliefs which are alluded to in the second and third parts. 'You
were silly like us' is echoed by the words of the 'Public Prosecutor'
('But, you may say, he was young; youth is always romantic; its
silliness is part of its charm'), and is more seriously explained by the
'Council for the Defence', who tries to show that Yeats's interest in
fairies and Anima Mundi was in a sense a search for a binding force
for society in the face of social atomism. The poem's answer in
Part II ('Ireland has her madness and her weather still,/For poetry
makes nothing happen: it survives/In the valley of its making') is
further enlarged upon by the Defence Counsel: '. . . art is a product
of history, not a cause. Unlike some other products, technical
inventions for example, it does not re-enter history as an effective
agent, so that the question whether art should or should not be
propaganda is unreal. The case for the prosecution rests on the
fallacious belief that art ever makes anything happen.'

Auden does not deliver judgment in the article. And indeed he
delivers a convincing case for the prosecution, which believes that
'a working knowledge of and sympathetic attitude towards the most
progressive thought of his time' is one of the three requirements of a
great poet. Three stanzas of Part III, now omitted, showed how this
requirement might be circumvented: Time, who worships language,
therefore 'with this strange excuse/Pardoned Kipling and his views,/
And will pardon Paul Claudel,/Pardons him for writing well'. It is
not clear whether Auden omitted these stanzas because he no longer
adhered to this doubtful belief, or in fact to indicate that the pardon
is effectively complete. Nor is it clear whether, in Auden's view, the
eve-of-war hatred and political malaise described in Part III is
effectively redeemed by art which takes little account of the real
circumstances of that malaise. No doubt the omission of the stanzas
does assist the reader to accept more easily the real point about the

value of art that Auden is making, that it teaches 'the free man how to praise', i.e. how to begin to value order above disorder, even though the order is only the order of art (cf. 'New Year Letter', ll. 78–79: 'Art is not life, and cannot be/A midwife to society').

'In Memory of Ernst Toller' [*New Yorker,* 17 June 1939; AT; CP, p. 124; CSP50; CSP, p. 143], which follows the essentially grand and musical Yeats elegy, is more intimate in tone. Toller, the expressionist playwright, hanged himself in New York on 22 May 1939. He had fled from Nazi Germany, was perhaps uncertain of his future and certainly short of money, but on the other hand had talked of suicide long before. He once wrote: 'If an intellectual man yields to death, the compelling motive will be the need of knowledge.'[2] Auden uses as an image of Toller's thoughts of suicide the pair of swallows that had nested in his cell in the summer of 1922 in the Stadelheim prison in Munich, where he had been imprisoned in 1919 for his part in attempting to set up a soviet republic in Bavaria. It was here that he wrote most of his plays, and also *Das Schwalbenbuch,* a book about the nesting swallows. In the third stanza Auden wonders what psychological or political reason could account for Toller's death. The questions are purely rhetorical, for Auden's real answer is contained in the fatalistic seventh stanza ('We are lived by powers we pretend to understand': cf. 'New Year Letter', l. 1649, 'the powers/That we create with are not ours').

'Voltaire at Ferney' [*Listener,* 9 Mar. 1939; AT; CP, p. 6; CSP50; CSP, p. 144], with its picture of the collaborators in *L'Encyclopédie* as rebellious school-children, assumes a subtly damaging attitude to its subject-matter. Voltaire is presented as the 'cleverest of them all', and his model estate at Ferney, with its agricultural experiment, social progress and benevolent concern for the local inhabitants, is only one aspect of his desire to defeat 'the infamous grown-ups', the superstitious and fanatical Establishment of his day. Auden had been reading N. L. Torrey's *The Spirit of Voltaire* (his review of it appeared in *The Nation,* 25 March 1939). The 'blind old woman' is Mme la Marquise du Deffand. Of the writers with whom Voltaire is compared in stanza 4, D'Alembert 'was in essential agreement with Voltaire's point of view, but . . . was "under the monster's claw", was drawing a pension from the

Court, and did not dare to compromise himself' (Torrey, p. 173).
Pascal, according to Voltaire, was someone who, like Plato, had
mistaken his vision for the truth: 'Voltaire admired the mysticism
and the style of his great predecessor, and at the same time he saw
in him the doctrinaire whose influence it was most important for
him to combat' (Torrey, p. 185). Diderot's materialistic atheism
seemed too narrowly systematic to Voltaire, while Rousseau had
given in by becoming a sentimentalist, a rather puritanical defender
of the goodness of God.

In his stand against 'superstition', Voltaire becomes a near relation of Herod in *For the Time Being,* except that Auden still at this
date seems to see such humanism as a possible stance. Its relevance
to the period just before the outbreak of the Second World War
is obvious: 'still all over Europe stood the horrible nurses/Itching to
boil their children' (a sly piece of Struwwelpeter, this: they are
doubly horrible, because boils itch). Voltaire is right to try to
prevent them, but is he not guilty (according to Auden's later
beliefs) of denying 'the Multiplicity, asserting that God is One who
has no need of friends and is indifferent to a World of Time and
Quantity and Horror which He did not create . . .'? (*For the Time
Being,* p. 183.) The poem ends with a bland and limiting comment on
such purely secular efforts to achieve the Just Society: 'Overhead/
The uncomplaining stars composed their lucid song.'

'Herman Melville' [*Southern Review,* Autumn 1939; AT; CP,
p. 146; CSP50; CSP, p. 145] refers to the fact that, after his
adventurous youth, Melville settled down as a New York customs
inspector. Auden sees this 'extraordinary mildness' as a kind of love,
a state of achieved goodness which could be reached only by
exorcizing the terror which produced his early books (a terror also
seen as Moby-Dick, 'the rare ambiguous monster that had maimed
his sex'). The storm had to blow itself out, a metaphor which also
effectively describes Melville's literary career (six books in six years).
Billy Budd was written in his last years, and presents the discovery
that 'evil is unspectacular', i.e. that we are all Claggarts, that we all
help to crucify Christ (Billy) and cannot escape from our destiny.
In the final stanza God is seen as a projection of parental images:
Melville's friendship with the older Nathanael Hawthorne prompted

his discovery that 'his [i.e. Melville's] love was selfish', that the real love is Agape, the Christian charity, and that man must surrender to this love so that the City of God can be reformed (' "The Godhead is broken like bread. We are the pieces" ').

'The Unknown Citizen' [*Listener*, 3 Aug. 1939; AT; CP, p. 142; CSP50; CSP, p. 146] sketches in, with the lightest of ironies, some details of 'the average man . . . put through the statistician's hoop' ('New Year Letter', ll. 1366–70). Bureaucracy cannot be concerned with the happiness of the individual, cannot indeed be concerned with any of the things that make him individual. Thus the title of the poem (parodying the grave of the Unknown Soldier) suggests an administrative chimera, whose predictability Auden wittily laments.

'The Prophets' [*Southern Review*, Autumn 1939; AT; CP, p. 99; CSP50; CSP, p. 147] and the following poem, 'Like a Vocation', are, in oblique terms, about Auden's returning need for belief (though the imagery suggests an amatory context; cf. 'Heavy Date', CSP, p. 151: 'When I was a child, I/Loved a pumping-engine,/Thought it every bit as/Beautiful as you'). In 'The Prophets' he uses autobiography to show how a sense of the numinous may be present even when not properly understood. In *The Dyer's Hand* (p. 34) he comments that his reading in adolescence consisted of books like *Machinery for Metalliferous Mines* or *Lead and Zinc Ores of Northumberland and Alston Moor*. The 'worship' mentioned in the poem was really a matter of reading 'the technological prose of my favourite books in a peculiar way. A word like *pyrites*, for example, was for me, not simply an indicative sign; it was the Proper Name of a Sacred Being, so that, when I heard an aunt pronounce it *pirrits*, I was shocked. Her pronunciation was more than wrong, it was ugly. Ignorance was impiety.'

In the same way, deserted industrial landscapes later had a meaning for Auden, but they let it be, as it were, the meaning which he at the time was prepared for; they taught him 'gradually without coercion'. They are like Rilke's *Dinge*. The *Ding* 'is ready to simplify everything, made you intimate with thousands through playing a thousand parts, being animal and tree and king and child, – and when it withdrew, they were all there. This Something, worthless as it was, prepared your relationships with the world, it guided you into

happening, and among people, and, further; you experienced
through it, through its existence, its anyhow appearance, through its
final smashing or its enigmatic departure, all that is human, right
into the depths of death' (Rilke, *Puppen,* quoted in *New Year Letter,*
p. 93). The concluding section shows how the 'answer' is revealed in
terms of the human love which could not be given by the 'book' or
the 'Place'; only this can lead to the love which is not selfish ('vain')
or unrewarded ('vain').

'Like a Vocation' [*Southern Review,* Autumn 1939: 'The Territory
of the Heart'; AT; CP, p. 82: 'Please Make Yourself at Home';
CSP50; CSP, p. 148] addresses divinity directly, and refers to the
poet in the third person as 'that terrified/Imaginative child who only
knows you/As what the uncles call a lie'. The poem appears to ask
for revelation in terms of individual choice ('like a vocation')
because anything else seems to involve an imposition upon the
country of spirit (in terms of the metaphor, the dictator and the
tourist of the first stanza would be revealed religion and deism).
Thus 'politeness and freedom' are, as spiritual qualities, merely
superficial, and the regimented devotion of the masses in organized
religion has even less to do with the truth. The obscurities of this
poem possibly indicate a certain tentativeness in dealing with the subject: a tentativeness shortly to be abandoned in the conceptual ease
and metaphysical disquisitions of the longer poems of the 'forties.

'The Riddle' [*New Republic,* 26 July 1939: 'The Leaves of Life';
AT; CP, p. 149; CSP50; CSP, p. 149] concerns man's double
nature in relation to God. This idea is best explained in Auden's
own words in his essay in *Modern Canterbury Pilgrims* (ed. James A.
Pike, 1956):

As a spirit, a conscious person endowed with free will, every man has, through
faith and grace, a unique 'existential' relation to God, and few since St
Augustine have described this relation more profoundly than Kierkegaard.
But every man has a second relation to God which is neither unique nor
existential: as a creature composed of matter, as a biological organism, every
man, in common with everything else in the universe, is related by necessity
to the God who created that universe and saw that it was good, for the laws of
nature to which, whether he likes it or not, he must conform are of divine
origin.

Thus the 'Duality' of the first stanza is the duality of freedom and necessity, whose origin is located with the fall of man in the Garden of Eden. Auden's ideas on this subject are more fully expounded, and clarified, in Simeon's speech in *For the Time Being,* and lie at the back of many of the poems of the 'fifties. Eden in this poem is portrayed in visual terms reminiscent of Dürer's engraving *Adam and Eve.* In imagination, the angelic sword guarding Eden against Adam and Eve's return becomes 'bayonets glittering in the sun': the judgment of God turns into the human judgment of 'soldiers who will judge' because the world of Necessity, a world linked to the laws of nature, does not involve the individual in a personal reward of Grace (i.e. 'the Smile'). In his free existential relationship with God (the 'vocation' of the previous poem), the individual must act out of love and conviction of the truth, but in the world of necessity this is not so: 'Even orators may speak/Truths of value to the weak,/Necessary acts are done/By the ill and the unjust'. This duality ('the Judgment and the Smile') is unavoidable. The Kingdoms of the Short and the Tall in the third stanza remind us of the Truly Weak and the Truly Strong Man (see p. 32), a concept which Auden revived in metaphysical terms in his sonnet sequence 'The Quest' in *New Year Letter.*

As with many of Auden's half-lyrical, half-philosophical poems of this sort, it turns in the last stanzas into a love poem. The inevitability of the duality prompts the argued reflection that Eros is thus the essence of human life. This is both because it is our greatest contentment, and because it shows us this limitation ('That we love ourselves alone') as a preparation for a spiritual development which the poem is not concerned with exploring, but which lies suggestively behind it: that reconciliation which is the subject of the related poem 'As He Is'.[3]

'Heavy Date' [AT; CP, p. 105; CSP50; CSP, p. 151], with its insistent trochaic rhythm and brief lines, achieves an effect which is appropriately careless, a kind of halting intellectual patter evading the demands of the metre. Indeed, the fact that the syllabic pattern is absolutely regular suggests that the poem is not really intended to be read with an eye to the traditional prosody that it is still theoretically invoking. Though the poem pretends to be the 'purely random thinking' of the poet as he awaits a prearranged sexual encounter, it does emerge as a perfectly coherent discussion of the nature of love.

Beginning with Malinowski's anthropological observation that the typical Oedipus dream of killing the father and committing incest with the mother occurs only in patriarchal communities (cf. 'The Good Life' in *Christianity and the Social Revolution,* 1935, p. 46), Auden concludes that the erotic object is purely relative and subjective, and may develop in unpredictable ways. Spinoza's idea of the 'intellectual love of God' demands that the individual recreate in his own mind some part of the self-creative activity of Nature, and thus transcend his mortality. This objective may have suggested the argument of the remainder of the poem, that 'Love requires an Object',[4] although Auden is playful: 'When I was a child, I/Loved a pumping-engine,/Thought it every bit as/Beautiful as you.' Love, he goes on, does not merely require an object: it requires mutual need, and the poem bows gracefully out by observing that the actuality of sex has nothing whatever to do with intellectual justification of it.

'Law Like Love' [AT; CP, p. 74; CSP50; CSP, p. 154] is based on Auden's distinction between human and natural law, which is also treated in *New Year Letter,* l. 761*n* (p. 138). Awareness of this distinction prompts the lovers to avoid the bland assertions used by other members of society ('Law is . . .'), and to state only 'a timid similarity' ('*Like* love . . .'). Man cannot step outside necessity to discover rules about his condition: 'In Natural law . . . there can be no opposition between the will of the whole and the separate wills of the parts' *(New Year Letter).* Thus to say that the Law is 'like love' is a reasonable approximation, reinforced by the verse's nursery didacticism (stanza 4, for example, is pure A. A. Milne). 'The Hidden Law', the rondeau which follows, may be found in the 'Notes' to *New Year Letter* (line 761*n*).

'Twelve Songs'. No. I: 'Say this city has ten million souls' [*New Yorker,* 15 Apr. 1939: 'Song'; *New Writing,* Autumn 1939: 'Refugee Blues'; AT; CP, p. 227; CSP50; CSP, p. 157] is one of Auden's most successful uses of a popular form. He well knew of the difficulties facing refugees from Nazi Germany: in 1936 he had married Erika Mann (daughter of Thomas Mann), merely in order to provide her with a passport. The refrain skilfully accommodates a varying tone of resignation, disturbance and menace. No. II: 'Driver, drive faster and make a good run' [AT; CSP, p. 158] was the last of the group of cabaret songs for Hedli Anderson in *Another Time,* and was omitted from later collections. Its exuberance and rhythmical oddity give it a charm which was well worth retrieving: the import of poems like 'Heavy Date' or 'Law like Love' attains here an emotional simplicity which is much more moving, despite the roughness of the calypso form.

No. III: 'Warm are the still and lucky miles' [AT; CP, p. 238; CSP50; CSP, p. 159] is an ecstatic lyric in which the epithets are just a little too easy, the inversions a little too relaxed, for the incisiveness it really needed, though the regenerative power of love is felt and the feeling conveyed. No. IV: 'Carry her over the water' and No. V: 'The single creature leads a partial life' [CP, pp. 199 and 230; CSP50; CSP, p. 160] are both from the Auden–Britten opera *Paul Bunyan,* performed at Columbia University in May 1941, but afterwards suppressed and never published.[5] No. V is a trio showing the shared loneliness of man and his pets. The Dog and the two Cats (coloratura- and mezzo-sopranos) were introduced to provide the only female voices in the opera (see Hoffman, p. 188). No. VI: 'Eyes look into the well' [From *The Dark Valley* in *Best Broadcasts of 1939–40,* ed. Max Wylie (1940); CP, p. 201; CSP50; CSP, p. 161] is from the radio play that Auden derived from his cabaret sketch *Alfred* (published in *New Writing,* Autumn 1936) and maintains its fantasy by evoking doom from a cento of fairy-tale images. No. VII: 'Jumbled in one common box' [*Nation,* 29 Mar. 1941; CP, p. 206; CSP50; CSP, p. 161] proposes that human life ('Orchid, swan and Caesar' represents love, art and politics) cannot escape from time; there is no order, only a debasement of philosophy and art, a sinister calm before a pointless disorder represented by the final tongue-twister. The mechanical virtuoso rhyming accentuates the blankness of this poem.

No. VIII: 'Though determined Nature can' [CP, p. 231; CSP50; CSP, p. 162] objectifies the selfishness of Eros into the Accuser, the One whose name is Legion, the Devil. The repeated qualifications of the poem ('Though . . .') make this summoning involuntary, but it is none the less real, and reflects man's duality ('Who is passionate enough/When the punishment begins?'). Almost as a corollary comes No. IX: 'My second thoughts condemn' [CP, p. 215; CSP50; CSP, p. 163], a rather more resigned and sympathetic tussle with the demands of desire in the guise of romantic love. The notion in the first stanza is one that Auden was fond of producing at awkward moments (cf. 'Dichtung und Wahrheit' in *Homage to Clio,* p. 50: ' "I will love You for ever", swears the poet. I find this easy to swear too. *I will love You at 4.15 p.m. next Tuesday:* is that still as easy?'). The point here is that such an extravagant gesture belongs very much to the world of time in which it may be forgiven for being dichtung and not wahrheit, but that outside time the Truth sits in continual judgment ('All flesh is grass, and all the goodliness thereof is as the flower of the field ... but the word of our God shall stand for ever', Isaiah xl) and no one 'on earth' can really measure the consequences.

No. X: 'On and on and on' [*Atlantic,* Nov. 1947: 'Serenade'; N; CSP, p. 164] objects to the demands of the libido with a pleasantly weighted humility. The 'shouts' or 'salute' of the first stanza (the aggression of the waterfall, the comic Dogberry nature of man) give place to the 'asks neighbourhood' of the final stanza: since the poem is more or less a sexual invitation ('my embodied love'), the poetic sleight of hand in the culminating gentleness has a sly metaphysical conviction. No. XI: 'Sing, Ariel, sing' is from *The Sea and the Mirror,* and No. XII: 'When the Sex War ended' is from *For the Time Being.*

'In Memory of Sigmund Freud' [*Kenyon Review,* Winter 1940; AT; CP, p. 163; CSP50; CSP, p. 166] is more discursive than some of the other elegies which accompanied it in *Another Time,* and for that reason seems less occasional, though possibly it is thereby a greater tribute. Auden wished to 'place' the role of psychology more exactly within the ideas he was developing about the importance of moral choice. Freud 'showed us what evil is, not, as we thought,/deeds that must be punished, but our lack of faith'. That is to say, psychotherapy can reveal the distinction between causal necessity and logical necessity more clearly,[6] so that the responsible moral choice can be disentangled from circumstances which

confused it. Freud was 'doing us some good' by helping to turn
tribulations into temptations, as any good scientist should.

The secondary theme of the poem, developed in the last half-
dozen stanzas, is that Freud also helped to 'unite/the unequal
moieties' of body and mind, and it is for this reason that he is
mourned by 'the household of Impulse', the sexual motive that both
binds men together socially and creates discord between them
personally.

This poem seems, incidentally, to be the first that Auden wrote in
syllabic metre, largely under the influence of Marianne Moore (see
The Dyer's Hand, p. 296). *Another Time* appeared on 7 February
1940, thus clearly antedating the Prologue and Epilogue to *New
Year Letter* which were first printed on 10 May and 7 December
1940 and which use the same stanza pattern (11/11/9/10). Blair
(pp. 150–1) had suggested these as the first syllabic poems, and
Spears (p. 222 and note), following G. S. Fraser, had put forward
Alonso's syllabics in *The Sea and the Mirror,* but this is much too
late.

'Another Time' [AT; CP, p. 41; CSP50; CSP, p. 170] is the
title poem of Auden's 1940 collection, and supports that volume's
acute sense of the present moment and its demands upon the
individual to justify his way of life. Those who live in the past,
respecting the established forms which are in fact breaking up around
them, are living a lie; though it is not 'as if they were wrong/In no
more wishing to belong'. The poem might perhaps be compared
with a much earlier one, 'The Questioner Who Sits So Sly' (CSP,
p. 31). 'Our Bias' [AT; CP, p. 118; CSP50; CSP, p. 171] similarly
exposes man's deviousness in respect of Time, as distinct from the
straightforward behaviour of other forms of life. There is a possible
ironic allusion in the original first line ('. . . lion's paw') to Shakespeare's nineteenth sonnet.

'Hell' [*Harper's Bazaar,* Jan. 1940; AT; CP, p. 51; CSP50;
CSP, p. 171], which begins with the Renaissance commonplace
about a personal hell (cf. Marlowe and Milton), goes on to expose
the sheer effort involved in most forms of human weakness. Relying
on the reader's inability to remember whether six monkeys and six
typewriters could or could not in time produce the works of Shake-

speare, Auden uses the example to undermine the real relevance of language altogether: it contrives, the ensuing stanzas say, to assist pride in its role as a supporter of man's pretensions to heroic grandeur (that Hell exists to contain him). Thus man theatrically revels in his supposed wretchedness, whereas if we were really wretched 'there'd be no living left to die'.

'Lady Weeping At The Crossroads' [from *The Dark Valley* in *Best Broadcasts of 1939–40*, ed. Max Wylie, 1940; CP, p. 207; CSP50; CSP, p. 172] is rather like 'The Lady of Shallott' in reverse: the lady is successful in enduring the tasks of the quest, but when she sees herself as she is in the mirror, she is forced to kill herself, for her heart is false.[7] Auden's sureness of touch in ballads of this kind is without question: one admires particularly the way that its relentless pace is made more weighty and sombre by the device of relating the narrative in the second person.

'Anthem for St Cecilia's Day' [*Harper's Bazaar,* Dec. 1941: 'Three Songs for St Cecilia's Day'; CP, p. 203; CSP50; CSP, p. 173], in which Auden revives the Augustan tradition of the St Cecilia's Day ode, makes use of the Renaissance theory of the divine power of musical harmony, not to redeem man, but to show him his lost innocence: before the Fall we could hear the music of the spheres. Music does not 'translate', it is 'pure contraption' ('The Composer', CSP, p. 125), and is therefore not able to make moral statements about the world. Its power is to draw forth the emotions, not to represent them.

The poem is appropriately dedicated to Benjamin Britten, whose birthday falls on St Cecilia's Day. Britten set the poem in 1942 for 'a small chorus of about fifty voices'. The italicized stanza in Part I is repeated at the very end of the setting, and the italicized lines in Part III are sung by a soprano solo (Cecilia).

Part I begins with an Edith Sitwell touch, and continues with curious hints of bawdy (Spears, p. 161, suggests that the metre of the first two stanzas alludes to 'The Groves of Blarney', No. 167 in the *Oxford Book of Light Verse*). Dryden's 'Alexander's Feast' had shown the power of the different modes to evoke different emotions in the listener. Aphrodite is appropriate here because Cecilia's vows of celibacy ('like a black swan') suggest that the kind of music she is known for (as supposed inventor of the organ, she was proclaimed the patroness of church music in 1584) is a sublimation of the erotic. The tone of these stanzas is not as unserious as critics make out, because really Auden is trying to introduce an extraneous cultural comment on the nature of the baroque.

After the invocation to Cecilia, Part II introduces the voice of music itself – terse, immediate, riddling, whispering – which, in the first two stanzas, contrasts its nature with that of man, and, in the following two, says that it is a product of man's life at the point where emotion has exhausted any possibility of action. Thus (as Part III goes on to show) it is able to fix and transform the emotions into something like their pure state, whereas in real life man is pathetically unconcerned about the civilization he is destroying ('ruined languages') because that civilization is a bizarre and irresponsible product of his fallen nature. It is like something thrown up by biological freak, a reasoning animal ('Impetuous child with the tremendous brain'). Cecilia's words, however, show great tenderness for the mortals who pray to her. They are like children who, with charm, gaiety and resilience, can learn to defy causal necessity by learning to love ('O wear your tribulation like a rose'). The last stanza creates a complex dialogue of soloist and chorus in a passage imitative, in Dryden's fashion, of various musical instruments. These instruments, in turn, symbolize the determined transformation of the emotions of Sorrow, Hope and Dread that were introduced at the beginning of the section.

'The Dark Years' is the 'Epilogue' to *New Year Letter*. 'The Quest' is from *New Year Letter,* and 'Shorts', 'No Time', 'Diaspora', 'Luther', 'Montaigne', 'The Council', 'The Maze' and 'Blessed Event' are all from the 'Notes' to the same poem.

'At the Grave of Henry James' [*Partisan Review,* July/Aug. 1941; CP, p. 126; CSP50; CSP, p. 197] contains a plea to the novelist for a spiritual as well as an aesthetic discipline ('there are many whose works/Are in better taste than their lives'). The visit to the Master's grave originally prompted twenty-eight stanzas of stock-taking which were much more personal and local (much about the war, for instance) than the ten-stanza elegy that we now have. Emphasized much more in this shorter version (axed by over half

from CSP50;) is the need for spiritual and artistic exclusiveness:
James's heart, 'fastidious as/A delicate nun' remained true to his
art, and ignored the 'Resentful muttering Mass,/Whose ruminant
hatred of all that cannot/Be simplified or stolen is yet at large'.

In a sense this devotion to truth is admirable, but there is a good
deal of snobbery in it, a snobbery that lurks elsewhere in the poem:
we all indeed say our 'a-ha to the beautiful, the common locus/Of
the Master and the rose'. In itself, 'this is a beautiful description of
the triangular schema of the artistic process, but is it really a
characteristic of 'that primary machine, the earth', this implied
identity of 'the clumsy and the sad' with the gawping audience?

There is a good bit of Caliban in the tone adopted for this poem
(not restricted to the mild Jamesian pastiche), and it comes out, too,
in the feeling that there is something unmanageable about life, and
that therefore the writer should avoid any temptation to manage it
(e.g. the reference to Julien Benda's attack on intellectuals, *La
Trahison des Clercs,* in the last line). In its cut version, Auden seems
to be trying out a case (perhaps for Ariel *v.* Prospero; cf. *The Dyer's
Hand,* pp. 337ff), rather than defining a felt position; but the ingenious and articulate figurative movement of the poem still comes
across with great power.

'Alone' [*Harper's Bazaar,* 15 Mar. 1941; CP, p. 35: 'Are You
There'; CSP50; CSP, p. 199], a series of jottings on the demands
and objectives of Eros, is built around the ambiguity of 'own' (i.e.
both 'self' and 'possess') and explores the nature of love as a relationship. Without their repeated lines, the enclosed stanzas of the
villanelle seem even more gnomic than usual, because the lyrical
element of the form's artifice has been removed. Marianne Moore
(in *Predilections,* 1955, p. 85) thought the poem rather like Ogden
Nash, viz:

> Each lover has a theory of his own
> About the difference between the ache
> Of being with his love and being alone.

'Leap Before You Look' [*Decision,* Apr. 1941; CP, p. 123;
CSP50; CSP, p. 200] similarly uses alternate key words at the end
of each stanza, and manages ingeniously to ring all possible changes

on the quatrain arrangement of two rhymes (nine of each in the whole poem). Such technical shadow-boxing seems neither as bland nor as menacing as a poet like William Empson could make it,[8] but the sense of circumspection nicely underlines the 'danger' which is the subject of the poem, i.e. the risk involved in making the existential choice of life. (The Kierkegaardian 'ten thousand fathoms' was to crop up again at the end of Prospero's speech in *The Sea and the Mirror*.) An Empsonian flatness also haunts the villanelle 'If I Could Tell You' [*Vice Versa,* Jan./Feb. 1941; CP, p. 135: 'But I Can't'; CSP50; CSP, p. 201]. It does, however, lean towards the lyrical (fully expressed in Miranda's villanelle in *The Sea and the Mirror*) and is not, in places, far removed from the kind of sentiment found in the popular commercial song.

In 'Atlantis' [CP, p. 20; CSP50; CSP, p. 202] the quest for Atlantis is so obviously a metaphor for the individual's quest for spiritual truth that the reader tends to assume at first that Auden's account is a generalized didactic one addressed to him. In fact, as the last stanza shows, the poem is addressed to a personal friend ('dear', even, in the first version), and thus its admonitions acquire a certain concern, even a kind of charm. The Mediterranean metaphor is supported by describing humanistic philosophy as Ionia, religious enthusiasm as Thrace (i.e. the cult of Dionysus) and hedonism as Corinth or Carthage (cf. Augustine's *Confessions*). These pitfalls encountered on the quest may be turned to its advantage, even if the result is only a 'peep at Atlantis/In a poetic vision'.

'In Sickness and in Health' [CP, p. 29; CSP50; CSP, p. 204], as its title indicates, is in the nature of an epithalamium, but it is an epithalamium with a difference: the poem begins by demanding humility in love because the self which is offered should be recognized as a waste land 'where dwell/Our howling appetites' (there is a probable allusion in this second stanza to Isherwood's travel book *The Condor and the Cows*). Love is destructive and demanding, and creates the 'syllogistic nightmare' of the false alternatives of Tristan and Don Giovanni,[9] loves that seek to escape the demands of time and the body either by rejecting them or by destroying them, and in their double failure produce the sublimation of Eros into political violence ('reject/The disobedient phallus for the sword'). Both types in this poem suggest the homosexual predicament: on the one hand the 'great friends' who 'make passion out of passion's obstacles', and on the other the 'unhappy spook' who 'haunts the urinals'.

In stanza 8, Auden introduces into the chaos of 'our stupid lives' (Kierkegaard's 'we are always in the wrong') the idea of the 'absurd' redemption of Christ: 'Yet through their tohu-bohu comes a voice/ Which utters an absurd command – Rejoice.' Not only do these lines seem to allude to Yeats's 'The Gyres' ('What matter? Out of cavern comes a voice,/And all it knows is that one word "Rejoice" '),[10] but they turn the idea to a specifically religious acceptance of the world by using the Hebrew *tohu-bohu,* which is the very word used in Genesis i.2 (translated as 'without form and void') to describe the chaos out of which God created the world (though *tohu-bohu* was no doubt a direct borrowing from Rimbaud's 'Le Bateau Ivre').

The italicized stanza which follows elaborates the creativity of God, and the poem continues by praising the real form of love, which is the love of God, and through him of the individual ('you and I,/ Exist by grace of the Absurd'). Stanzas 11 and 12 recapitulate the Tristan/Don Juan polarity in twin prayers to the 'Essence of creation' and to Love to guard the lovers from the extremes of 'sublimation' or 'animal bliss', and to 'permit/Temptations always to endanger' their love so that they may 'love soberly', preserved 'from presumption and delay'. Although the poem's conclusions (owing much to Kierkegaard) are argued out in religious terms, this remains essentially, like so many of the poems of the early 'forties, a love poem. The context of Auden's spiritual need is frequently, in the most humane sense, erotic: fate is addressed as 'O Felix Osculum', and the implied God of Genesis, who *'showed the whirlwind how to be an arm',* also *'gardened from the wilderness of space/The sensual properties of one dear face'.*

'Many Happy Returns' [CP, p. 68; CSP50; CSP, p. 208], a birthday poem, similarly wishes, for its seven year-old recipient, a path between extremes ('Tao is a tightrope' – Tao being the path of virtuous conduct in Confucianism). The tone of the poem shares something of the occasional impromptu soliloquizing of 'Heavy

Date' (CSP, p. 151), whose form it adopts, taking it much nearer to
the jagged precipitation of syllabics. Although Auden wishes for
the boy a 'sense of theatre', he is well aware that such self-consciousness (which in a good sense can lead to self-understanding) is also
the occasion for human pride, the feeling that one can control one's
destiny. With a comfortable avuncular twist in the argument (there
is a lot of half-apologetic sermonizing in this poem) Auden allows
such pride its small holidays (like 'birthdays and the arts') because
by playing at being gods we are admitting that we are men. Auden
runs through the qualities which will instil spiritual alertness with a
pleasant enough air of improvisation, and the *via media* is tied up
finally with an existentialist ribbon ('Follow your own nose', perhaps
alluding to another Johnny, Keats's 'Song of Myself').

In 'Mundus et Infans' [*Commonweal,* 30 Oct. 1942; CP, p. 72;
CSP50; CSP, p. 211] the fine comic distinctions and tea-table
syntax (this is a very Marianne Mooreish poem) disguise with charm
a serious qualification about human nature: we have unlearnt the
technique of existing without shame that we had as babies, so that
now only a saint is comparable with a baby as 'someone who does
not lie'. There is a pleasant vein of tenderness in much of the poem.
The natural processes are praised ('his seasons are Dry and Wet')
with a certain wry air of conscious unfastidiousness: these become
an image of our own needs that we are so reserved about, since
'we had never learned to distinguish/between hunger and love'.
The title of the poem is borrowed from an early sixteenth-century
play.

'Few and Simple' [CP, p. 161; CSP50; CSP, p. 213] plays with
the idea that love is not independent of that assortment of mental
and physical facts which make up memories. Thus thoughts of an
unfulfilled love are as familiar and intimate as though it had been
fulfilled, and the body is obedient to desire even if there is no
reasonable object or outcome to that desire. The mind and the
flesh are therefore the raw material of our subjective experience,
'enough/To make the most ingenious love/Think twice of trying to
escape them'.

'The Lesson' [CP, p. 116; CSP50; CSP, p. 214] describes three
dreams. Auden's dream poems do carry conviction (in *Letters from*

Iceland he reveals his habit of noting them down in the middle of the night), and these three, despite literary echoes of Kafka and *Alice Through the Looking-Glass,* have the right kind of emotional coherence to be half-genuine.

'A Healthy Spot' [CP, p. 134; CSP50; CSP, p. 215] says that liberals are nice but unhappy, through, it seems, refusing to acknowledge their 'hunger/For eternal life', or their own fallen natures. Since the pay-off lines of the poem involve a doubtful theory about the real nature of the 'smoking-room story' as a symbol of spiritual need, and since the real unicorn of *New Year Letter* and 'Kairos and Logos' is already beginning to look like a shibboleth, the reader doesn't feel inclined to take the poem very seriously. It is certainly one of Auden's smuggest, in its exposure of average bourgeois spiritual timidity.

'The Model' [*Dodo* (Swarthmore College), Feb. 1943; CP, p. 45; CSP50; CSP, p. 216] is again reminiscent of Marianne Moore. If 'the body of this old lady exactly indicates her mind', is it really clear that speculation about her past is quite irrelevant (stanza 3)? The essential human element which her body provides cannot be divorced from the experiences which that body has undergone and which have contributed to physical habit, stance, expression and so on. Yet Auden wishes to show that what is essentially human ('She survived whatever happened; she forgave; she became') lies beyond measurable experience, and certainly beyond the investigations of the psychiatrists (Rorschach's blots, or the IQ test pioneered by Binet). And he is making this point in the context of graphic art, which must rely upon the physical presence to evoke the human nature beyond it. 'Three Dreams' are from *The Age of Anxiety*.

In 'The Fall of Rome' [*Horizon,* Apr. 1947; N; CSP, p. 218] the comic world of surrealistic decadence and bureaucracy is familiar from earlier Auden, but the analogy between the fall of Rome and the decline of modern civilization is to become more characteristic in his post-war period. The first few stanzas recall the 'Journal of an Airman' in *The Orators.* Auden is inclined to prefer the endomorphic type to either the ectomorphic ('Cerebrotonic Cato') or the mesomorphic ('muscle-bound Marines'). The dedication to Cyril Connolly is appropriate because Connolly, as editor of *Horizon*

(where the poem appeared), was himself a great prophet of doom
for the Western world. The beautiful final stanza lifts the poem out
of its atmosphere of absurd apocalypse to suggest the mysterious
inevitability of natural processes which take no account of human
power (the allusion would seem to be both to Germanic migrations,
and to some sort of epiphany).

'Nursery Rhyme' [*Mademoiselle,* Oct. 1947; N; CSP, p. 219]
is simply an exercise in cheerfully sinister nonsense, elaborately
linked by rhyme, phrase and refrain. Its particular kind of suggestiveness would seem to owe something to Graves.

'In Schrafft's' [*New Yorker,* 12 Feb. 1949; N; CSP, p. 220] is a
more serious poem. The 'globular furore' which the eupeptic smile
of the anonymous lady in a restaurant is blandly ignoring might well
be said to be about food, the international haves and have-nots.
But this is not a foretaste of Auden's Brechtian tag 'Grub first, then
ethics', for in a mysterious way the lady's smile is explicitly beatific:
this is a poem about innocence, an apotheosis of the mundane, like
Salinger's fat woman who is Jesus Christ. It also perhaps glances at
the epicure's assurance in Sydney Smith's 'Recipe for a Salad'
('Fate cannot harm me, – I have dined today').

'Under Which Lyre: A Reactionary Tract for the Times' [*Harvard
Alumni Bulletin,* 15 June 1946; N; CSP, p. 221] is one of Auden's
best light poems. In the post-war world, when 'Ares at last has quit
the field', the perennial conflict between two other Greek gods
becomes once more of primary concern. The *Hymnus Homericus ad
Mercurium* is the source for Hermes' invention of the lyre on the first
day of his life, and for his conflict with Apollo, his elder brother.
Horace uses the phrase 'Mercuriales viri' as a term for *literati* in the
Odes (II, 17, ll. 29–30), though Hermes as the messenger of the gods
is more usually associated with dreams and the underworld. Apollo
was traditionally associated with codes of law and the inculcation
of high moral and religious principles: Auden sees his 'lyre', therefore, as only an authoritarian simulacrum of the genuine Hermetic
one (stanza 13), and his art as consequently official and factitious.
The distinction is similar to that between Apollonian and Dionysiac
poetry developed by followers of Graves in the 'fifties; Auden,
however, does not limit his ingenious categorizing to the sphere of

the literary, but uses it to express his personal advocacy of the generous, disorganized, instinctive life as against the humourless pedantry and authority of the self-important. There are a number of good academic jokes, appropriate to the poem's occasion, but it survives, with a sympathetic insistence, its witty after-dinner tone. It is a serious protest against bureaucracy, against the 'managers' of life, whether they be dictators or diet-faddists, and in its last lines suitably borrows from Auden's favourite Sydney Smith ('Take short views, hope for the best, and trust in God', *Lady Holland's Memoir,* Chap. 4).

'Music is International' [*American Scholar,* Autumn 1947; N; CSP, p. 226] shows the ornate conversational style which Auden began to adopt in the 'forties at its most exhibitionist. And, after all, a poem that calls itself a Phi Beta Kappa poem (Phi Beta Kappa being the honorary fraternity of the American academic elite) needs to be a kind of exhibition. Though the style seems factitious, it can be extremely exhilarating, even when it is not relying on wit or the obscurer gems from the *Oxford English Dictionary.* The whole thing is a splendidly contorted display of quick-thinking, well served by the syllabic form and the Skaldic rhymes (used in the following two poems as well).

Auden seems rather dubious about music's role here. It compares oddly with the line taken in poems like 'Anthem for St Cecilia's Day' or 'The Composer', in that the art is seen as a potentially wish-fulfilling drug ('the mornes and motted mammelons' – i.e., the small hills and wooded hummocks – give the bourgeois Eden a rather Gothicly erotic air). Even so, 'the jussive/Elohim are here too, asking for us/Through the noise'. 'Jussive Elohim' actually means 'demanding Hebrew gods', though the phrase contrives to sound gentle and vulnerable like some kind of shy horse. I suppose this is one way in which Auden's verbal playfulness has a useful density and deceit about it. His examples of valuable behaviour to which music yields in importance are, however, so apparently trivial ('feeding strays or looking pleased when caught/By a bore or a hideola') that our sense of the increasingly moral persuasiveness of the argument yields uncertainly to the earlier comic tone, and I doubt if anyone is much convinced by the rather Wordsworthian ending ('We may some day need very much to/Remember when we were happy', etc.). Despite all this, the controlled excitement of tone carries its own kind of conviction, so that one is inclined to pardon the poem's mixed cynicism and piety.

'The Duet' [*Kenyon Review,* Autumn 1947; N; CSP, p. 228] is one of the most ingeniously suggestive and inventive of Auden's post-war poems. It says that time can be redeemed only by full acceptance of all that it brings, and contrasts the lady's cloistered and self-indulgent *lacrimae rerum* with the exposed and deprived beggar's joyful acceptance of life. One could see the lady's 'warm house' as the body: she is the self-regard that sees no further than the mutability she laments. The beggar, on the other hand, could represent Agape, quite outside the body, seen ironically therefore as a 'runagate', but therefore blessed ('We know the time and where to find our friends'). The seasonal symbolism is powerful, too, and the poem moves beautifully on its concrete, descriptive level. One might say that the poem was a kind of Christian answer to Auden's earlier song about the six beggared cripples (CSP, p. 87).

In 'Pleasure Island' [*Commentary,* May 1949; N; CSP, p. 229] the process by which the amoral holiday island ('where nothing is wicked/But to be sorry or sick') becomes 'this/Place of a skull', i.e. Golgotha, the place of crucifixion, is as mild and leisurely as the pace of life on the island itself. Nemesis arrives with appropriate insidiousness as a kind of Mephistophelean highwayman, although it is not altogether clear whether 'Miss Lovely' is merely the poet's pleasure-seeking persona, or whether she is in fact a real pick-up.

In 'A Walk After Dark' [*Commonweal,* 11 Mar. 1949; N; CSP, p. 231], the poet, stocktaking in middle-age, praises the 'clockwork spectacle' of a starry night for keeping pace with his age and moods. Now the galaxy may be seen as middle-aged too, because astronomy has discovered that the red light emitted by the furthest stars that are going away from us at great speeds can be used as an indication of their age, and that they are often so far away and so old that they may not even exist any longer. Yet despite these thoughts, 'only the young and the rich/Have the nerve or the figure to strike/The *lacrimae rerum* note' (cf. 'The Duet'). The poet, on the other hand, stresses his responsibility towards the truth, which involves not only the 'wronged' and their political disasters being ignored, but also the possibility of miraculous interference in the natural law (stanza 7) heralding a second coming which will deliver final judgment on 'My person, all my friends,/And these United States'. The poem is a fitting farewell to the American period.

10   The Age of Anxiety

Although this, the fourth of Auden's long poems of the 'forties, did not appear in England until well into the post-war period,[1] 'a substantial part . . . was written by 1944, and at least half by 1945' (Spears, p. 230). The war itself plays an important part in the poem, through the radio announcements which continually break in upon the characters' explored consciousnesses to remind them of the violence and frivolity of the material world. The setting, a New York bar on the night of All Souls, thus provides an atmospheric link with other wartime meditations of Auden's, 'September 1, 1939' and *New Year Letter*. Here, though, he is not much concerned with rationalizing the immediate predicament of the individual or the world, or of applying to it the terms of art, philosophy or Christian revelation. It seems to me a sign of the highest invention and genius that Auden should have produced so soon after *The Sea and the Mirror* and *For the Time Being* another major poem which embodied his convictions in such radically different terms, those of Jungian psychology and the allegorized interior consciousness.

The principal idea of the poem (that of representing the four faculties of the fragmented psyche by four different characters) was not, I have suggested, a new one for Auden (see my discussion of *The Ascent of F6*, p. 92). What he seems to have done here is to elaborate a hint from *For the Time Being* (CLP, p. 141), where a morality-play personification of these four faculties allowed him to demonstrate how the Fall destroyed the wholeness of man's personality, and how the separate faculties allow him only glimpses of the redeemed life which his fallen nature denies him. In *The Age of Anxiety* this Christian application is not stressed. Auden is much more interested in the complex relationship between the four faculties indicated by Jung's *t'ai chi t'u,* a diagrammatic representation of the processes of the psyche,[2] and in embodying the relationship in the thoughts of the four 'real' characters who represent the faculties. This interior nature of the work makes it in parts almost as difficult as *Finnegan's Wake* (published in 1939 and evidently an influence on Auden here), and allows his talent for fantastic and symbolic landscape its full rein.

The poem is subtitled 'A Baroque Eclogue', and the traditional pastoral concerns may be intermittently glimpsed throughout its six parts. The baroque element makes reference to that appeal to the senses characteristic of the religious art of the seventeenth century known as baroque, and seems an appropriate term for Auden's ingenious discovery of metaphor applicable to the elusive states of mind he is concerned with. In poetry, the baroque uses wit as an instrument of vision, and works upon the reader through extravagance and shock.[3]

The four characters are Malin, a medical officer in the Canadian Air Force who represents Thinking; Rosetta, a Jewish department-store buyer who represents Feeling (these according to Jung are the rational, evaluative faculties); Quant, an elderly Irish shipping-clerk representing Intuition; and Emble, a teenaged naval recruit representing Sensation (these are the irrational, perceptive faculties). At the allegorical level, these four closely follow in attitude and sensibility the various mental processes they represent. They do, however, exist as characters in their own right, and the nature of their encounter is the classic pastoral one (the erotic triangle Malin-Emble-Rosetta evoking, say, Spenser's Hobbinol-Colin-Rosalind). It is also a mystical encounter like that described by Auden in his Introduction to Anne Fremantle's *The Protestant Mystics* (1964), p. 26, where four schoolteachers experience a mysterious communal awareness. Auden had already described such an experience in his poem 'A Summer Night' (CSP, p. 69), so it was a real one for him, and, as he goes on to say in *The Protestant Mystics* (where he characterizes the experience as a Vision of Agape), it is of a kind which could lead directly to Christianity.

The need for an extra-human solution to the problems which the poem explores seems to be appreciated only by Malin. The 'anxiety' of the title – according to such Protestant theologians as Niebuhr, by whom Auden was much influenced at the time – is itself a characteristic of the human condition indicating an awareness of the need for God, a characteristic identifiable with the 'dread' of Kierkegaard or the 'angst' of Kafka. Niebuhr saw man as living a two-dimensional existence of necessity and freedom; he is both a spirit, and a child of nature, compelled by its necessities: 'In short, man, being both free and bound, both limited and limitless, is anxious. Anxiety is the inevitable concomitant of the paradox of freedom and finiteness in which man is involved. Anxiety is the internal pre-condition of sin. It is the inevitable spiritual state of man' (*Nature and Destiny,* I, 194–6). It is interesting to compare with this Malin's long final speech (pp. 352–3): the Christian choice is his, and is therefore seen by Auden (as we have seen in *New Year Letter*) as essentially an intellectual choice.

However, the spiritual is (as so frequently even in the Christian Auden) subservient to the psychological, and this emphasis links the poem firmly with earlier works concerned with the quest for integrity, like *The Orators* or *The Ascent of F6*. Seen from this point of view, the central figure is not Malin but Rosetta, the representative of Feeling, who leads the others in the central journey through the unconscious in the important third part of the poem, 'The Seven Stages'. Her personal quest is for an emotional fidelity to experience (in this case her childhood in England, which she glamorizes and misrepresents); but the larger quest (suggested perhaps by Dante's seven cycles of purgation and the vision of Paradise in Canto XXVIII of the *Purgatorio*) leads to the hermetic gardens which each of the characters in their roles as mental faculties has power to glimpse (cf. 'New Year Letter', ll. 860ff). The Vision of Agape, uniting the faculties in mystical communion, brings them to the hermetic gardens, as to a lost Eden which the fragmented psyche has left behind.

In his acutely perceptive article 'Allegory in Auden's *The Age of*

Anxiety' (Twentieth Century Literature, Jan. 1965), Edward Callan suggests the following interpretations of the characters' names: *Rosetta* from the Rosetta Stone, suggesting, through the link with the mouth of the Nile and prehistory, the feminine principle, the past, the unconscious. *Malin* from the French *malin,* meaning clever, mischievous. *Quant* from quantum, referring to the intuitive perception of things as wholes. *Emble* from emblem, which makes concepts manifest to the senses (as in emblem books, characteristic of baroque literature).

The 'Prologue' describes the characters, and charts their gradual process of awareness. Their initial monologues reveal the habits of thought which are most typical of their natures. Quant's quizzical interrogation of his mirror-image as he sits drinking in the bar (p. 258) shows how he is sharply aware of possibility. Auden has some fun with this looking-glass world. As Martin Gardner has shown in *The Ambidextrous Universe* (1967), p. 133, the line 'What flavour has/That liquor you lift with your left hand?' makes a serious point, because alcohol contains carbon compounds called 'esters' which give it flavour, and most of which are asymmetrical. Thus Gardner concludes: 'No one knows what flavour Looking-glass liquor might have.' Malin rationalizes man's predicament in scientific aphorisms which cut bluntly across the alliterative lines of the verse: this is familiar Auden subject-matter, here introduced to stress man's peculiarity as an inquisitive, self-conscious creature, and to prepare for Malin's application in his final monologue of the idea of the inexplicable enrichment of 'novelty', the fact that 'Nature rewards/Perilous leaps', to Christian thought. Even at this stage of the poem, the leaps seem insistently Kierkegaardian.

Rosetta describes her ideal landscape, a stylized and cute version of pre-war England: this is her obsession, as unreal, say, as the English sets of the Americanized Hitchcock, but representing symbolically an important fantasy about her deepest feelings and origins. Auden has dropped a clue about his intention here by referring the reader to English detective stories (p. 257) and their 'lovely innocent countrysides' into which a 'horrid corpse' suddenly intrudes. As the earlier poem 'Detective Story' (CSP, p. 102) makes clear, Auden looks upon these elements of the genre as representative of the archetypal awareness of sin and guilt, even as a type of the lost Eden. Rosetta's awareness in her final long speech of a need for a paternal deity resolves her self-delusions, and explains their symbolism. Emble's speech (p. 260), as is proper to the representative of sensation, analyses the spiritual loneliness which he does not really share.

The radio breaks in upon their soliloquies at this point, making them aware of the world around them. Malin's reaction (p. 262) is an interesting application in a realistic context of the mythical inventions of *Paid on Both Sides* and other early poems, but his role as airman has little significance in the poem as a whole, except to corroborate his representation of the high-flying intellect (similarly Rosetta as buyer for a store is fulfilling her role as representative of taste and feeling, and Quant as a clerk that of the literary imagination). The verse takes on an epic colouring in the Old English manner (compare 'Many have perished; more will' with 'þaes ofereode, þisses swa maeg' in *Deor*, a rare instance of a refrain in Old English poetry). Quant may imagine the war he has not experienced, and Emble has the disasters of a convoy to recount with all the brashness of his youth (victims of a torpedo are 'exposed to snap/Verdicts of sharks'), while Rosetta's thoughts naturally turn to a besieged England and an occupied Europe.

They begin their dialogue (p. 266) by applying the general principle of the failings of the human will to the specific situation of the war. Emble describes the passing of cultures in the face of the barbarian, while Malin points out that the Nazis are not in this sense barbarians, but a product of modern civilization (p. 268):

> He was born here. The
> Bravura of revolvers in vogue now
> And the cult of death are quite at home
> Inside the city.

Thus the point of this argument, and Rosetta's consequent avowal of personal guilt and responsibility, is essential (*a*) to the conditions which the 'Prologue' is concerned to elaborate as urging and defining the investigations of the poem which follow, and (*b*) to Auden's own

principal reason for rejecting the liberal humanism which had failed
to prevent Nazism, and could of itself provide no real validity for its
values (cf. his essay in *Modern Canterbury Pilgrims,* ed. James A.
Pike, 1956).

Malin proposes a conversation: shall it be about past or future,
atom or star? They decide instead to discuss 'the incessant Now of/
The traveller through time', who is 'in quest of his own/Absconded
self' – that is, his real self, which, like the elusive law of God
(cf. 'New Year Letter', ll. 751–86), remains hidden from him by
reason of his sin. They propose, then, to investigate man's nature
and his guilt in time, so they leave their bar-stools and move to a
booth.

The second part of the poem, 'The Seven Ages' (p. 274), examines
the condition of man at both the generic and the personal level,
with the Shakespearean hint providing a bold metaphorical brilli-
ance. Malin leads the investigation. He introduces each stage, which
the other characters then describe in relation to their own experience.
The theme is the loss of innocence. Malin's terms ('that ban tempts
him;/He jumps and is judged') are quasi-theological, and the
individual developments are all concerned with the vagaries of the
will and of love, the paradoxes of 'anxiety' (p. 279: 'So, learning to
love, at length he is taught/To know he does not'). The verse in this
section is among the most striking in the poem, ranging from Quant's
surrealist vision of an adolescent's sexual discovery (pp. 279–80) to
the neat, symbolic songs from the Wallomatic (a device, like the
radio in the 'Prologue', which enlarges the significance of the statements to include the social ambience of the psychological organisms:
in a sense the baroque in the poem evokes the specific world of the
bourgeois United States).

Rosetta's song (p. 280) shares some of the syntactical pastiche of
Ferdinand's sonnet in *The Sea and the Mirror,* while Emble's is a
clever application of the terms of the game 'Consequences': both
destroy the illusions of romantic love, the first by describing a brief
affair of unequal love, the second a 'sensible' divorce. This process of
disillusion in the first three stages yields in the fourth to 'the real
world of/Theology and horses' (an allusion to Swift's *Gulliver's
Travels,* as is 'Fanatics of the Egg', three lines later[4]), a world where

commitments must be made, but where a pattern is missing, 'We are mocked by unmeaning'. The speeches here (pp. 282ff) show man's growing awareness and expectation of the Kairos of 'the Absolute Instant'. This is itself reflected in the strange communion which the characters experience, but in this fifth age the young adult is aware of the numinous merely in terms which reflect back on his own needs and ego, 'that Generalized Other/To whom he thinks and is understood by' (Malin, p. 284); the 'Personal Call/ From Long Distance . . . the low voice that/Defines one's future' (Emble, p. 284); 'the wheel' (Quant, p. 287). Quant's long speech here tells how man has always been like this, how his failed aspirations are reflected in the stories of Narcissus, Polyphemus and Orpheus (mythology is one of Quant's specialities) and condemn him to the eternal revolutions of the wheel.

The sixth age introduces the doubtful poise of middle age, where 'clandestine under/The guilt and grime of a great career,/The bruise of his boyhood is as blue still,/Horrid and hurting' (p. 288). This makes man pine 'for some/Nameless Eden', which the characters describe in terms of their personal quests. In Quant's case, failure is described in terms very reminiscent of 'Journal of an Airman' ('on the thirteenth day/Our diseased guide deserted with all/The milk chocolate'), with a gallery of eccentric allegorical characters, representing the selfish postures of the will, and a landscape of spiritual endeavour nearer to C. S. Lewis than to Bunyan. Quant has only one glimpse of the Good Place, and then he wanders back, 'whistling ruefully' (p. 290). For Rosetta, the Primal Age she is nostalgic for is symbolized by the dolls, who are simply themselves 'so clearly expressing . . . the paternal world'. The child is like a mechanical doll wound up by the father (who is also God) and working through nature. To her, as Feeling, the lost condition of Being is symbolized by images of dancing animals from childhood and myth, and the failure to obtain it is symbolized by the decay of the great country house, and the unwinding of the clockwork doll. Emble (p. 291) takes up this idea when he says that he has lost 'the key to/The garden gate', an image by *Burnt Norton* out of *Alice in Wonderland,* and one that has already appeared in Auden (cf. *New Year Letter*). The Eliotelian note is maintained when Quant refers to reproaches 'emanating from some hidden centre . . . The Accuser crying in a cocktail glass' (p. 291).

Such a glance at the bourgeois limbo is a cue for another song from the Wallomatic, a dense and witty encapsulation of the Fall of Man ('jilted his heirs') and of the Seven Ages, reviewing man's desire, will and intellect (stanzas 2–4) and concluding that his mortality is the most significant thing about him (stanzas 5 and 6). Malin's brief description of the seventh age ('he/Joins the majority, the jaw-dropped/Mildewed mob and is modest at last') underlines this. The discussion ends, and while fresh drinks are fetched, the characters review their obsessions: Rosetta's parody world of the pre-war English upper-class, Emble's fear of fading into the crowd like his contemporaries, Quant's fear of age. Malin then asks Rosetta to show them the path to 'hope and health'. He does this in somewhat whimsical terms of pastoral chivalry, but Rosetta comments that she has no special gifts to lend them in their next journey: 'the sole essential a sad unrest [i.e. anxiety]/Which no life can lack' (p. 295).

Auden's prose comment at this point re-establishes the mystical terms of the quartet's experience, and the following part, 'The Seven Stages', represents their search 'as a single organism' for 'that state of prehistoric happiness which, by human beings, can be imagined only in terms of a landscape bearing a symbolic resemblance to the human body'. Thus the spiritual quest by the psyche in the process of overcoming its division into the four faculties can be represented or understood only in quite other terms, as intimate physiological allegory, for instance, or in fairy-tale images ('Grandmother's House' in Rosetta's speech refers us to *Red Riding-Hood,* itself capable of a psycho-sexual interpretation).

Their 'urge to find water' (p. 297) probably represents their establishment of the Jungian collective unconscious as a field of exploration. The mountainous district into which they all, from their several starting-points, begin to advance is represented (as before in Auden) as man's first mammary objective, contrasted with Emble's 'inedible hills' in their fallen, war-torn landscape. Appropriately it is given to Rosetta to describe these 'twin confederate forms . . . white with lilies': the mother's breasts represent that solace 'Where the great go to forget themselves,/The beautiful and boon to die' (p. 299). It is here, as Quant's 'dream' suggests, that myth originates (the little monks in a landscape of 'doomed hills' and 'wild volcanoes' are attempting to retain the child's innocence by translating their vision of sexuality, the brides and the robbers, into terms appropriate to civilized life), and it is from the mother's breasts that there comes the contrary motivations of the 'pilgrims' puffing 'Up the steep bank' (i.e. the religious impulse as a continual regret for the experience of weaning) and of Emble the sensualist running 'in the other direction,/Cheerful, unchaste' (p. 300).

From there, the travellers proceed to the heart ('the tumbledown Mariners Tavern . . . miles inland'), from which they see railroads and rivers running east and west (i.e. veins and arteries). Here they split up – Rosetta with Emble to the left, Quant and Malin to the right – to reach 'the rival ports' (lung and liver), which completes the second stage of their journey (p. 303). Their lyrics here are purely evocative of the self-confrontation which the landscape induces. Emble, in the metre used by Matthew Arnold in 'Heine's Grave' and 'Rugby Chapel', shows the individual at odds with the apparently settled world he moves through; Quant becomes aware of his earliest parental relationship; Rosetta contrasts her aristocratic illusions with the encroachment of 'plainer minds'; Malin finds the proximity of the 'ocean' (blood) suggests something 'about time/And the anxious heart/Which a matter-snob would dismiss' (p. 306).

In the third stage of their journey they move, from their contemplation of the ocean of the blood, inland again towards a common goal, the city (brain), where they are together again, though as Quant says: 'What mad oracle could have made us believe/The capital will be kind when the country is not' (p. 309). In other words, there have been no rational solutions to man's anxiety.

The fourth stage is their experience of the brain's 'facetious culture' (Malin's speech at p. 310 was first printed as 'Metropolis' in *Commonweal,* 20 Dec. 1946). Civilization demands a Niebuhrian emphasis on sin ('How are these people punished?') and finds the supreme ironical expression of man's independence of will in the likely self-destruction of the recently exploded atomic bomb ('the artful/Obliterating bang').

From here they travel on to the fifth stage of their journey, the big house (i.e. the womb, which, like the breasts, it is left to Rosetta to describe). She runs in eagerly, for here is the very matrix of the human psyche: but all she sees is the isolation and selfishness of created things, 'a World that is fallen,/The mating and malice of men and beasts,/The corporate greed of quiet vegetation,/And the homesick little obstinate sobs/Of things thrown into being' (p. 314).

In reaction to this disappointment, they race on to the sixth stage of their journey, 'the forgotten graveyard' (i.e. the skeleton which should act as *memento mori*). This is presented as a 'still museum' exhibiting 'the results of life' (p. 315). The next part of their journey is heralded by a fresh pairing, Rosetta with Quant, and Emble with Malin. In this way, their erotic objectives (Quant's for a 'daughter-wife', Malin's for a 'son', Emble and Rosetta for each other) are prepared for as they arrive at the seventh stage.

This last stage is the 'hermetic gardens' (the genitals, on the physiological level of the allegory). This is presented as the Earthly Paradise where man's fallen nature may temporarily be redeemed: 'The ruined rebel is recreated/And chooses a chosen self.' Love is seen as conferring Being upon Becoming, a means for the timeless to meet with time: 'the sudden instant/Touches his time at last' (p. 319). This whole section is a dramatic elaboration of a passage from 'New Year Letter' (ll. 860ff) which stressed the dangers of man imagining that these glimpses of the timeless (visions of Agape) could in any sense be permanent. Here 'the extraordinary charm of these gardens begins to work upon them also. It seems an accusation.' Their joy turns to an uneasy awareness of their defects, Quant's of the imagination which makes him dissatisfied with what he has; Emble's of his Don Juanism; Rosetta's of her snobbery; and Malin's of his intellectual narcissism. They turn away one by one into a labyrinthine forest of guilt, where fragments of their sorrowful songs are heard.

The whole process here re-enacts the Fall, since their defects are all forms of pride, the archetypal sin. This leads them into the Desert, the place of trial (cf. *For the Time Being*), where their doubts assail them: Emble says he would have no reason to believe 'the wrinkled/ Reports of explorers' (i.e. saints) who claim that 'this desert is dotted with/Oases where acrobats dwell/Who make unbelievable leaps' (cf. Kierkegaard). Thus the religious solution does not present itself, the hero takes up his 'defiance of fate', and the 'gentle majority' assume a Bosch-like placidity (p. 325). This speech of Emble's retraces the autobiographical passage about the exceptional child for whom a deep 'Urmutterfurcht' provides the drive towards 'knowledge' from 'New Year Letter' (ll. 1087–1152). But this drive is itself an evasion, a hope for a 'last landscape' where 'number is unknown', and is to be disappointed.

The real world 'from which their journey has been one long flight rises up before them now as if the whole time it had been hiding in ambush'. This intrusion of reality scatters the quartet 'to the four coigns', or corner-stones, of the Jungian *t'ai chi t'u:* they are again divided, and the phantasmagoric journey ends as themes of war and chaos accompany their ascent into consciousness. In fact, it is now closing-time, and the bar-tender is turning off the lights. Only a faint memory of their experience in the hermetic gardens remains for Emble and Rosetta: she invites them all back to her apartment, hoping that Malin and Quant will refuse (but they don't).

Part Four, 'The Dirge' (p. 330), appears to be an elegy for Franklin D. Roosevelt converted into a generalized lament for the passing of secular lawgivers who are the heroes of the City. Thus 'our colossal father' is in immediate terms President Roosevelt as executive of the modern paternalist state in America in the pre-war years of the New Deal (the 'seven years' of stanza 2, i.e. between 1933 and 1940), when he 'reformed the weeds/Into civil cereals and sobered the bulls'. Roosevelt thus becomes ironically representative of a substitute God, a 'semi-divine stranger with superhuman powers, some Gilgamesh or Napoleon, some Solon or Sherlock Holmes', and yet again we are reminded of *The Orators* (e.g. the second part of Book I). The passing of such a liberal humanist hero symbolizes the merely ephemeral sanctions of the secular point of view, a recurrent aspect of Auden's religious theme.

Part Five, 'The Masque' (p. 333), takes up the pastoral mode of the work more deliberately. The characters are now trying to make something exciting happen, when all they really want is to go home to bed. Thus the growing attraction between Rosetta and Emble seems to them of great importance, for in this way they may all (and Malin and Quant contribute some vicarious bawdy and whimsy) try to recapture the vision of the hermetic gardens. Rosetta and Emble dance, and sing as a duet a drottkvaett (a verse form used in Old Norse poetry[5]), while Malin invokes Venus with a little altar of sandwiches (p. 335).

Rosetta's and Emble's prayers and vows have a touching innocence which is none the less belied by their illusions and experience as revealed in the poem, and Malin's blessings similarly increase the air of self-delusion that the Earthly Paradise is at hand. But their notion of this paradise is held in terms of Rosetta's 'mad gym-mistress, made to resign/Can pinch no more', a touch of Mortmere which colours their pastoral idyll: hate and suffering, as Auden clearly indicates in his prose comment, cannot be dispelled merely by 'alcohol, lust, fatigue, and the longing to be good'. This Rosetta begins to realize in the long speech (p. 344) which she makes after Quant and Malin have been seen to the elevator and she finds Emble has passed out on her bed.

She stresses their cultural and racial differences ('You'll build here, be/Satisfied soon, while I sit waiting/On my light luggage to leave if called/for some new exile') and alludes to Naaman's conversion in 2 Kings v when she says that if they married he would continue to feel gentile when he joined in 'The rowdy cries at Rimmon's party', even if, like Naaman, he had asked for the Lord's forgiveness in advance (p. 345). To see WASP society as an Assyrian god is a measure of the imaginative sympathy which Auden projects here into Rosetta's Jewish position.

The speech contains a good many Joycean puns and allusions, as indeed does the whole work ('mind your poise/And take up your cues, attract Who's-Who,/Ignore What's-Not. Niceness is all and/The rest bores'), but its extended intent is one of seriousness, for not only does it show up Rosetta's illusions about her father and all she made him stand for, but it predicates the Jewish God whose omnipresence is a precondition of the Christian solution which Auden demands. The faith of the persecuted recognizes the will of God even in the most terrible adversity ('our bodies are chucked/Like cracked crocks on to kitchen middens', p. 346), and Rosetta's acceptance of her real origins ('the semi-detached/Brick villa in Laburnum Crescent') and her real father ('How appalling was your taste in ties') is a paradigm of this. Her speech ends with the Hebrew prayer 'Hear, O Israel, the Lord our God, the Lord is one.'

The 'Epilogue' (p. 348) demonstrates that although Rosetta's recognition of a paternal deity may reflect an emotional need for God, it is left to Malin (and therefore to the intellect) to make the Christian choice. As Malin and Quant part, their counterpointed lyrics probe the illusory nature of human progress, though only Malin is sharply aware of the need for change and man's avoidance of it: 'We would rather die in our dread/Than climb the cross of the moment/And let our illusions die.' This choice is not easy because it is 'too obvious and near to notice', and because man's double nature continually demands allegiance to the primitive forces which are the only ones really recognized by 'the poor muddled maddened mundane animal/Who is hostess to us all'. Malin is the scientist, the intellectual, and as such is liable to lapse into philosophical jargonizing, but even so, his long last speech does clearly reflect the central concern of the work, the conditional reasons for man's anxiety (pp. 352–3):

> Temporals pleading for eternal life with
> The infinite impetus of anxious spirits,
> Finite in fact yet refusing to be real,
> Wanting our own way, unwilling to say Yes
> To the Self-So which is the same at all times,
> That Always-Opposite which is the whole subject
> Of our not-knowing . . .

Perhaps Auden, in bestowing beliefs upon fictional characters who are also personified faculties, is avoiding direct commitment here. Certainly the baroque style, with its paradoxical remoteness from, and direct grasp of, the here-and-now, presents a solution to the condition of anxiety as defined by Niebuhr. As in *The Sea and the Mirror,* it is the richness and candour of art which by implication continually absolves men from solving their insoluble predicament. Malin's last words stress the irresponsible childishness of men, but Auden's poem is such a subtle and generous effort of understanding that this speech, with its appeal to the traditional Judao-Christian God, paternal and inscrutable, seems like an historical pose suited to the years of Belsen and Hiroshima; it is itself a poetical trope less artistically moving than that 'noble despair of the poets' which Malin condescendingly mentions (p. 350). Actually, *The Age of Anxiety* is rich not only in noble despair, but in a kind of inner glee and inventive response to the conditions of life which is the mark of great literature.

Part Four

LATER POEMS

11 The Libretti

Auden's own view of a libretto as not being addressed to the public but as acting as 'a private letter to the composer' and then being 'as expendable as infantry to a Chinese general' (*The Dyer's Hand,* p. 473) is a somewhat overstated version of an unexceptionable belief in the supremacy of the musical share of operatic collaboration. And the kind of inaudibility he finds in an opera's words is again probably exaggerated (one word in seven is usually heard, he says in 'The World of Opera' in *Secondary Worlds,* p. 90). Even so, an opera libretto is much less accessible to criticism than the text of a play, simply because it is far less complete when studied in isolation from a production. I shall therefore deal only with the three major libretti written in collaboration with Chester Kallmann, *The Rake's Progress, Elegy for Young Lovers* and *The Bassarids,* and only briefly at that. I shall not deal at all with *Paul Bunyan* (written by Auden for Britten in 1941 and remaining unpublished), *Delia* (written with Kallmann, published in *Botteghe Oscure,* Vol. XII, 1953, and unset) or the translations of Schikaneder and Giesecke, Da Ponte and Brecht (also written with Kallmann). Kallmann's role has been quite extensive (nearly half of *The Rake's Progress* and about three-quarters of *Elegy for Young Lovers,* according to Spears, p. 341), and it is indicative of the low-keyed style of these libretti that it is almost impossible to tell which parts are Kallmann and which parts Auden.

The libretto of *Elegy for Young Lovers* contains a postscript, 'Genesis of a Libretto', and there are interesting comments on the origins of the three major libretti in 'The World of Opera' (*Secondary Worlds*, pp. 97–115). On the writing of *The Rake's Progress*, the volume *Memories and Commentaries* by Stravinsky and Robert Craft (1960), pp. 154–66, should be consulted.

The Rake's Progress [1951]: Stravinsky wanted to write a moral fable in Mozartian form, and had become interested in the famous paintings by Hogarth of 'The Rake's Progress'. The action was worked out scene by scene, and the musical numbers plotted, by Stravinsky and Auden together. Auden and Kallmann completed the libretto in four months in 1948. The first performance was in 1951.

Auden seized upon the opportunity afforded by the opera's eighteenth-century pastiche to write about a religious predicament in terms of the rationalization of appetite with which that century was obsessed. His manic-depressive hero, Rakewell, is a gloomy and Byronic exemplar of the human will struggling to be free of necessity. Even his pleasures disgust him. Only the memory of an ennobling love haunts his ruinous career, and finally saves him. Auden uses a variety of myths to suggest that Rakewell is an archetypal hero. Like the quest-hero, he has three wishes. The first ('I wish I had money', p. 7) is answered by news of a fortune which whisks him away from the opening pastoral idyll with his true love, Anne. The second ('I wish I were happy', p. 21) is answered by a proposal from his Mephistophelean servant, Nick Shadow, that he should deny both reason and desire, and marry a bearded lady from St Giles's Fair. And the third (of a magical dream: 'I wish it were true', p. 33) is answered by Shadow's unveiling of the bread-making machine which is to bring about his final bankruptcy and ruin. All these wishes represent false illusions of life, manifestations of Rakewell's (or Everyman's) fallible nature. The third may even be intended as a bizarre version of one of the temptations of Christ, here applied to the delusions of material progress affecting capitalist society.

The use of the Faustian myth may conceivably have been suggested by Jung, whom Auden was influenced by at the time:

The character that summarizes a person's uncontrolled emotional manifestations consists, in the first place, of his inferior qualities or peculiarities. Even
people we like and appreciate suffer from certain imperfections of character
that have to be taken into the bargain. When people are not at their best, such
flaws become clearly visible. I have called the inferior and less commendable
part of a person the *shadow*. We have met with this figure in literature; for
instance, Faust and his shadow Mephistopheles. (*The Integration of the
Personality*, 1940, p. 20.)

Thus, although Rakewell is motivated by his desires, he is aware of a
deeper desire to be free of them. His marriage to Baba the Turk is an
acte gratuit, but only perhaps in Gide's sense of 'un crime immotivé',
like Lafcadio's in *Les Caves du Vatican*. As Sartre was keen to point
out, the freedom and choice of humanist existentialism belong
always to a total situation, and not to mere caprice (*L'Existen-
tialisme est un Humanisme,* 1954, p. 74). No doubt Auden had
existentialism in mind, however, and it is clear that Rakewell's
absurd marriage is only a grotesque parody of the true Christian
choice. This choice is symbolized later in the opera when, on the
suspended stroke of midnight after the year and the day allowed
him by Shadow, he irrationally chooses the Queen of Hearts for a
second time as a gesture towards Anne's love which still haunts him.
Shadow is cheated of his human soul by the sublimated power of
love, although in revenge he makes Rakewell mad.

The rest of the opera elaborates the symbolism of Bedlam as a
purgatory in which transfigured love (Anne as Venus) has power to
redeem the human soul from torment (Rakewell as Adonis) in a
scene which ironically relates to the opening idyll (also presided
over by 'the Cyprian Queen'). A Christian significance of Innocence
and Experience is implicit here, and Anne's last barcarolle seems
nearer to the Shelley of *Prometheus Unbound* than to the neo-
classicism whose terms the opera's language has so closely followed.
In a sense, the work is pulled in two directions here, for its symbolism
is essentially Romantic in colouring.

Elegy for Young Lovers [1961], written for Hans Werner Henze,
has, by contrast, much of the perfectly reasonable and inventive, but
primarily melodramatic, characterization of a play like *On the
Frontier*. No doubt, this is eminently suited to the artifice of opera;

the methods of construction as recounted in the postscript seem ideally to reflect Auden's notions about characters in opera ('persons who insist on their fate, however tragically dreadful or comically absurd', *Secondary Worlds,* p. 94).

The central character is a great poet whose sexual potency is maintained by frequent injections, and whose poetry is largely inspired by the transcribed visions of a madwoman. The self-confessed theme also derives from Yeats:

> The intellect of man is forced to choose
> Perfection of the life or of the work.

Mittenhofer chooses the latter, and thus needs to be pampered and humoured like a baby. All the other characters are made to serve his needs, even the unfortunate young lovers, whose 'illusory but rhymable love' is the substance of Mittenhofer's latest poem, which, since it is to be an elegy, must demand their actual destruction. The character of Mittenhofer (and the whole paradox of the nineteenth-century artist-genius) is treated with a lightness and humour very reminiscent of the plays of the 'thirties. More ambitious is the symbolism of love's illusions. This is managed by a curious juxta-positioning at the end of Act I of the discovery of the madwoman's dead bridegroom, lost for forty years in a glacier, and the coming together of the young couple. This symbolism is maintained at the climax of the opera, when the couple, dying on the mountain, imagine they have been married for forty years, and discover that their love has little meaning as they 'say farewell to a real world'. The symbols and images of this central theme are insistently sacri-ficial: the madwoman prophesies the couple's death in terms like these (p. 15):

> To the Immortal, high
> On their white altar,
> Mortal heat neither
> Simple nor wicked
> Lamb-like is fed.

And one feels that the madwoman's bridegroom (cf. 'the lolling bridegroom' in '1929', CSP, p. 34) is a sacramental victim, too. The point remains that human love is subservient to divine love, and yet is an image of it, particularly of Christ's (p. 42):

> One who dare break the barrier . . .
> His own . . . who only will turn, will move to
> Reach for and bless their happiness,
> Shall heedlessly enter Eden too.
> They bring us a gift from afar:
> A fragile, an eternal flower.

This greater love and greater reality seems somewhat imposed upon the action by the librettists, while the question of Mittenhofer's genius is evaded by the musical representation of his elegy. It is intended to be a great poem, but we are not clear that Mittenhofer has any great understanding of these religious issues behind the events.

The Bassarids [1966] was, like *Elegy for Young Lovers*, written for Hans Werner Henze, and is also about human motivation in a religious context, though Christian symbolism is curiously less in evidence (Dionysus/Christ offers much, but the offer is not taken). In Euripedes's *Bacchae*, of which *The Bassarids* is a free adaptation, Dionysus takes his revenge upon Agave and Pentheus for denying his divinity. The librettists are less concerned with Dionysus as a type of religious force, though much play is made with his power to reveal unconscious motivation. His manipulation of Agave and Pentheus actually tells us more about the strange maternal relationship at the centre of the opera than his portrayal as a languid Regency dandy might suggest.

Dionysus is a catalyst, a presence by which the other characters can assert their religious positions. To Agave he provides a meaning in life which she has lost, an identification with nature (see her aria on p. 28). To Pentheus, a stoic-humanist, he represents the instinctual life which he has repressed in his rational pursuit of 'the True Good'. The other characters in their various ways relate to the Dionysiac cult as to a religious choice (Cadmus is unwilling to commit himself, Tiresias is merely being fashionable, and so on), but in the case of Pentheus, the sexual challenge is significantly present ('Here you may do,/Do, do,/Do the forbidden/Shameless thing', p. 23).

In allegorical terms, this would imply that Pentheus's puritanical suppression of the cult represents the familiar ascendancy of the Ego over the Id (stressed by the stage's division in depth into Thebes and Mount Cytheron), and that the final implacable triumph of Dionysus represents the dangers of not allowing the instinctual life its expression. Auden discusses the damaging results of repression in *Secondary Worlds,* and compares Pentheus with Sarastro in *The Magic Flute:* 'Suppose, we cannot help wondering, there had been no Tamino and Pamina to provide a tidy and happy conclusion, would Sarastro have enjoyed his happy triumph for long?' Auden reminds us that today we again understand how it is possible for whole communities to be demonically possessed, and in the Epilogue to *The Bassarids* he embodies the Dionysiac triumph in a vision of two enormous fertility idols on Semele's tomb in the ruins of Thebes, with the Bassarids in adoration. The child with the doll that says 'mama' smashes it in glee, repeating, in conscious worship, the unconscious murder of Pentheus by his mother.

The implication is clear. Pentheus had wished for knowledge of his mother's sexual nature, and his repression had stemmed from this hidden wish. When he is given her mirror by Dionysus, what he 'sees' is the comic Intermezzo, a piece of pastoral whimsy in which the Olympian appetites are portrayed in neo-classical terms, alternately rakish, coy and vulgar. Agave plays for the handsome Captain, a Dionysus-surrogate and, significantly, an administrator who has already stood in for Pentheus in his political role and here would seem to represent Pentheus's own desires. Pentheus is disappointed at the vision, and wishes he could have 'Seen the raw deed plainly'.

From this point he is caught, and determines to observe the Bassarids at their supposed orgies by visiting Mount Cytheron himself. In this ensuing voyage into his real subconscious he is, like Ransom in *The Ascent of F6,* symbolically destroyed by his repressed instincts, here again embodied in the aggressive mother. The scene (p. 55) in which he struggles with his Dionysus-nature, and comes to some understanding of his psychic identity, is rather obscure, as many of the key moments of the opera are, but is evidently intended as a revelation of lust which destroys him effectively even before he is actually dismembered by his mother.

The setting of the opera is a deliberate farrago: the Bassarids are hippies, Tiresias an Anglican archdeacon, and so on. The result is a rather striking reappraisal of Euripedes in Audenesque terms, but the writing does not seem particularly incisive. Indeed, it is interesting to see that the libretto is often more diffuse than the text actually used in the score, and its staccato impressionistic flow (in, for instance, the rather Hopkinsian syntax of Dionysus) does not allow for many poetic set-pieces.

12   Poems 1948–1957

In this period (one of the most relaxed and sympathetic of Auden's career) he began to spend his summers on the Mediterranean island of Ischia. Although his activity in opera and criticism increases a great deal in these years, his shorter poems show no slackening of development. Indeed, in assurance of tone and subject (especially now in classical and medieval history) they are among his most impressive. They originally appeared in the collections *Nones* (1951), *The Shield of Achilles* (1955) and *Homage to Clio* (1960). Now, gathered together as the last section of the 1966 *Collected Shorter Poems,* their real substance (and shared concerns) is more apparent.

'In Transit' [N: 'Air Port'; CSP, p. 237] shows man as a fugitive from his environment. The two fears may be both the two flights that the airport connects, and the common concern for safety of the general staffs and engineers: in both cases the uneasiness of post-war travel is economically sketched in. With the unreality of the airport waiting-room, more of an Inferno than a community, Auden contrasts the reality of those places that have meaning because life is lived there, and that are, as it were, under the protection of a *deus loci;* places also where the choices and revelations of life are unquestionably present (an allusion perhaps in the fourth stanza to Goethe's Italian journey?). Again airborne, Auden sees spring's processes of renewal, and in a familiar image (the literal debacle of a river, the breaking up of the spiritually constricting ice) forecasts the hope which real possession of even a congested surface can bring. This is the renewal of the will to live, pardon for 'the maculate cities'.

The poem inaugurates a new period in Auden's verse when, with spiritual explorations largely behind him, he turns to questions of domestic virtues and the Horatian life.

'In Praise of Limestone' [*Horizon,* July 1948; N; CSP, p. 238], not only in the formula of the title, but in its tone and concerns, also suggests Horace. Auden establishes with elegiac sweetness and modesty the proposition that human virtue depends, in part, upon a simple assertion of the common values of life and their appetites, that limestone inconstancy may in another sense (as the poem's argument enacts) be limestone innocence.

It is not merely a tribute to an Italian landscape which embodies Auden's particular Eden, where man's expeditious control of stone and water becomes a paradigm of art (statues and fountains) seen as a wish to please the *Urmutter.* It is a statement of the spiritual temptations, and of the eternal opposition between those who recognize the demanding reality of sin and death, and those who feel that virtue and human happiness are within man's reach. 'We ... the inconstant ones' (intellectuals) are homesick for the limestone land-scape because it suggests exactly what 'we' can no longer really believe in: the immediacy of Nature and the self-sufficiency of a people who can control their environment and relate their appetites to their ultimate well-being. These are 'the band of rivals', a 'they' who, in a Pelagian certainty, are 'adjusted to the local needs of valleys/Where everything can be touched or reached by walking' and 'have never looked into infinite space/Through the lattice-work of a nomad's comb'. Auden's play with symbolic landscape and symbolic cate-gories is casual but ingenious. 'We' like limestone because it, like 'us', dissolves in water. 'They' like limestone because 'they' can control it as water controls the stone.

The temptations are real, as Auden sadly acknowledges, and are maintained in the same metaphor: the granite wastes lure the putative saints; clays and gravels lure the seekers of power (an allusion here to Goebbels: 'If we are defeated, we shall slam the doors of history behind us'?); the sea lures the 'really reckless'. The paradox is that although these voices cumulatively represent the forces of arrogant spiritual nihilism,[1] they do represent the alternative urge in man to face the unknown and to face death:

> They were right, my dear, all those voices were right
> And still are; this land is not the sweet home that it looks . . .

The tone of regret, gentle humour, affection, and personal resolve mingle brilliantly in this passage as Auden ties his threads of argument together: the temptations to spiritual exploration (away from the limited comprehensible ways of the 'backward/And delapidated province') involve both the best *and* the worst, and between these extremes of which the poet is consciously and ambiguously aware still remains the 'worldly duty' of the common life. Even in a context of sin and death and their hoped-for conquest ('a faultless love/Or the life to come') this worldly duty remains as a simple talisman of the innocence (however self-regarding) which attracted Auden in the first place.

The development works on a number of levels: even the streams themselves, at first chuckling through 'a secret system' of caves as though they are hiding from the visitor their real intention, become by the end 'the murmur/Of underground streams', as though their secret has been won and they share with the recipient of the poem the poet's endearments ('My dear', 'dear'). It has taken its place among readers, after all, as a kind of love poem: it seems to be about the lovers exploring a habitat conducive to their attempt to transcend time. The poet has shared his fear of losing time (it is this that gives the relevant lines their personal tone which wholly convinces), but it is as if he comes to half believe that time may be conquered only in time, not escaping but accepting: 'The blessed will not care what angle they are regarded from,/Having nothing to hide.' It is an important poem, foreshadowing much in Auden's method and concerns in the 'fifties.

'Ischia' [*Botteghe Oscure,* Vol. II, 1948; N; CSP, p. 241], a tribute to the Italian island where from 1948 Auden rented a house in which to spend each summer,[2] amplifies the Horatian tone. The change of heart is presumably the fact that the era of Mussolini is over (seen with rich irony in the first stanza as the Leader of Eliot's 'Triumphal March'). The poem expresses the *otium* of Auden's Mediterranean period with an agreeably relaxed humour, the only darkening of the scene being a donkey who 'breaks out into a choking wail/of utter protest at what is the case' (i.e. the world, see Wittgenstein's

Tractatus). The syllabic form (13/12/7/8) is adapted from the form of the Freud elegy and the 'Epilogue' to *New Year Letter,* and seems particularly appropriate to the kind of local descriptive-meditative poem that this is.

'Under Sirius' [*Horizon,* Oct. 1949; N; CSP, p. 243] deals with a theme that Auden returns to again and again in this period: the cultural parallel between the decadence of the later Roman Empire and of the post-war western world. Here the traditional reign of madness under Sirius, the dog-star, is represented particularly as a decline in the art of poetry: 'the Sybil utters/A gush of table-chat'. The stream of inspiration is drying up, 'the baltering torrent/Shrunk to a soodling thread'. (Incidentally, 'soodling' has taken some hard knocks as an instance of Auden's nonce-words, though – *pace* G. S. Fraser – it is not one, having been used by John Clare. It is marvellously appropriate in context, with suggestions of 'doodling', 'soothing' and 'footling', all the marginal qualities of the kind of minor verse which Auden wishes to evoke.)

It is plain that Auden is in some sense talking about his own development here, as typifying the general cultural scene. The poem's address to 'Fortunatus' is more than a mere piece of classical atmosphere, since Venantius Fortunatus (*c.* AD 530–600) was the last Latin poet of Gaul, a charming *bon viveur* and writer of occasional verses, who took holy orders in later life. It is therefore clear that Auden's spiritual interrogation is in some sense a self-interrogation, however good-humoured the tone. It is a qualification of the suggested parallels in 'The Epigoni' (CSP, p. 302) and uses the comfortable diction and tone which its questions undermine in order to set up a tension between a Fortunatus making the most of his limitations, and a Fortunatus whose glimpses of divine Grace make him fear divine Judgment. The 'pantocratic riddle' is the question which lies behind everything: 'Who are you and why?' In many of Auden's poems of the 'forties it becomes a kind of Christian touchstone against which the Horace–Auden or the Fortunatus–Auden may set the classical virtues. Here Auden plainly condemns those who refuse their chance, but it seems that under Sirius (as in the Desert of *For the Time Being*) the chances are not easy to see.

'Cattivo Tempo' [*Horizon,* Oct. 1949; N; CSP, p. 245] dramatizes the mental and moral depression brought by the Sirocco, a subject that has also been described by Graves.[3] The minor devils Nibbar and Tubervillus seem to correspond to the twin aspect of the Sirocco, whether it blows over sea (thus hot and moist: 'ga-ga and bêtise') or over land (thus desiccating and dusty: 'gossip and spite'). These are pitfalls for the poet, since his poetry and table-talk suffer, and mere silence is no remedy. The light, successful touch of such a moral exercise seems itself a good enough remedy for the enervating wind and its insolent demons. See also 'The Cave of Making' (*About the House,* p. 18) for these 'lip-smacking/imps of mawk and hooey').

'Hunting Season' [*Third Hour,* 1954; SA; CSP, p. 247] elaborates the proposition that the wooing of lovers is analogous to the hunting instinct. This is done in the first two stanzas with typical Audenesque deftness and economy. The third stanza, however, does little more than add an irrelevant comic flourish: the 'deathless verse' can be completed only if the poet 'Postpones his dying with a dish/Of several suffocated fish'. The connection is understood, that behind ideals lie instincts, and there is something pleasantly witty about the poet acknowledging this with the kind of ponderous gentility that leads to such wry circumlocutions.

'Fleet Visit' [*Listener,* 3 Jan. 1952; SA; CSP, p. 247] seems to go against a statement which Auden once made that 'the sailor on shore is symbolically the innocent god from the sea who is not bound by the law of the land and can therefore do anything without guilt' (*The Enchafèd Flood,* p. 122). For here the 'natives pass with laws/And futures of their own', and the sailors (who have come out of their hollow ships, not as masterful intruders out of the Wooden Horse, but as 'mild-looking middle-class boys/Who read the comic strips') 'look a bit lost'. The ships themselves, however, are 'far from looking lost': Auden's defence of their presence, on the purely aesthetic grounds that they look beautiful, is an interesting by-product of the Pax Americana, as though the purpose of NATO could really be disregarded for a second in 1952, however striking the 'pattern and line' of the ships in the harbour.

'An Island Cemetery' [HC; CSP, p. 248] offers an interesting parallel to Housman's 'The Immortal Part', as Spears has pointed out (p. 325). Probably an allusion to Valéry is intended, too. Anyway, the tone is light, approving the clinical impersonality of the skeleton, being rather offhand about the afterlife, toying with the idea of burial as a kind of agriculture, and refusing to play Hamlet to the Ischian gravediggers.

'Not in Baedeker' [N; CSP, p. 249] begins with a beautiful though surely questionable expression of permanence ('Is there a once that is not already?'), as Auden indulges in a travel-book excursion into his dream Eden (cf. *The Dyer's Hand*, p. 6). The poem is interesting to compare with such an early appraisal of the nostalgia of lead-mining as 'Lead's the Best' (*Oxford Outlook*, May 1926). Though some details are similar, the two are worlds apart, and nowhere so much as in the note in the later poem of 'the accidental' seen as a species of the historical: the imitation of a clergyman with a cleft palate becomes a curious symbol of the poet's genius wasted on triviality. As a piece of ironical autobiography, the poem is flatter and chillier than most, though as an application of that sense of the telescoping of time it is accurate and moving. One would guess that the Larkin of 'Church Going' had read this poem.

In 'Ode to Gaea' [*Listener*, 15 Dec. 1954; SA; CSP, p. 251] 'this new culture of the air', which has provided Auden with so much fresh material for panoramic views of the earth and its occupants, is responsible for a meditation of great virtuosity (like 'Ischia' in a 13/12/7/8 syllabic stanza, though rhymed, with a manner of procedure reminiscent of the Horatian ode). The aeroplane allows a view of Spring, season of love, as a seasonal movement of natural masses, a 'vernal plunge' in which 'her desolations' are 'glamorously carpeted/with . . . delicious spreads of nourishment', and where on land the mating of creatures begins (Auden's talent for sedate riddling here is at its best):

> . . . in her realm of solids, lively dots expand,
> companionship becomes an unstaid passion and
> leaves by the mile hide tons of
> pied pebbles that will soon be birds.

The view of Gaea (the earth) that science provides (in contrast with the unknown monsters beyond the boundaries of the cartographer's Christendom) seems even more mysterious, because less concerned with man than with the inanimate, such as water, sketched in a brilliant phrase: 'she joins girl's-ear lakes/to bird's-foot deltas with lead-blue squiggles'.

In response to this neglect, man must cultivate his sense of order and good manners (stanzas 10 on). Auden shows that it is natural to invent a wilful Olympian deity who may tire of the Greeks and become interested in the Scythians (the Hippemolgoi, the mare-milkers), and whose destructions, therefore, are unpredictable and inevitable. Thus it is that 'manners, maybe, will stand us in better stead/ . . . than a kantian conscience' (i.e. than believing that your behaviour is good only when it is consciously obeying the moral law), and thus it is that

> perhaps a last stand in the passes will be made
> by those whose Valhalla would be hearing verse by Praed
>   or arias by Rossini
>   between two entrées by Carême.

Which is an ideal elaborated with less challenging mock-effeteness in a later poem, 'Grub First, Then Ethics' (*About the House*, p. 33), which culminates in a similar stand of gourmets at Thermopylae. Even so, Gaea is impersonal – 'She has never been moved/except by Amphion' (who drew stones after him with his magic lyre) and finds human ideals irrelevant.

The seven 'Bucolics' [SA; CSP, p. 255] were recorded by Auden on 12 December 1953, and therefore must all have been written before this date. Each geographical phenomenon is invested not only with all the characteristics that Auden's categorizing and descriptive talents afford, but with a serious moral identity as a *genius loci* which assists or detracts from his notion of the Good Life.

In 'Winds' [*London Magazine*, Nov. 1954] he begins boldly with wind as the 'holy insufflation' of God the Creator breathing into man's nostrils the breath of life. Metropolis is the Fallen City, the product of man's asserted will. 'I am loved, therefore I am' is taken not in the sense of God's love being a necessary condition for well-being, but as a pseudo-Cartesian argument for self-sufficiency (cf. Diaghilev in 'September 1, 1939'). Thus the lion is not lying down with the kid (Isaiah xi.6), perhaps because of the bubble-brained creature God chose (an extinct fish, an insect or crab or so forth, might have made a better job of it, and not brought death into the world).

Such theological musing is lightly replaced by the wind as weather, and how concern for the weather can be 'an image/For our Authentic City' (as opposed to the Fallen Metropolis of the first stanza). This merely acts as a bridge passage to the longest and final stanza, the poet's invocation to 'Goddess of winds and wisdom', i.e. the Muse, to bring him inspiration, save him from writing nonsense and remind him of the purity of the subjects he celebrates: 'Earth, Sky, a few dear names'.

In 'Woods' [*Listener,* 11 Dec. 1952] Auden turns to a rhymed iambic formality as if to comment ironically on society's prized decorum which has treated woods as the residue of the primitive and dangerously numinous ('Crown and Mitre warned their silly flocks/The pasture's humdrum rhythms to approve/And to abhor the licence of the grove'). The rhythms of the poem are far from humdrum, and in the last stanza take on a rib-prodding Empsonian menace. The argument is that woods constitute, not merely a location for bizarre rites or easy seduction, but a concentrated expression of man's basic condition (some brilliant descriptions here of sounds, as cuckoos, doves, fruit and leaf enact their symbolism of generation and death), and that a society's attitude towards its trees is a good sign of its health.

'Mountains' [Faber and Faber Ariel poem, 1954] takes a curiously jaundiced view of its subject. The fastidious tone supports the investigated notion of safety and comfort running through the whole series, the difficulty of managing 'the Flesh,/When angels of ice and stone/Stand over her day and night who make it so plain/They detest any kind of growth'. Mountains have always represented some kind of challenge in Auden's poetry, but in this poem response to the challenge breeds fanatics and hermits (there is an unusually sharp vignette of mountaineers), and it is suggested that mountains are best appreciated from a distance.

In 'Lakes' [*New Poems by American Poets,* ed. R. Humphries, 1953], the lakes that Auden is concerned with are charmingly described in family-sized terms. Anything larger, though potable, is, he says, an 'estranging sea', borrowing the phrase, via Arnold's 'To Marguerite', from the Horatian 'oceano dissociabile' (*Odes*, I, 3). The 'lacustrine atmosphere' breeds good manners. The first ecumenical council of the churches (at which Constantine made Arianism heretical) was held on 'the Ascanian Lake' at Nicaea in Bithynia, and lakes are, Auden claims, ideal places to hold peace talks. The modest scale of a lake is even flattering to a drowning man's sense of fatalism, and so the examples continue in Auden's best essay-manner, culminating, in the penultimate stanza, with an acknowledgment that one is likely to defend one's ideal landscape aggressively (as Wordsworth resented the growing popularity of the Lake District) because it represents a Paradisal retreat which no appeal to common humanity ('amniotic mere' = womb) can make one wish to share. It is this wrily critical point which governs the final stanza's conscious whimsy about one's daydreams:

> Moraine, pot, oxbow, glint, sink, crater, piedmont, dimple . . .?
> Just reeling off their names is ever so comfy.

Critics read this (as they read much of Auden, but this is a notorious example) as unconsciously twee.[4] But surely Auden is adjusting, as he continually does, the tone and diction of his meditation to suit the meaning, and the meaning here is that such Paradisal retreats are a dangerous illusion (that Nature is benign, that they can be defended by savage dogs and man-traps, and so on) and that contemplation of owning one is not only a *comfortable* activity, but, with all the social overtones of the phrase, *ever so comfy*.

'Islands', by being in short quatrains, seems more evidently a catalogue-poem than the others, pointing out without great wit that on islands are to be found saints, pirates, convicts, natives (despite Hobbes, innocent natural man ousted by civilized man), tyrants, poets and sunbathers. Elba, Lesbos, Capri and Ischia are blandly linked as examples of the Ego's habitat.

'Plains' [*London Magazine,* Apr. 1954] provides a landscape without form or direction. Plain-dwellers are without choice in

love, and are at the mercy of the strong who 'chamber with Clio' (i.e.
make history, history, as Auden remarked elsewhere, being the
'realm of man's freedom and of his sin', *Theology,* Nov. 1950). Thus
plains are a nightmare landscape of victimization to the poet, who
is not a man of power (though he would like to own a cave with two
exits). They are a reminder of the extensiveness of evil. Not even in
poetry is anything 'lovely', and poetry is not even real ('the case', i.e.
the world, an allusion to Wittgenstein already used in 'Ischia').

In contrast to the nightmare of 'Plains' is the idyllic love-vision
of 'Streams' [*Encounter,* June 1954] whose water is (as in 'In Praise of
Limestone' or 'Ode to Gaea') 'pure being', an eternally innocent
presence unrelated to size ('unchristened brooks' as much as the
Brahmaputra, the great river of north-east India). Water may
provide national barriers (stanza 5) and ridicule the human motivation that makes use of them (stanza 7), and in this role it is beyond
man's power to spoil. But as a sacramental blessing upon his
nobler ideals it seems, as a prompter of the dream (the sound of
Kisdon Beck), to be almost a sign of grace.

'Shorts' [Nos. 4, 5: N; Nos. 1, 2, 3, 6, 9, 11: SA; Nos. 7, 8, 10:
HC; CSP, p. 268] is a collection of brief epitaphs, dedications and
mottoes, and limericks from the 'fifties. 'Behold the manly meso-
morph' and 'Give me a doctor, partridge-plump' were originally
entitled 'Footnotes to Dr Sheldon', referring to W. H. Sheldon's
work on human physiological types. Auden had already expressed
his preference for the endomorphic type rather than the ectomorphic
or (here particularly) mesomorphic types (cf. 'The Fall of Rome',
stanza 4). 'Fair is Middle-Earth . . .' was the motto to 'Bucolics'
(for Middle-Earth, see J. R. R. Tolkien's *Lord of the Rings*), and
'Guard, Civility . . .' the motto to the central miscellaneous section
of *The Shield of Achilles.* The warning that 'Any lout can
spear with ease/Singular Archimedes' had a particular meaning in
the period of the McCarthyite witch-hunts. Auden's injunction has
thus a certain nobility, despite its brevity. The two limericks from
Homage to Clio (originally entitled 'History of the Boudoir' and 'The
Aesthetic Point of View') both retail a sly truth about human
aspirations of a certain kind, though their camp tone has not been
well taken by critics. The last two shorts (the dedications of their

respective volumes) both refer, as do a number of poems of this period, to Auden's awareness of a drying-up of poetic inspiration and the corresponding value of the lucky truth at a time of sterility.

'Five Songs': No. I: 'Deftly, admiral, cast your fly' [*Horizon*, Nov. 1948; N; CSP, p. 271] is an excellently anecdotal song which again uses the properties of Auden's Roman analogy. The admiral and ambassador, retired functionaries of the Empire, are powerless to stop the unwanted love-affair between their children, just as they have been powerless to prevent the destruction of the fleets or the invasion of the Chateaux by 'unshaven horsemen'. The irony (splendidly dramatic and lyrical) is that the pair of lovers themselves can likewise do nothing to avoid the Furies who 'With claw and dreadful brow/Wait for them now.' In No. II: 'The Emperor's favourite concubine' [N: 'Music Ho'; CSP, p. 271] the doom of the Empire (palace intrigue, mutiny in the provinces and apocalyptic signs) seems to its inhabitants merely boring: it is a story they have heard before. Even the 'Transformation Scene' (the metaphor is of a dramatic performance) provides only 'a rather scruffy-looking god'.

No. III: 'A starling and a willow-wren' [*Encounter*, Nov. 1953: 'The Willow-wren and the Stare'; SA; CSP, p. 272] is a ballad in Auden's old manner offering a delicate and touching scepticism about human motivation in love:

> *Is it only that?* said the willow-wren;
> *It's that as well*, said the stare.

When the lover on the grassy bank wakes from his gratification and talks about standing 'upon the shining outskirts/Of that Joy', the birds wonder whether he knew what he meant, and when the starling says *God only knows* we can take this as humorous resignation at the inscrutability of the events they have witnessed, or we can perhaps take it literally. At any rate, the criticism is gently made. We are reminded of Auden's belief that 'Agape is the fulfilment and correction of eros, not its contradiction' (*Theology*, Nov. 1950, p. 412).

No. IV: ' "When rites and melodies begin" ' [*Times Literary Supplement*, 17 Sept. 1954: 'The Trial'; SA: 'The Proof'; CSP, p. 273] is based on the trials of Tamino and Pamina in Act II, scene v, of *The Magic Flute*. Their love is seen by Auden as a type of Grace, won only by Tamino's perseverance and Pamina's faithfulness. In the opera it is the flute, given to Tamino by Astrafiammante (representing the instinctual life opposed to Sarastro's rule of reason) which tames the elements (the 'fermatas' here are musical pauses). There are hints that Auden sees their love as a symbol of the regaining of Paradise. 'Innocent? Yes. Ignorant? No' glances at C. S. Lewis's comment on Milton's prelapsarian Adam and Eve (*Preface to Paradise Lost*). In No. v: 'Make this night loveable' [S A: 'Nocturne II'; C S P, p. 274] the appeal to the moon (symbol of the imagination) to make absent friends accessible 'in dreams' turns into a charm against jealousy.

'Three Occasional Poems': No. i: 'To T. S. Eliot On His Sixtieth Birthday (1948)' [*T. S. Eliot: A Symposium,* ed. R. March and M. J. Tambimuttu, 1948; N; C S P, p. 275]. Auden first read Eliot in 1926 (see the account of his tutor, Nevill Coghill, in the above symposium), so that this tribute to what would seem to be an analysis of a spiritual malaise ('the crime' = original sin) has the benefit of hindsight. The poem may be compared with 'Detective Story' in *Letters from Iceland* (C S P, p. 102), with the ideas in Auden's essay 'The Guilty Vicarage' in *The Dyer's Hand:* 'The interest in the detective story is the dialectic of innocence and guilt' (p. 147), and with 'New Year Letter' (ll. 233ff). The subservience of even a great detective to the ultimate processes of the Law would seem to imply the inferiority of poetic activity to the divine truth. The Shakespeare allusion adds a moral piety that takes the poem even further, to my mind, from the real Eliot.

No. ii: 'Metalogue to *The Magic Flute'* [*Listener,* 26 Jan. 1956; *The Magic Flute,* English version by Auden and Kallmann, 1957; H C; C S P, p. 276], spoken between the two acts of *The Magic Flute* in an American television production in 1956 (the Mozart bicentenary) for which Auden and Kallmann had translated the libretto, serves as a constructive deflation in the manner of an Augustan epilogue. The jokes outweigh the tribute, but they are good, and the whole piece forms an elegant pastiche of Dryden. The translation of the characters to an academic background for speculations on their modern significance is a brilliant stroke.

No. iii: 'Lines addressed to Dr Claude Jenkins' [H C; C S P, p.

279] is all that survives in the *Collected Shorter Poems* of the appendix of 'Academic Graffiti' in *Homage to Clio*. Jenkins had been one of Christ Church's six Canons over thirty years previously, when Auden first went up there as an Exhibitioner in Natural Sciences. This Common Room tribute, from the then Professor of Poetry, slight as it is, has a genuine warmth.

In 'Their Lonely Betters' [N; CSP, p. 280] the generalizations about man and nature are rather subdued and quasi-Frostian. The poem contains a personal rebuke: speech provides man with an awareness of time, and with the possibility of lying, so that love (which is so instinctive and helpless in the case of the robin or the flowers) is often a matter of deceit and frustration. Thus the longing for letters implies an unkept promise in the final stanza: the feeling is beautifully and stoically understated.

'First Things First' [*New Yorker,* 9 Mar. 1957; HC; CSP, p. 281] is another love poem, again contrasting inarticulate nature with the human urge to make linguistic sense of the universe, to translate the storm's 'interjectory uproar' into the name of the loved one. It is a poem, too, of touching and dignified loneliness: the storm *has* power to evoke the sacred image, but in the cold light of morning it is seen that all it has really done is to fill the cistern ('Thousands have lived without love, not one without water').

'The More Loving One' [HC; CSP, p. 282] seems merely to be an extravagant way of coming to terms with an unreciprocated love: how much worse it is to be the loved one who cannot return the affection. The absence of all 'stars' may be contemplated, like the absence of desire, with only a precarious equanimity. In 'A Permanent Way' [SA; CSP, p. 282] the 'choice one might have made' can be imagined without undergoing actual risk: this poem is in praise of a settled love, even when enforced by 'dogma'.

In 'Nocturne' [*Botteghe Oscure,* Vol. VIII (1951): 'A Face in the Moon'; *Third Hour,* 1954: 'The Moon Like X'; SA: 'Nocturne I'; CSP, p. 283] the mind admits to the heart that 'both are worshippers of force'. Thus the moon, mockingly invoked as a supernatural talisman, a love-goddess, is seen to be only a myth or a machine, since Eros is an appetite with its own unaffected compulsions. The lover is real, though, and his moon-substitute on a purely practical plane might be any other real person belonging to the world of natural appetite (merely 'x', an algebraic representation of human possibility) who can, as he thought the moon could, 'Make/Or break you'. This element of fortuitous influence in a real, as opposed to mythological or mechanical, world is seen wryly as a counterbalance to a dangerous solipsism: 'My world, the private motor-car/ And all the engines of the State.' Compare Auden's ideas in his essay 'The Virgin and the Dynamo' in *The Dyer's Hand,* especially pp. 62–63. The terms were borrowed from *The Education of Henry Adams* and used by Auden as early as 'New Year Letter', l. 1466 and note.

'Precious Five' [*Harper's Magazine,* Oct. 1950; N; CSP, p. 285] enjoins the five senses ('Be patient . . . Be modest . . . Be civil . . . look straight . . . Praise . . . the Earthly Muse . . . Be happy') to serve the Natural Law, and in so doing to concur in the Divine Law, whose singular command is *'Bless what there is for being'.*

The nose is seen as the organ which is aware of time (perhaps as a tribute to Proust?). It is asked to persist 'Up the storm-beaten slope/ From memory to hope' even though the 'calm enchanted wood' of childhood has gone.

The ears are the poet's 'ear' for poetry, 'spoiled darlings', he modestly proclaims, in an 'undisciplined' age. There is a pointed criticism of his public when he says that 'It cannot take pure fiction,/ And what it wants from you/Are rumours partly true', and he concludes the stanza by admitting the need for inspiration. His ears must go back to school and drudge, but even then poetic success is a 'luck' which the ears celebrate but cannot predict.

Hands are the instruments of action and power, but in a funny contrast between 'hairy wrists/And leg-of-mutton fists' and 'A tight arthritic claw/Or aldermanic paw' Auden appeals to hands to be exploratory and generous, not merely to evoke the authority of the past.

Eyes are instruments of intelligence (beware of mirrors: no self-deception is possible) and in 'living men' complement the heart (seat of feeling) in a 'mutual undeceiving'. 'True seeing' is not merely a matter of 'sight'.

The tongue is the instrument of praise of 'the Earthly Muse', praise for just that daily quality of life enjoyed by the tongue's 'old self' as instrument of taste, and of its twin, the penis. The tone of quiet meditative acceptance which brings the faculties under control is maintained in the final stanza, where any 'anger and despair/At what is going on' is shown to be useless: the theological position is one of Leibnizian optimism. The trimeters (as usual in Auden) have a pace and gravity that link the poem with some of the philosophical lyrics of the 'thirties.

'Memorial for the City' [*Horizon*, Nov. 1949; N; CSP, p. 289] is dedicated to the memory of Charles Williams, some of whose ideas appear in it. The City is the Christian community, and Auden's Memorial is consciously written in the years after Auschwitz. 'The crow on the crematorium chimney' and 'the camera's candid eye' provide the bleak evidence of human sin that in Homer's world remains marginal to the large unconcerned processes of Nature, but which in a Christian system is a central necessity of man's predicament. 'We know without knowing there is reason for what we bear,/That our hurt is not a desertion'. This is the Christian *felix culpa*, the redeemed sin which carries an eternal significance so that (as the contrasts of Part I are meant to show) to the Christian 'the crime of life is not time', and the 'meaningless' moments of violence and despair are not lost in 'the hard bright light' of actuality, because the realms of nature (necessity) and of history (man's freedom) are distinct.

The epitaph from Juliana of Norwich underlines this point by showing that the kingdom of God is not something wholly removed from the real world: *'In the self-same point that our soul is made sensual, in the self-same point is the City of God ordained to him from without beginning.'* This quotation had been used by Charles Williams in *The Descent of the Dove* (p. 224), with the comment that natural justice is a necessary preliminary to all charity. The notion of 'the Post-Vergilian City' also derives from Williams (p. 79), who contrasted the use of literary Latin in Christendom with the 'elegancies' of Virgil.

In Part II of the poem (where there is a much greater use of the internal rhyming borrowed from Williams) Auden provides an adroit potted history of Christendom. He begins by describing the precarious equilibrium of Pope and Emperor, each, according to medieval theory, one half of the indivisible God. Behind the simple unifying power of a secular and temporal authority ('Fear of the stranger was lost on the way to the shrine') lies the idea that if Byzantium had been absorbed, we would never have had Prussia. More important is the comfortable symbolism of medieval life in matters of religion: the 'double meaning' that divided authority represented becomes in the second stanza a matter of jest and parody, in the sense that the spiritual life more and more came to be embodied in the secular and the representational ('Limbs became hymns' as tangible images of the supposedly miraculous cure; aggression was worked out in the crusading spirit; and astrology expressed the fatalism of an anthropocentric universe).

In the third stanza this is developed into a description of the praiseworthy attempts to establish 'the Sane City', where a supra-national network of letters and travel ('Scribes and innkeepers') combined with the rationalizations of dogma (a reference in lines 3 and 4 to the Nicaean Council, perhaps) are aspects of that urge for order which may be found in the treatment of landscape in the religious paintings of the early Renaissance. But this kind of control of the 'dry rocks' is seen in the following stanza as producing the reaction of the Reformation: the dry rocks, like Luther's 'sandy province', clearly represent man's sense of sin, which is not ulti-mately appeased by 'the machine that so smoothly forgave and saved/If paid'. The mechanical indulgence could not bridge the 'grinning gap' between man and God which Luther perceived. The Sane City had become the Sinful City, and 'her conclusions were to include all doubt' (all this Auden had expounded in greater detail in *New Year Letter*).

The fifth stanza (the internal rhyming steps up here significantly) describes the ascendancy of art in the Renaissance; the sixth, the growth of science ('Nature was put to the Question') and a polite culture. In the seventh stanza, secularism is taken to its extreme in the ideals of the 'Rational City', with its egalitarianism and utilitarian-ism. The shift to Romanticism is cleverly done here, as 'her pallid affected heroes/Began their hectic quest for the prelapsarian man' (an allusion to the Godwinism of Shelley, perhaps). The remainder of this part describes religious exploration of the Romantic tradition in terms of the sea-voyage and its disasters: it is clear that Auden is thinking of the ideas that he was expounding in his Page-Barbour Lectures (given at the University of Virginia in 1949), which are reprinted in *The Enchafèd Flood*.

Part III returns to the present, to the bombed landscape of the 'Abolished City'. The omnipresent barbed wire is man's pride and will which destroys his community. The ultimate image of man ('behind the wire/Which is behind the mirror') is an expendable automaton, a creature of the flesh responsible for the wire and the ruins and owing no allegiance to the weeping soul.

Part IV describes, in the form of a riddle, man's redeeming qualities of innocence and humility (ironically introduced as *'Our Weakness'*). Though the forces of power ('Metropolis', the fallen city) are ascendant, 'I shall rise again to hear her judged'. The message of this poem, with an optimism elaborately prepared for and skilfully embodied in a grave and measured style, is none the less a little too dense and didactic to be wholly convincing in its context.

'The Shield of Achilles' [*Poetry,* Oct. 1952; SA; CSP, p. 294], by contrast, puts the post-war scene into just the kind of oblique and dramatically archetypal context that brings out both its full horror and its religious meaning. Thetis looks for the classical virtues on her son's shield (see the *Iliad,* Book XVIII). She looks for order and good government but finds only its negative image, a spiritless totalitarianism; she looks for religion, but finds only a military execution parodying the crucifixion; she looks for art, and finds only an aimless violence:

> A ragged urchin, aimless and alone,
>   Loitered about that vacancy, a bird
> Flew up to safety from his well-aimed stone:
>   That girls are raped, that two boys knife a third,
>   Were axioms to him, who'd never heard
> Of any world where promises were kept,
> Or one could weep because another wept.

The quiet pace and feeling in this poem, and its conscious simplicity of diction, give it a moving conviction and grandeur. Thetis's dismay is counterbalanced by the fated shortness of Achilles's life (see the *Iliad*, IX, 410ff), so that Hephaestos's provision of such a shield seems significantly like the Christian God's provision of man's free-will, as though the landscape of evil were a necessary condition for redemption. Any optimism in the thought of the death of the 'Iron-hearted man-slaying Achilles' is beautifully and ironically understated in the conclusion of the poem, so that it is enabled to concentrate instead on the bleak inevitability of the 'unseemly deeds' which he represents.

'Secondary Epic' [*The Mid-Century*, No. 7, Dec. 1959; HC; CSP, p. 296], a move from Achilles's shield to Aeneas's shield (made by Vulcan, i.e. Hephaestos, in Book VIII of the *Aeneid*), represents a shift of interest generally noticeable in *Homage to Clio*, from the moral to the historical. Here Auden is interested in the fact that prophetic scenes on the shield could naturally not extend further into the future than 31 BC (the latest reference in the poem, the date of Octavian's campaign in the East after Actium). He imagines some 'refugee rhetorician' adding a later gloss about the fall of Rome to the barbarians (this done in a minor eighteenth-century blank verse like that of, say, Dyer), and at the end of the poem he exposes the prophecies of Anchises in Book VI for mention-ing Romulus and Augustus, but not disclosing 'the names pre-destined for the Catholic boy/Whom Arian Odovacer will depose'. This refers to the barbarian ruler Odovacer, or Odoacer, who in AD 476 deposed the ironically named Romulus Augustus, last Emperor of the West. There is a fine scornful passage about the unworthy 'Momyllus Augustulus' in Gibbon, Chapter 36.

'Makers of History' [*The Old Man's Road*, 1956; HC; CSP, p. 297] was one of seven poems on historical themes published in a limited edition in 1956, and later collected in *Homage to Clio*. 'Serious historians', it asserts, care less for the powerful rulers, who so often have become legendary, than for the craftsmen and artists who are responsible for the tangible remains of their civilizations, without which even the legend could not be understood.

'T The Great' [HC; CSP, p. 299] is such a ruler. Auden's ana-grammatic riddle underlines the essential anonymity (and lack of real importance) of such a bogey as Tamburlaine, who is eventually succeeded by 'N' (Napoleon), who in turn is replaced by 'S' (Stalin). Thus in a sense the poem is more about Stalin than about Tamburlaine, and may have been written not long after his death.

'The Managers' [*Horizon,* Nov. 1948; N; CSP, p. 300] contrasts with the rulers of the past the grey faceless rulers of the present, the managers, children of Apollo (cf. 'Under Which Lyre', CSP, p. 221), to whom the exercise of power is a compulsion like a game: 'the fun/Neither love nor money/But taking necessary risks, the test/Of one's skill, the question,/If difficult, their own reward'. Thus they are not to be pitied. The poem drifts forward on its Skaldic rhyming with an extemporizing air.

'The Epigoni' [*The Old Man's Road,* 1956; HC; CSP, p. 302] examines literary Alexandrianism. The epigoni (a succeeding and less distinguished generation, so called after the sons of the Seven against Thebes) are here the Latin poets of the declining Empire, involved in just that cultural predicament which Auden had already likened to our own: an impotent expectation of barbarianism, and the poetic choice of 'dramatizing their doom' or 'expiring in preposterous mechanical tricks'. They sensibly chose the latter, 'epanaleptics, rhopalics, anacyclic acrostics', forms which 'can safely be spanked in a scholar's footnote' but which have in the circumstances a kind of nobility. If we call them shallow, it is because our generation would not conform to Auden's touchstone for critics (see *The Dyer's Hand,* p. 47).

In 'Bathtub Thoughts' [*The Old Man's Road,* 1956: '*c.* 500 AD'; HC; CSP, p. 303] the same cultural bond is more ironically presented, in this case as a mathematical relationship between two numbers in a sequence whose length 'chance only knows', since the words which Auden imagines the Romano-Briton addressing to him are also the words which Auden is addressing to an unknown 'future friend': the civilization which is symbolized here by plenty of hot water may be destroyed more than once.

'The Old Man's Road' [*Perspective,* No. 14, Winter 1956; *The Old Man's Road,* 1956; HC; CSP, p. 304] is the road of spiritual self-discovery which ignores all the established positions of religious orthodoxy. Those who follow it have freed themselves from the bonds of history even though they are 'assuming a freedom its Powers deny', because for Auden history is, in fact, the realm of man's freedom and of his sin. The old man's road, therefore, belongs very much to the world of nature, the realm of necessity and of obedience to God's creation: in other words, the Quest that the road represents is the quest for innocence or 'authenticity of being'.

'The History of Science' [*New Statesman,* 9 June 1956; *The Old Man's Road,* 1956; HC; CSP, p. 305] uses the myth of the lucky Third Brother in fairy-tales to postulate a Fourth Brother, milder even than the third, who ignores the offered advice, choosing the heroic 'North', and yet discovers 'a wonderful instead' which is as satisfactory as the original object of his quest. The point is that science proceeds as much by chance and error as by enlightened direction. By contrast, 'The History of Truth' [HC; CSP, p. 306] proposes that the truth in a pre-scientific era was a given fact, a reality which its artifacts could mirror simply by existing, since 'being was believing'. Our ephemeral products barely exist (like paper-dishes) and therefore imply an anti-model, an 'untruth anyone can give the lie to'.

In 'Homage to Clio' [*Encounter,* Nov. 1955; *The Old Man's Road,* 1956; HC; CSP, p. 307], in a spring setting ('Our hill has made its submission and the green/Swept on into the north'), Auden reflects upon the difference between the human world and the natural world ruled by the twin urges of sex ('Provocative Aphrodite') and hunting ('Virago Artemis'). The point about humanity is that it is aware of itself as a multitude of individual consciousnesses whose desires are historically conditioned. If life were merely a matter of instinct (like the 'cock pronouncing himself himself/Though all his sons had been castrated and eaten'), we would be like any other species, making our 'tribal outcry' at the proper season.

Our individual awareness is presided over by Clio, 'Muse of Time', 'Madonna of silences', who creatively intervenes between us and the 'magical centre' of the absolutely natural instinctual life which the animals enjoy, symbolized in the poem by noise. Artemis and Aphrodite are 'Major Powers', whose rule we must obey, but birth and death for us are 'unique historical fact':

I have seen
Your photo, I think, in the papers, nursing
A baby or mourning a corpse . . .

It is the secular tyrants who defy Clio ('The Short, The Bald, The
Pious, The Stammerer' are the nicknames of kings; the Laxey
Wheel is in the Isle of Man, cf. *Letters From Iceland,* p. 254) and are
thus, like the children of Artemis, victims of time.

'The Love Feast' [N; CSP, p. 310], concerned with the erotic
possibilities of a late-night party, has disturbed some critics with its
final flat, unrecalcitrant use of St Augustine's 'Make me chaste,
Lord, but not yet' (*Confessions,* VIII, 16). In fact, the religious imagery
pervades the poem (especially in the notion of the new arrivals as
catechumens, or candidates for baptism, and the allusion in stanza 4
to Dante's 'L'amor che move il sole e l'altre stella') and seems plainly
intended by Auden as an assertion of the validity of Eros. In *Theology,*
November 1950, p. 412, he complained: 'In some circles recently
there has been a tendency to see the notion of love as eros or desire for
getting and the notion of love as agape or free-giving as incompatible
opposites and to identify them with Paganism and Christianity
respectively. Such a view seems to me a revival of the Manichean
heresy which denies the goodness of the natural order.'

'The Chimeras' [*Times Literary Supplement,* 9 Mar. 1951; N;
CSP, p. 311] are any of those illusions that we have about life which
ignore the truth of the individual, and are beautifully and delicately
half-personified in the Auden manner. Similarly, 'Merax & Mullin'
[*The Old Man's Road,* 1956: HC; CSP, p. 312] are illusions about
Eros which lie in wait for those who, as it were, want to escape from
the realm of Clio to the realm of Aphrodite (compare 'who would
unwish themselves' with the 'mere commanders' of 'Makers of
History': 'What did they do but wish?'). 'Wishing' is thus to assert
one's freedom and one's propensity to sin; it becomes a characteristic
of jealousy and impotence to deny this in oneself and yet to ascribe
its perversions to others, just as in a war (very much the activity of
those who 'wish') a world of unobliging objects is comically assumed
to be sexually aberrant. Almost as a footnote to this is described a
'nastier, more deadly' devil, who urges 'laodicean' (i.e. indifferent)
lovers to 'swear/Undying love'. The dangers of such a delusion were

elaborated by Auden in 'Dichtung und Wahrheit' (the prose 'Unwritten Poem') in *Homage to Clio.*

In 'Limbo Culture' [*Atlantic,* Nov. 1957; 'HC; CSP, p. 312] the comic definition of Limbo culture (no words for *yes* or *no,* no pronouns distinguishing between persons, and so on) looks like a covert needling of a prevaricating lover, the eternal maybe. This love for inexactness seems to indicate only a self-love ('For that, we know, cannot be done exactly'), and here, perhaps, the religious parallel suggested by the name 'Limbo' asserts itself: exactness, and unselfish love, would suggest the state of grace that only 'baptism' could bring (cf. *Inferno,* Canto IV).

'There Will Be No Peace' [HC; CSP, p. 313] and 'A Household' [N; CSP, p. 314] examine real cases of the kind of self-regard that is the ultimate Limbo objective. Spears (p. 327) reports Auden as saying at a reading that 'There Will Be No Peace' 'seems to be about paranoia', and certainly the sense of motiveless persecution which characterizes the paranoiac delusion is carefully evoked from the patient's point of view by the speaker's quiet and insistent elaboration of how he feels. 'A Household' similarly shows how self-possession can be built upon delusion: the clubbable but lonely managerial figure maintains a family myth which, if it were true, would destroy him.

The title of ' "The Truest Poetry is the most Feigning" ' [*New Yorker,* 13 Nov. 1954; SA; CSP, p. 315] is a quotation from Touchstone's remark to Audrey in *As You Like It* (III. iii), a kind of inverted syllogism naïvely betraying his own doubtful motives in wooing her: poetry is the language of lovers, and what lovers swear in poetry they feign, thus poetry is most typical ('truest' in that sense) when it is most feigning. Auden plays with Touchstone's meaning in his elaboration of the poet's 'ingenious fibs' about his feelings, culminating in his splendid example of the all-purpose encomium hastily adapted (with the modification of epithets like 'lily-breasted' into 'lion-chested') to praise a Franco. But ultimately he takes the sense of 'truest' to imply 'conveying the truth', as we might expect, by showing that it is poetry's very trickery that reveals its awareness of the fact that the truth is unknowable. This was even so in the case of the love-poem pure and simple ('No metaphor, remember, can express/A real historical unhappiness') and is doubly so in the case of 'truth in any serious sense', which, 'like orthodoxy, is a reticence' (cf. *The Dyer's Hand,* p. 21).

'We Too Had Known Golden Hours' [N, dedication; CSP, p. 318] provides another way of looking at the relationship between poetry and truth. It similarly uses the term 'glory' apparently to describe the authentic note of poetic inspiration, but complains that language has been debased, and that 'the old grand manner' will no longer do. Now the only civil style to have survived is 'the wry, the sotto-voce,/Ironic and monochrome'. The implied apologia here explains much in Auden's later conversational manner, even though 'the old grand manner' is commoner than one tends to think. Auden put his feelings plainly in the *Kenyon Review,* Winter 1964: 'In so much "serious" poetry, poetry, that is to say, which is neither pure playful song nor comic, I find an element of "theatre", of exaggerated gesture and fuss, of indifference to the naked truth, which, as I get older, increasingly revolts me. This element is mercifully absent from what is conventionally called good prose.' The point is put in Christian terms in the dedication to the *Collected Shorter Poems* (1966), originally the motto to Part II of *Homage to Clio.*

In 'Secrets' [*Ladies' Home Journal,* Aug. 1950; N; CSP, p. 318] Auden exposes a love of secrets as a love either of the excitement of dramatic irony (stanza 1) or of social power (stanza 2). In either category, and in all the cases that Auden so entertainingly elaborates the categories with, the motive is unworthy: 'our commonest fault' is the Professor's own short-sightedness translated to the moral sphere, i.e. our lack of pity, pity being conquered by our desire for superiority. Ironically, Auden goes on to define love in terms of sharing a secret, albeit, in the Christian context which the last lines rather tamely introduce, one which is as irrelevant to Agape as it is to the animals 'who . . . have nothing to hide'.

'Numbers and Faces' [N; CSP, p. 319] carries overtones of an Eros-Agape contrast (compare 'To ask if it is big or small proclaims one/The sort of lover who should stick to faces' with the equation of big pricks, big money and big bangs in *Marginalia,* 1966). Lovers of big numbers are conformist power-maniacs; lovers of small numbers are mild eccentrics: both concentrate on the inhuman. Love demands concern for a different kind of number, i.e. one which 'is always real' (the individual). None could be called good except Infinity (God), which is not really a number at all because boundless. The ideas in the poem probably owe a great deal to Rudolf Kassner's *Zahl und Gesicht* (1919), which Auden had been reading at the time (see his introduction to *The Living Thoughts of Kierkegaard*, 1952).

There is a certain air of extemporized 'fiftyish flatness in the following three sonnets from *Homage to Clio*, which in places suggests deliberate pastiche (e.g. the offhand Empsonian 'There is less grief than wonder on the whole'). 'Objects' [*Encounter*, Jan. 1957; HC; CSP, p. 320] proposes that animals' acceptance of death does not make their lives any the less rich: their self-sufficiency is some guarantee of Life's value. Indeed, our loss, as human beings, is concerned only with 'our bestial substance', which, with the soul, makes up the 'person': our mourning is in fact for a division unknown to animals.

'Words' [HC; CSP, p. 320] uncovers the twofold nature of the relationship between language and truth. First, language is true in itself, as being an enclosed system ('Words have no word for words that are not true': evidently Auden had been reading Wittgenstein). Second, it is true as being the natural form that the truth takes, a fact that explains the urge to gossip and the chance symbolizing of 'our fate' in words, 'As rustics in a ring-dance pantomime/The Knight at some lone cross-roads of his quest.'

'The Song' (HC; CSP, p. 321] consists of two determinedly unpunctuated sentences, which are less syntactically obscure than they at first appear. In a harmonious dawn landscape, a bird is racing with its own reflection in a lake. Its double is quite as daring, but the bird's rebellious will compels a struggle which is unnecessary, since natural beauty is effortless. The morning 'can cope with' the bird, because it has no need to be concerned: when the bird (representing the poet) climbs to song (art here as compensation), it 'lacks all picture of reproach'. Thus both the beauty and the drabness are without moral significance, and the bird finally merely sings in harmony with the dawn and with nature.

In 'One Circumlocution' [*Third Hour*, 1951; N; CSP, p. 322], an appropriately indirect piece of writing, the 'one circumlocution' disguises the 'blank' statement 'I love you', which only seems to be acceptable in poetry, since in reality it 'is not what we are here for', and is 'bound to re-occur', and 'is nothing therefore that we need to say'. The real problem, Auden goes on to say, is of giving the phrase the inevitability that we feel it has (a problem investigated in 'Dichtung und Wahrheit' in *Homage to Clio*), and he casts doubt on the traditional portents. The poem shares with 'The Song' and 'Objects' a kind of careless oddity and density of style which is rather unlike Auden, and clearly some attempt is being made to enlarge meaning by suggestiveness.

'Horae Canonicae' [SA; CSP, p. 323] is a sequence based on the canonical hours, the Church's set times for prayer and meditation. The framework, in itself, thus supplies the necessary devotional intensity, leaving the actual poems free to range widely in their attempt to define that continual awareness of the guilt and sacrifice which is the foundation of the Christian's efforts to re-establish any temporal community (cf. the significantly chance rhymes of *will* and *kill* in 'Nones'). The poems are about the nature of such a community, glimpsed through the daily recreation of the events of Good Friday.

In 'Prime' [N], the first of the series (see Spears, p. 317), the body wakes at 6 a.m., dispelling the dreams of the active subconscious and thus symbolizing the creation of Adam, 'without a name or history'. As soon as the will comes into play (moving an arm, breathing), human nature is assumed and the Fall is re-enacted ('Paradise/Lost of course, and myself owing a death').

'Terce' [*Catholic Worker,* Jan. 1954] finds at 9 a.m. that the anonymous individual of 'Prime' has become the specific hangman, judge or poet who will, unknowingly, participate in the coming crucifixion. The daily prayer of the working man is ironically answered: 'not one of us will slip up', and 'by sundown/We shall have had a good Friday'. The unconcern of the numerous deities leaves responsibility firmly with man, even though the Christian paradox of God's omnipotence and man's free-will is briefly raised in parenthesis.

Indeed, the whole sequence is concerned with the contribution which the individual is asked to make to the scheme of guilt and redemption. 'Sext' (12 noon) treats in three parts the social organisms

necessary for the sacrifice: agents, authority and the crowd. These
are also the constituent elements of civilizations: first, the idea of a
vocation which leads men to ignore 'the appetitive goddesses'
(Aphrodite, Artemis) and yields the 'notion of a city'; second
(contrasting with this, as does Apollo with Hermes in 'Under Which
Lyre', or the tyrants with the true 'makers of history' in the poem of
that title), the executives, representatives of the will, without which
the courtesies of the city could not exist; third, the crowd, the
negative witnessing crowd ('its existence is chimerical', *The Dyer's
Hand,* p. 63). Without the last of these, man would ironically be no
better than 'the social exoskeletons', ants or bees, whose society can
never develop into the community which must be based on 'worship
[of the] Prince of this world'.

   In 'Nones' [N], by 3 p.m. the deed is done, and in the terrible siesta
time which follows, the individual tries to come to terms with his
responsibility. He cannot blame the crowd, which has dispersed.
The presence of the Madonna symbolizes man's betrayal of his
potentiality: the building of the city is only half-finished, and it
seems impossible that it should ever be completed by men who
themselves feel like discarded artifacts. The fourth stanza suggests,
in noticeably Eliotelian terms, that the betrayal is the betrayal of
Eros: 'We shall always now . . under/The mock chase and mock
capture,/The racing and tussling and splashing,/The panting and the
laughter,/Be listening for the cry and stillness/To follow after'.
Auden yoked love and violence together in several poems at this
period (cf. 'Nocturne', 1. 12, or 'Memorial for the City', 1. 18). The
guilt is a dilemma of man's nature, though the will may dream of
evading its responsibility (stanza 6 is a splendidly atmospheric
nightmare) and the flesh may be technically 'wronged' (stanza 7),
just as awed by the betrayal as the watching animals (Auden introduces such details like a Renaissance painter).

   'Vespers' [*Encounter,* Feb. 1955] returns, at 6 p.m., to man's urge
to build the Just City, whose beginnings were defined in 'Sext'.
Auden contrasts the Arcadian with the Utopian, his own ideal Eden
and the materialist's New Jerusalem, in terms that remind us of the
Hermetic-Apollonian categories of 'Under Which Lyre' (CSP, p.
221) and possibly, too, of the distinction between a community and a

society in *The Enchafèd Flood,* p. 36. He has defined his distinction elsewhere: 'In their relation to the actual fallen world, the difference between Eden and New Jerusalem is a temporal one. Eden is a past world in which the contradictions of the present world have not yet arisen; New Jerusalem is a future world in which they have at last been resolved' (*The Dyer's Hand,* p. 409). The distinctions in 'Vespers' wear an air of lightness, but they act as a reminder to each idealist of the peculiar paradox that the Christian *felix culpa* embodies ('but for him I could forget the blood, but for me he could forget the innocence').

At 9 p.m. 'Compline' returns us to sleep, as an image of death ('the end, for me as for cities,/Is total absence'), and as a state in which the heart's motion, like that of the stars, merely obeys necessity. In the last stanza, Auden shifts the sequence into its role as prayer by quoting the mass and asking for forgiveness for himself and 'dear C'; the final image is of 'the dance' of the Trinity. 'Lauds' is merely a decorative postcript, borrowed from *Delia (Botteghe Oscure,* Vol. XII, 1953), but providing a splendidly musical sense of the commanding presence of the Christian communion. Spears (p. 320) has shown how its verse form is borrowed from the Spanish *cossante.*

The whole sequence contains much striking poetry, but shows, I think, that Auden's real talent (and real interest) in this period is less for religious poetry than for poetry on the themes of nature and history, language and truth, friendship and landscape. The secular 'fifties thus contrast very much with the exploratory (and often theological) concerns of the 'forties, and 'Horae Canonicae' betrays at its centre a certain blurring of definition which the other major poems of the decade ('Bucolics', 'Memorial for the City' and so on) do not have. The secular themes, and such interesting characteristics as the reliance on a personal pantheon of classical and invented deities, seem to have been stimulated by his residence in Ischia: the 'fifties were very much a 'Mediterranean' period.

In 'Good-Bye to the Mezzogiorno' [*Encounter,* Nov. 1958; HC; CSP, p. 338] he marks the end of a phase in his poetic as well as his domestic career, and incidentally the end of his *Collected Shorter Poems,* at which point he started 'a new chapter of [his] life which is not yet finished'. Auden brings to his contrast between the 'gothic North' and the 'sunburnt otherwhere' just that contrast which his readers feel between the poetry of his New York and his Mediterranean periods, between 'those who mean by life a/*Bildungsroman* and those to whom living/Means to-be-visible-now', between (predominantly) anxiety and happiness. Even to 'a certain *Monte'*, the landlord who would not sell him his Ischian house,[5] Auden is grateful:

> though one cannot always
> Remember exactly why one has been happy,
> There is no forgetting that one was.

13   About the House

Not included in the 1966 *Collected Shorter Poems* were a number of poems from *Homage to Clio* (1960) that were written after 1957, and the subsequent collection *About the House* (1966). Omitted from *Homage to Clio* were 'Reflections in a Forest', 'Hands', 'The Sabbath', 'Dame Kind', 'Walks', 'Friday's Child' and the academic clerihews. These, no doubt, will be candidates for a later edition of the *Collected Shorter Poems*.

'Reflections in a Forest' [*Depauw Alumnus,* Dec. 1957; *Listener,* 23 July 1959] follows the familiar Auden procedure of contrasting man with nature (in this case, trees) and underlining the paradoxical advantages of duplicity. 'Hands' is a lighter, more inventive physiological essay: these are our distinctive feature, whose language is international and whose characteristics (fingerprints, handwriting) are individual and exact. The contrast here with the human mind which does not acknowledge limitations (praying to the hidden god of its intuitions not to the finite god of purpose), and which is aware of absence and time, is casually and persuasively sketched. 'The Sabbath' [*Observer,* 6 Sept. 1959] shows that only man among the creatures shares in the divine purpose: the poem is engagingly offhand about man's persistence, and contrasts our late appearance in terms of the geological time-scale with our importance as biblical lords of creation. 'Dame Kind' [*Encounter,* May 1960] is like Aphrodite, Mrs Nature and other Audenesque personifications of the sexual instincts. The poem is a quirky colloquial rampage, intended to be 'slightly unpleasant perhaps' in a reaction against the problem

of writing the truth about love (see *Homage to Clio,* p. 51), a delicate
verbal qualification of the sentiments of homage, in which 'the
Chi-Rho' (the Christian fish symbol) is a signal for academic retreat,
and Petrarchan love is a 'hypochondriac/Blue-Stocking'. 'Walks'
takes the circular stroll as a symbol for larger experience (no need to
decide when to turn back). 'Friday's Child' [*Listener,* 25 Dec. 1958]
is the martyred Christ, and the nursery rhyme suggests a tacit answer
to the weighed anger or compassion of stanza 3: 'loving and giving'
must be a key to the Christian justice of the Judgment Day that even
'conscious unbelievers' feel quite sure of. Here on earth he 'leaves/
The bigger bangs to us': this is a freedom of choice that we have
never quite understood. Auden's God in this poem is absolved from
capriciousness precisely by that refusal to save appearances which
led to the Incarnation and Redemption: the theology is thus somewhat circular in argument.

The first part of the collection *About the House* is a sequence about
the various rooms in Auden's Austrian house, glossed by a quotation
from the Vulgate: 'etenim hereditas mea praeclara est mihi' (Psalm
16). Gratitude for this goodly heritage bubbles over wittily as Auden
takes us round his study, the cellar, the attic, the lavatory, the bathroom, the kitchen, the guest-room, the dining-room, the bedroom
and the living-room. He is well aware of the dangers of a public
celebration of the domestic virtues, and thus the poise and humour
of the sequence pleasurably steer a tasteful course between intimacy
and sermonizing. Happiness is not often creative: here the dogmas
of the household gods (that you must never 'borrow' stamps, p. 37,
and that it is a good omen to start the morning with a 'satisfactory
dump', p. 26) are necessarily concerned with the trivia of morality
which are found in that borderland where privacy may be inspected
and found to be natural. Such domestic aphorisms don't need
to do more than assert and suggest the minor sanctity of the common life, the 'here and now' of the dedicatory verse to the whole
volume.

The *hereditas* seen in such mundane terms in 'Thanksgiving for a
Habitat' is rather new in Auden's work: one can see the concern in
earlier poems taking a generalized symbolic form (in, say, 'Bucolics'),
but for the first time the daily circumstances of the individual's life

are seen not only to be symbolic of that individual's existential nature, but to have meaning in themselves, perhaps as an assertion of the values of the body against the 'Manichees'. However, the symbolic suggestiveness is still there, as 'Prologue: The Birth of Architecture' [A H, p. 13] reveals: man as architect is governed not only by technology ('concrete or grapefruit') but by potentiality, which is why nature ('that Immortal Commonwealth') 'won't quite do'. It is in the postscript that Auden implies, though comically, that the 'second nature of tomb and temple' is in fact man's religious sense, his awareness of identity and morality, and that what we build is our own soul which doesn't take easily to fraternization.

'Thanksgiving for a Habitat' [*New Yorker,* 17 Aug. 1963; A H, p. 15] examines the nature of the creature who is to inhabit it. We are at the mercy of 'the flesh/Mum formulated' and of our social circumstances, too. We cannot, as William Randolph Hearst tried to do when he built his palace at San Simeon, recreate a nobler past. Auden justifies his asserted privacy (as a kind of modest Hearst, shuddering at, but tolerant of, 'the race of spiders') by an ornithological tag and a developing comic tone in the poem. The humour of this (and other poems in the volume) lies in the hideous possibilities that are envisaged: of, for instance, being destroyed in a thousand millionth of a second 'at the nod/of some jittery commander'.

Despite this, 'The Cave of Making' [*Listener,* 1 Oct. 1964: A H, p. 18] asserts that 'More than ever/life-out-there is goodly, miraculous, lovable'. The assertion comes at a point where Auden is retracing some old autobiographical ground in this memorial poem for Louis MacNeice, and we are reminded that for Auden the failure of liberal humanism and consequent reminder of the truth of original sin was due to the triumph of totalitarianism in the 'thirties: 'we shan't, not since Stalin and Hitler,/trust ourselves ever again: we know that, subjectively,/all is possible'. Auden once taught a course called 'Romanticism from Rousseau to Hitler': romantic possibility is clearly a danger that the Horatian virtues celebrated in the sequence emphatically repudiate. 'The Cave of Making' restates poetry's doubtful relation to the truth, its manipulation by 'lip-smacking/imps of mawk and hooey' (cf. 'Cattivo Tempo', CSP, p. 245), and its status as the only art which demands either serious attention or to be ignored. Material that didn't quite get into the poem is arranged in the 'Postscript', an interesting clue to Auden's method of composition, for many longish poems have the air of being compiled from similar aphorisms arranged according to theme.[1] In this 'Postscript', Auden takes up the notion of the poet as a necessarily good man (cf. Marianne Moore quoted in *The Dyer's Hand,* p. 305: 'rectitude *has* a ring that is implicative, I would say'), and we are given the doubtfully appalling vision of God reducing him to tears on Judgment Day by reciting by heart the poems he would have written had his life really been good. At the same time, however, Auden is clear that vice has been inspiring, that he knows 'what imagination/can owe temptation/yielded to,/that many a fine/expressive line/would not have existed,/had you resisted'. The moral ambiguity is an interesting one, and none the less serious for being capriciously expressed.

Symbolical meanings are lightly touched on in the next pair of poems in the sequence, 'Down There' and 'Up There' [AH, pp. 24, 25]. The cellar is the deep area of our resources, our 'safe-anchor' ('A father sends the younger boys to fetch something/For Mother from down there'), but such a journey suggests less a psychological quest than a piece of controlled spiritual husbandry, whose counterpart is the attic's disorganized detritus of the past which the feminine instinct has hoarded.

'The Geography of the House' [AH, p. 26] blends some familiar observations about the psychological role of excretion with some ingenious double meanings that lend the poem a comic lightness of touch. 'Encomium Balnei' [*Encounter,* Aug. 1962: AH, p. 29], itself formally resembling the 'mallarmesque/syllabic fog' it refers to, takes up where 'Bathtub Thoughts' (CSP, p. 303) left off in its allusions to 'the caracallan acreage'. The kind of escapism that the bathroom provides combines a classical comfort with the sacrosanct political right of withdrawal and privacy derived (Auden elaborately proposes) from the desert saints, who didn't actually believe in washing. To take a bath is to feel good, to feel at one with the body.

'Grub First, Then Ethics' [*New Yorker,* 7 Mar. 1959: 'On Installing an American Kitchen in Lower Austria'; HC; AH, p. 33] has the

Brecht epigraph from *Homage to Clio* translated and promoted as
the new title. There is a distinction to be made here between the good-
naturedly epicurean solidarity of Auden, and the Marxist accusation
of Brecht:

> . . . Jew, Gentile or pigmy,
> he must get his calories
> before he can consider her profile or
> his own, attack you or play chess . . .

This physiological truism leads Auden to a number of bright,
characteristic generalizations ('a cook [can be] a pure artist'; 'in
murder mysteries/one can be sure the gourmet/didn't do it') in his
most fluent and conversationally occasional manner. However, the
new title forces us to remember the real context of the Act II finale
of *The Threepenny Opera,* with all the desperate but exultant relent-
lessness of Weill's setting:

> Ihr, die ihr euren Wanst und unsre Bravheit liebt
> Das eine wisset ein für allemal:
> Wie ihr es immer dreht und wie ihr's immer schiebt
> Erst kommt das Fressen, dann kommt die Moral.
> Erst muss es möglich sein auch armen Leuten,
> Vom grossen Brotlaib sich ihr Teil zu schneiden.

> 'You who love your own belly and our honesty,
> Once and for all learn this single thing:
> However you twist it and however you get round it,
> Feeding comes first and then comes morality.
> First it must be possible for poor people, too,
> To cut their share of the big loaf.'

Brecht is showing how the exploitation of the poor by the rich is
accompanied by just the kind of moral preaching to them that keeps
them subservient. The irony is that when the poor do get their slice
of cake, then society will be able to see what morality is really about.
The Brecht tag in Auden is as surprising as if we had, for instance,
discovered that he somehow approved of the Hollywood daydreams
of his six beggared cripples (CSP, p. 87). The religious analogy is
worked up in the poem into something far more meaningful than
metaphor. He says his kitchen is numinous, and later identifies an

omelette with the Eucharist (shades of Lilliput?). The citizens of the
Just Society admit to being a minority, and the poem ends by showing
how likely it is that they will be called upon to fight off the hordes at
'her Thermopylae'. 'Her vagabond forum/is any space where two
of us happen to meet/who can spot a citizen/without papers':
perhaps a necessary qualification to all the talk of territory and
status that lies behind the sequence.

After 'For Friends Only' [A H, p. 37], a visitors' book compliment
in reverse, written in a novel form of lines of seven and five words,
the sacramental implications of eating are continued in 'Tonight at
Seven-thirty' [A H, p. 39]. Here table-talk is seen as a way of life
('a laugh is less/heartless than tears'), and even as a reverent acknowledgment of an order other than human ('can see in swallowing/a
sign act of reverence,/in speech a work of re-presenting/the true
olamic silence', *olam* being the Hebrew word for eternity).

'The Cave of Nakedness' [*Encounter,* Dec. 1963; A H, p. 42]
returns, in a more informal manner, to the concern of the individual,
to the habitat as body. It reminds us of Auden's belief that Agape is
the fulfilment of Eros, while 'The Common Life' [*New York Review
of Books,* 26 Dec. 1963; A H, p. 46] completes such a line of thought
by paying tribute to a friendship and a style of living.

In the second section of the volume ('Ins and Outs') Auden takes
up the theme of man's uncertain respect for the present world in
which he finds himself. Man ought to be as grateful for this larger
habitat as the poet is for his personal bailiwick, but though 'even
melancholics/Raise a cheer to Mrs/Nature for the primal/Pleasures
she bestows', the larger responsibilities seem to have been mis-
managed.

'A Change of Air' [*Encounter,* Jan. 1962; A H, p. 51] is reminiscent
of some earlier poems of Auden's on spiritual enlightenment and
the way in which other people seem to regard it as having made no
difference to one (cf. Sonnet XVI in 'The Quest': one of the themes of
New Year Letter is that only God can really tell the saintly from the
suburban). Minor ailments are the psychosomatic symptoms of
'estrangement between your name and you'.[2] The persona-ego
problem signals a contrast between a person's inner and outer
biography: going 'Elsewhere' is the rather Eliotelian process of

withdrawing 'from movement', opposed to real and exotic acts of change (Rimbaud, in Greenland rather than Africa, is suggested), which are mere 'mollycoddling'. This is the Truly Strong Man over again, developed in this case, as Auden admitted, from incidents in the life of Goethe (it was the Grand Duke of Weimar who complained – not to his cousin – that Goethe was more aloof after his Italian journey). The Grand Duke here stands in for 'Society, Literary Critics, etc.', which implies that Auden after all has literary fame in mind in the poem.

'You' [*Saturday Evening Post,* 3 Mar. 1962; AH, p. 53] is the Mind's address to the Body, governed by a quasi-scientific observation that the two are split through having developed at different rates ('between two glaciers/The master-chronometer/Of an innocent primate/Altered its tempi'). Even so, this does not explain why it is Mind which feels guilt (corollary to the celebration of the corporeal life elsewhere in the volume), or why man's anxiety belongs wholly to his spiritual life.

The simple style in this poem contrasts strikingly with the rococo conversationalism of some of the longer-lined pieces in the style he acquired in the 'fifties. 'Et in Arcadia Ego' [AH, p. 55], using the haiku stanza, has a different kind of abbreviated purity of style which does not reject the old lexical deliberation. This is a fine poem, whose imagery co-ordinates without fuss a truth about the nature of evil with a truth about the holiness of nature in terms of modern Austria, where rurality (the ironic Arcadia of the title) still confronts technocracy and recent genocide:

> I well might think myself
> A humanist,
> Could I manage not to see
>
> How the autobahn
> Thwarts the landscape
> In godless Roman arrogance,
>
> The farmer's children
> Tiptoe past the shed
> Where the gelding knife is kept.

Similarly, Auden is inclined to value a landscape as yet unplundered by man. 'Hammerfest' [*London Magazine,* Mar. 1962; A H, p. 57] is in Norway, 'the northernmost township on earth'. It produces beer, and 'the best deep-frozen fish-sticks you can buy', and Auden does not disguise its obvious dreariness (symbolized here by its geological peculiarities in stanza 3). The skill with which he develops his particular argument is masterly: the poem is a chilling reminder of the most basic forms of human futility and self-deception. Yet Hammerfest has a kind of 'holiness', albeit of an admonitory kind:

> Whatever noise our species cared to make still mattered.
> Here was a place we had yet to disappoint.

Iceland, too, in 'Iceland Revisited' [*Encounter,* July 1964; A H, p. 59] is a place where 'all men are equal/But not vulgar – not yet'. The occasion, though, is one for feeling middle-aged and missing the comforts of civilization. The significance of Place is not approached with even the seriousness of 'Hammerfest', let alone with the power and relevance of the poem which most comes to mind, 'Journey to Iceland' (in the later poem, the three who 'slept well' were Auden, MacNeice and Michael Yates, on their earlier visit). Travel now for Auden is less an exploration than a tour of fame that reminds him of his deficiencies:

> He hears a loudspeaker
> Call him well-known:
> But knows himself no better.

The poetry-reading circuit appears more directly in the next poem, 'On the Circuit' [*New Yorker,* 4 July 1964; A H, p. 61], and provides a comic background to that Audenesque genre, the aeroplane poem. Here the poet's eye is not on the world below him; it is on his suitcase:

> *Is this a milieu where I must*
> How grahamgreeneish! How infra dig!
> *Snatch from the bottle in my bag*
> *An analeptic swig?*

Despite such feared deprivations, the poem ends (with deficient irony, one feels) with blessings for the USA, 'so large/So friendly, and so rich'.

The 'Four Occasional Poems' are, on the whole, as slight. 'A Toast' [AH, p. 64], in the manner of Praed, must have served well after a college dinner. 'A Short Ode to a Philologist' [*English and Mediaeval Studies,* ed. N. Davis and C. L. Wrenn, 1962; AH, p. 66] pays tribute to J. R. R. Tolkien, the Old English scholar, by elaborating comment on the proposition that the health of a society depends upon the health of its language, since language is the prime instrument of man's free will: the foundation of language is 'Dame Philology', and Auden takes an opportunity to salute again the fourteen-volume *Oxford English Dictionary* in his admirably devious route to his intended encomium. The 'Elegy for J.F.K.' [*Of Poetry and Power,* ed. E. A. Glikes and P. Schwaber, 1964: AH, p. 67] commemorates the assassination of President Kennedy with curiously little reference to its subject (unfortunate if we remember the confessed strategies of 'The Truest Poetry is the most Feigning'). It was written to be set by Stravinsky (see Igor Stravinsky and Robert Craft, *Themes and Episodes,* 1966, pp. 56–59). The ingenious compliment of 'Lines for Elizabeth Mayer' [AH, p. 68] has charm, not least by virtue of the playful sense of ephemerality that the opening stanzas establish. Miss Mayer was the dedicatee of *New Year Letter.*

'Symmetries & Asymmetries' [AH, p. 70] looks like notebook material that never quite became poems. Indeed, the little booklet *Marginalia* (Ibex Press, Cambridge, Mass., 1966) containing similar haiku aphorisms, shows the astonishing and casual fertility of Auden's sooterkins of wit in this period. The epigrams are discrete yet related: they gnomically confirm Auden's preoccupation with the comic spectacle of man sulking or dreaming in a world puzzled by 'Dame Kind's thoroughbred lunatic', and chronicle the ironies of his narcissism, pretentiousness and violence. The 'Four Transliterations' [last three in *Encounter,* April 1963; AH, pp. 76–81] are evidence of Auden's growing interest in translation and in Russian poetry.

'The Maker' [*Poetry in Crystal,* 1963; AH, p. 82] is a footnote to the craftsmen of 'Makers of History' (CSP, p. 297), who similarly in their extra-historical role teach 'the Quality . . . that charm is useless,/A threat fatal'. The Quality exert their power against the flux of history in vain: the allusion in the final stanza to the story in *Struwwelpeter* of the thumbsucker and the Scissor Man implies a psychological determinism behind the supposed authority of the will which only art (the sculptor, here) can understand and redeem. 'At the Party' [AH, p. 84] and 'Lost' [AH, p. 85] both cover old ground: only the latter, the merest trace of a dream, carries an authentic though understated fear.

'Bestiaries are Out' [AH, p. 86] returns to an idea from 'Prologue: The Birth of Architecture', where the admired bees are shown to be builders but not architects, in the sense that it is only man who self-consciously creates a habitat for his immortal soul. Bees provided behavioural analogies for human society in the eighteenth century ('Philosopher and Christian Preacher' are Bernard Mandeville and Isaac Watts), but today we see how different they really are, how indeed the only political model they provide is mechanical and totalitarian.

'After Reading a Child's Guide to Modern Physics' [*New Yorker*, 17 Nov. 1962; AH, p. 88] is healthily irreverent about science by asking what we want the knowledge *for* (here are echoes of ideas in *The Age of Anxiety*, CLP, pp. 270–1). True enough, but perhaps as a sentiment slightly upstaged by the portentous theological nudge in the final stanza. 'Ascension Day, 1964' [*London Magazine*, Aug. 1964; AH, p. 90] treats the Holy Thursday ritual of the risen Christ in terms of a lover's parting, caused, as it were, by the 'glum Kundry' in us all which sets out to impede the spiritual quest that Christ provides (see Wagner's *Parsifal*).

The final poem in the collection, 'Whitsunday in Kirchstetten' [*The Reporter*, 6 Dec. 1962; AH, p. 92], somewhat reverses the quotation from Karl Kraus which Auden had used as an epigraph in 'A Short Ode to a Philologist'. *Die Sprache ist die Mutter, nicht die Magd, des Gedankens* ('Language is the mother, not the handmaid, of thought') doesn't seem to hold for the ecumenical point that Auden wants to make when he writes:

> The Holy Ghost
> does not abhor a golfer's jargon,
> a Lower-Austrian accent, the cadences even
> of my own little Anglo-American
> musico-literary set (though difficult,
> saints at least may think in algebra
> without sin) . . .

The poem is much concerned with boundaries of this kind, and with geographical boundaries too, since the fact that the Anglican Auden is attending a Roman Mass implies a decline in the secular influence of the churches which is elaborated in the second part of the poem, and the early observation about which side of the Iron Curtain Niederösterreich happens to be on is taken up at the end in the meditations upon the Russians' cold war threats. A Russian conquest of the West is felt to be unlikely (a comfort encouraged by the general ecumenical goodwill in the poem). But what about the Chinese? What, indeed, about the Africans? Retreating wryness here does not dispel the real nervousness in the glum laugh about paying the price for an Imperialist heritage (rather less than goodly in this case):

> . . . to most people
> I'm the wrong colour: it could be the looter's turn
> for latrine duty and the flogging block,
> my kin who trousered Africa, carried our smell
> to germless poles . . .

14 Some Poems Outside the Canon

Auden has been much attacked for revising and suppressing poems.[1] I believe that however irritating it may be for a reader to find a well-known and even a well-loved poem missing, it is a poet's right to take decisions about the canon of his work (though he should in turn be prepared to admit that these decisions are not likely to be perpetually respected). I have taken the opportunity afforded by the recent *Collected Shorter Poems* (1966) and *Collected Longer Poems* (1968) to treat Auden's work as a somewhat pruned and considered œuvre. Bibliographical and ideological matters have in the past sometimes unfairly swamped critical treatment of Auden, and I hope I have kept this sort of concern to a minimum. Even so, I feel that in a guide of this kind there should be some indication of what poems have been lost in the latest editions, and some discussion of the most important of them.

Auden's self-criticism has been extreme. Perhaps only in a poet as fertile as he is could rejection of early poems be accompanied by such deliberate vehemence as that reported by Robin Skelton in his introduction to *Poetry of the Thirties* (1964). According to Skelton, in allowing him to use early texts of 'Sir, No Man's Enemy', 'A Communist to Others', 'To a Writer on his Birthday', 'Spain' and 'September 1, 1939', Auden asked that it be made clear that 'Mr W. H. Auden considers these five poems to be trash which he is ashamed to have written'. Auden has more moderately expanded on this attitude in his Foreword to Bloomfield's *Bibliography* (1964) and in his Foreword to the *Collected Shorter Poems* (1966). Here, omitted poems are categorized as dishonest, or bad-mannered, or boring, and it looks as though most of the poems that his readers will miss are intended to fall into the first category. One is up against the problem here of how far to respect a poet's claims (*a*) that he can remember clearly how he felt thirty years earlier, and (*b*) that he has never 'attempted to revise [his] former thoughts or feelings, only the language in which they were first expressed' (CSP, p. 16). Without allowing either of these claims, or even Auden's much-quoted dictum from Valéry, that a poem is never completed, only abandoned, the sympathetic reader will admit that Auden has been unkindly served by the parroting of accusatory material from such critics as Joseph Warren Beach, who, in *The Making of the Auden Canon,* seemed delighted to find ideological recantations even in misprints. Auden will one day get the full editorial treatment: meanwhile he may surely appear as the poet he wishes to be.

There exists, of course, a vast amount of unpublished and uncollected material. Some of the poems which remain only in periodicals are no less considerable than many which were collected, from such striking Oxford pieces as 'In Due Season' [*Oxford Outlook,* Dec. 1926] right up to 'Since' [*Encounter,* May 1965], which, though it missed *About the House,* may still, one hopes, be collected. Everyone has his favourites among these by now rather obscure poems, but the exuberant first part of 'A Happy New Year' [*New Country,* 1933] and the five sonnets in *New Verse,* October 1933, are among the most admired.

Of the seventeen poems from *Poems* (1928) that do not survive, five (Nos. ib, iii, iv, vii and viii) had a short public life in *Poems* (1930) before being dropped in 1933, and several of the others, as I have shown, were cannibalized in part. This first collection appears to be very roughly in chronological order, and shows the impact of Hopkins and Eliot at its most extreme. The first poem, No. ia–h (a sequence of eight very varied pieces), is a kind of farewell to the homoerotic romanticism of school, the 'dazzling cities of the plain where lust/Threatened a sinister rod' (f). One of the pieces (d), if we can trust Isherwood's accuracy here, was in existence at Christmas 1925 (*Lions and Shadows,* p. 187) and might therefore have been written while Auden was still at school, or just after. The first poem sets the scene:

> The sprinkler on the lawn
> Weaves a cool vertigo, and stumps are drawn;
> The last boy vanishes,
> A blazer half-on, through the rigid trees.

It is a sequence celebrating calm after intoxication, a calm which is none the less evasive, for these emotions will recur: 'This peace can last no longer than the storm/Which started it' (d) and 'if, though we/Have ligatured the ends of a farewell,/Sporadic heartburn show in evidence/Of love uneconomically slain' (f). The suggestions of a particular relationship here are born out by (c) and (e), the affair symbolized (curiously) by a buzzard (c):

> We saw in Spring
> The frozen buzzard
> Flipped down the weir and carried out to sea.

From the moment of birth, the mind and the body are divorced (b), and love cannot be entered upon freely, though the sexual pressures are cyclical (g):

> Amoeba in the running water
> Lives afresh in son and daughter
> 'The sword above the valley'
> Said the Worm to the Penny.

The phallic life (Worm) has only this rather extraneous power over the social life (Penny). The result, as one grows older, is the sentimentalism or shrivelled pedantry of (f): 'An evening like a coloured photograph,/A music stultified across the water.' Notions of duty obstruct the loved one's yielding: 'Ought passes through points fair plotted, and you conform,/Seen yes or no. Too just for weeping argument' (b).

Much of the difficulty of the early poetry is due to the compulsive allegorizing of the pervading theme of love. The allegorizing is begun in such poems from the first volume as No. XII, where four men, after aphoristically analysing their attitudes to love, 'sat waiting

the enemy', No. IX, 'Because sap fell away' (with its beautiful fragment 'Love, is this love, that notable forked-one' used in *The
Orators*), and No. X, 'The mind to body spoke the whole night
through'; and is most evident in the group that was later used in
Paid on Both Sides. By the time that love becomes a 'handsome raider'
or can be seen riding away from the farm, we are all set for the daring
symbols of *Paid*.

Of the poems that were new in the two editions of *Poems* (1930
and 1933), seven have been dropped: P30 No. II: 'Which of you
waking early'; P30 No. VI: 'To have found a place for nowhere';
P30 No. XIV: 'Sentries against inner and outer';* No. XXII: 'Get
there if you can and see the land you once were proud to own';
P30 No. XXX: 'Sir, no man's enemy, forgiving all';* P33 No. IX:
'It's no use raising a shout'; and P33 No. XXVIII: 'Under boughs
between our tentative endearments how should we hear'*.

Of these, 'Sentries against inner and outer'* is one of the most
powerful of Auden's love poems, depending for its effect on the
rather grave and reasonable tone of the couplets up to the moment
when the military metaphors yield gratefully to the splendidly erotic
close. You may 'parley' with the mouth, because only the mouth as
an erotic centre can subvert the implacable opposition to love of the
other features; but also because the mouth is the organ of speech,
and the poem is really (despite its coolness and deviousness) a wooing poem.

'Get there if you can' harangues the bourgeois 'dead' with great
high spirits in the metre of Tennyson's 'Locksley Hall'. The villains
are all those who have provided a reasonable escape from real life,
from (oddly enough) the very public Freud to the rather private
'Ciddy'.[2] These are the romantics, the pessimists, the authoritarians:
set against them are the cloak-and-dagger heroes all destroyed by
the puritan middle-class society that Auden is attacking from the
inside:

Lawrence was brought down by smut-hounds, Blake went dotty as he sang,
Homer Lane was killed in action by the Twickenham Baptist gang.

* Asterisks denote those poems which are still available in the first edition of the
Collected Shorter Poems (1950).

The poem threatens revolution, and holds out the alternative of psychological regeneration for the bourgeoisie in some of the plainest terms to be found in the early poems, while retaining a hectic invigorating diction that makes the poem excitingly bold, prophetic and assured.

One of the most-discussed poems in Auden's first book was the last one, 'Sir, no man's enemy'* ['Petition' in CP]. Auden has been fairly explicit about his reasons for dropping this poem since the 1950 edition of the *Collected Shorter Poems*. In the Foreword to the 1966 edition he writes: 'I once expressed a desire for "New styles of architecture"; but I have never liked modern architecture. I prefer *old* styles, and one must be honest even about one's prejudices.' Since the line 'New styles of architecture, a change of heart' suggests far more in the poem's context than being a fan of Gropius or whatever, this explanation seems a little disingenuous. Actually Auden had expressed serious doubts about the rest of that line (and it is the climactic line of the poem) as early as *The Dog Beneath the Skin,* p. 155, where the chorus say: 'Do not speak of a change of heart, meaning five hundred a year and a room of one's own,/As if that were all that is necessary.' Here there seems to be a pretty clear condemnation of the extravagant sentiments of a dependent adolescent who is not really aware of the selfish needs which he himself brings to the problem (at least, this is the way the chorus's meaning tends). But the earlier poem is no breathless gesture. On the contrary, it is one of the more clinically diagnostic of Auden's early poems, right from the initial Hopkinsian invocation ('God' forgives everything but man's will, which through sin has come to negate the divine will, and yet is asked to 'be prodigal', i.e. to forgive even that). The bulk of the imagery ('liar's quinsy' and so on) may be glossed by Isherwood's account of the effect of Layard's teachings on Auden (*Lions and Shadows,* pp. 229–304), so that it is hard to see whether the 'Sir' of the invocation is God seen as a psychiatrist or a psychiatrist seen as God (and both at one point become a sentry on the perimeter with a searchlight: 'Cover in time with beams, etc.'). Such a synthesis has made critics regard the poem as seminal, and one therefore regrets its absence.

Look, Stranger! (1936) is the volume from which Auden has

omitted most poems: No. I: 'O love the interest itself in thoughtless heaven';* No. xɪv: 'Brothers, who when sirens roar'; No. xv: 'The chimneys are smoking, the crocus is out in the border';* No. xvɪɪ: 'Here on the cropped grass of the narrow ridge I stand';* No. xvɪɪɪ: 'The sun shines down on ships at sea'; No. xɪx: 'To lie flat on the back with the knees flexed';* No. xxɪɪ (1): 'Night covers up the rigid land'; No. xxɪɪɪ: 'To settle in this village of the heart';* No. xxx: 'August for the people and their favourite islands';* and No. xxxɪ: 'Certainly our city – with the byres of poverty down to'.* The first three of these had originally appeared in *New Country* (1933), and the second at least shares with *The Dance of Death* of the same year the general adoption of the Communist position (and some incidental details, too: compare stanza 10 with *Dance,* p. 28, for instance). It was originally entitled 'A Communist to Others', and makes brilliant use of Burns's stanza to cover much the same ground as 'Get there if you can' from a more committed standpoint. 'Here on the cropped grass'* [*New Oxford Outlook,* Nov. 1933: 'The Malverns'] is one of the best poems of this period, a love poem of absence and resolution, as is 'The chimneys are smoking', and shares with that poem a fluid panoramic context of great beauty and inventiveness.

Of the rest of the *Look, Stranger!* losses, most important is 'August for the people'* [*New Verse,* Oct./Nov. 1935: 'To a Writer on His Birthday'], dedicated to Christopher Isherwood. More orotund and less technically flexible than 'The Malverns', it is none the less one of the key autobiographical poems, consciously, even programmatically, dividing early Auden from the Auden of the later 'thirties. Nine years before, he and Isherwood became absorbed (wrongly, he concludes) in the fantasy worlds of *Paid on Both Sides* and of Mortmere, both mere reflections of their environment. Isherwood has described Auden's visit in 1926 to the Isle of Wight, the poem's 'southern island,/where the wild Tennyson became a fossil':

I see him striding towards me, along Yarmouth Pier, a tall figure with loose violent impatient movements, dressed in dirty grey flannels and a black evening bow-tie. On his straw-coloured head was planted a very broad-brimmed black felt hat. . . . The black hat caused a considerable sensation in the village where I was staying. The village boys and girls, grouped along the inn wall by the bus stop, sniggered loudly as we got out of the bus. Weston was pleased: 'Laughter,' he announced, 'is the first sign of sexual attraction' (*Lions and Shadows,* pp. 188–9).

It is plain that such Freudianism is one key to Auden's early use of fantasy. The felt hat appears in the poem, too (stanza 5), but it is turned into part of the apparatus of the spy, a direct conflation of disguise and erotic challenge. In the same stanza we hear that 'one laughed, and it was snow in bedrooms'. The allusion is to drugs, for 'coke', another slang word for cocaine, is mentioned in the preceding line. No doubt Auden's abundant sense of the sinister and unconsciously meaningful demanded that the sniggers at his hat should have this sexual, even unlawfully sexual, significance.

But this is dismissed, and so is the maturer role that 'love' played in his Homer Lane period: 'five summers pass', and love becomes an easy panacea, taming even the dragon of fascism. The poem makes it clear that such 'flabby' fancies can no longer serve a poet who has responded to the urgency of social and political reality. It is almost suggested that poetry itself must yield to the documentary novel, to the 'strict and adult' pen of Isherwood, the task of making 'action urgent and its nature clear' (he also used this phrase in his introduction to *The Poet's Tongue,* 1935, where he was concerned to show how art must avoid being propaganda). However, the poem itself sweeps on to a strikingly personified anatomy of the current crisis (modelled on Shakespeare's Sonnet No. 66 or on the beginning of *The Dunciad,* Book IV) which entirely justifies the rhetorical skills of the poet. The whole poem is very Popean, with antithetical and sensually evocative lines, and a chaste and pictorial diction. The feeling of justice and satirical understanding that such a flavour imposes on the argument of the poem accounts for the simple authority with which it is able to demand as a substitute for adolescent daydreams a wholly committed literature.

Eight poems have been dropped from *Another Time* (1940). These are Part I, No. III: 'The Creatures';* Part I, No. XVI: 'Pascal';* Part I, No. XXIV: 'Where do They come from? Those whom we so much dread';* Part I, No. XXVII: 'Matthew Arnold';* Part II,

No. II (2): 'James Honeyman'; Part III, No. I: 'Spain 1937';* Part III, No. IV: 'September 1, 1939';* and Part III, No. VI: 'Epithalamion'.*

'Spain 1937'* had already been published as a pamphlet three years before, in May 1937. Auden had visited Spain from January to March, not, it appears, as an ambulance driver (as Spender reports in *The Atlantic Monthly,* Vol. CXCII, 1953), but with the desire at least 'to *do* something' (see Claud Cockburn, *The Review,* No. 11/12, p. 51). The poem's large rhetorical structure, contrasting past and future, necessity and the political will, fully supports the poet's call to action. 'History', the poem dramatically explains, means nothing without the clear decisions of individual responsibility:

> 'What's your proposal? To build the Just City? I will.
> I agree. Or is it the suicide pact, the romantic
>   Death? Very well, I accept, for
> I am your choice, your decision: yes, I am Spain.'

Thus the poem stirringly underlines the need for personal involvement and risk in the fight against fascism: 'but to-day the struggle'. Without this, the Just City, the whole premise of the needs of humanity, is an impossible dream. If the struggle fails (through the implied failure of the political will), then 'History to the defeated/ May say Alas but cannot help or pardon.'

In his Foreword to the 1966 *Collected Shorter Poems,* Auden quoted these concluding lines and wrote (p. 15): 'To say this is to equate goodness with success. It would have been bad enough if I had ever held this wicked doctrine, but that I should have stated it simply because it sounded to me rhetorically effective is quite inexcusable.' In context, of course, the lines could refer equally to Franco or the Loyalists. Since Franco won, the lines merely reinforce the previous treatment of history in the poem as the result, not the cause, of the actions of the human will. Auden is remembering the Marxist meaning of the lines, but you can't really conflate the two, since one merely provides a much larger context than the other.

What the poem really seems to be after (as a call to arms) is an exploration of the mechanics of success. Another example of this would be in the antepenultimate stanza, the line which originally read: 'The conscious acceptance of the necessary murder'. This was seized on by George Orwell (in 'Inside the Whale') as an example of that left-wing thought which 'is a kind of playing with fire by people who don't even know that fire is hot'. Orwell was stressing the gulf between murder as a word, and murder as a fact (which he had witnessed), but of course Auden was consciously involved in the poem in a serious train of argument: unless one is a complete pacifist, murder may well be the only means to a just end. And it should be remembered that Auden's immediate subject is *not* Marxist revolution in general, but the defence of the Spanish Republic against a fascist military insurrection. He later changed the line to: 'The conscious acceptance of guilt in the fact of murder'.

'September 1, 1939'* [*New Republic,* 18 Oct. 1939], whose title is the date of Hitler's invasion of Poland, is similarly centred upon the need to establish the Just Society, though it is naturally composed of different proportions of despair and hope. The basis of such a society is a universal love, the Christian Agape indeed, which appears to be denied by the Eros of the individual corrupted by sin (stanza 6):

> For the error bred in the bone
> Of each woman and each man
> Craves what it cannot have,
> Not universal love
> But to be loved alone.

Auden borrowed these last two lines from Nijinsky: 'Some politicians are hypocrites like Diaghilev, who does not want universal love, but to be loved alone. I want universal love' (*The Diary of Vaslav Nijinsky,* 1937, p. 44). The immediate evidence of this 'error' could be traced in theory by psychoanalytic investigations of Hitler's earliest experiences ('what occurred 'at Linz,/what huge imago made/A psychopathic god') or by a historical study of German nationalism ('the whole offence/From Luther until now/That has driven a culture mad'), but there is a simpler answer, with a strongly Christian flavour: 'Those to whom evil is done/Do evil in return'. Phyllis Bartlett and John A. Pollard take this to refer to Hitler's unhappy youth in Vienna (*Explicator,* Nov. 1955: the mention of Linz – Hitler's birthplace – they take to refer to the Anschluss). Actually, the mention of Luther was probably intended to indict far more than Nazism, for Auden at this time blamed the anxiety of modern life largely on those thinkers of the Renaissance and the Enlightenment who were responsible for Economic Man. A passage from Auden's preface to his *Poets of the English Language* (1950) bears a very direct relationship to the meaning of 'September 1, 1939':

The dualism inaugurated by Luther, Machiavelli and Descartes has brought us to the end of our tether and we know that either we must discover a unity which can repair the fissures that separate the individual from society, feeling from intellect, and conscience from both, or we shall surely die by spiritual despair and physical annihilation (p. xxx).

In the words of the poem: 'We must love one another or die'. In his Foreword to Bloomfield's *Bibliography,* Auden has justified his suppression of the poem as follows:

Rereading a poem of mine, *1st September, 1939,* after it had been published, I came to the line 'We must love one another or die' and said to myself: 'That's a damned lie! We must die anyway.' So, in the next edition, I altered it to 'We must love one another and die'. This didn't seem to do either, so I cut the stanza. Still no good. The whole poem, I realized, was infected with an incurable dishonesty – and must be scrapped (p. viii).

Since this is perhaps Auden's most notorious revision, it is worth pointing out that his statement here does not seem supported by the bibliographical facts. The stanza was omitted in the *Collected Poetry* (1945), whereas the variant 'and die' (which Beach thought must be a misprint) seems not to occur until 1955 in Oscar Williams's *New Pocket Anthology of American Verse*. The stanza concentrates all the Yeatsian postures of the poem, and is, moreover (despite its grandeur of tone), very simple and moving in its acceptance of the artist's role and limitations. It seems honest enough, though it is possible to understand how Auden could come to feel that it was a trifle ingenuous (though hardly, as he claims, positively mendacious).

From this point in time, Auden's omissions seem far less tendentious. Clearly, the intoxication of new ideas spilled over into an extraordinary technical virtuosity in the early 'forties, producing such chilly dazzling poems as 'Kairos and Logos'* (four sestinas) and

'Canzone'* (a poem of sixty-five lines using only five end-words). There seems almost a fear here of an emotional commitment. Form uses up energy: there are a few authentic neo-Rilkean moments, but the diction is parnassian for the most part. These two poems, together with 'In War Time',* ' "Gold in the North" came the blizzard to say'* and 'Christmas 1940',* are those that Auden has omitted from the poems first published in the *Collected Poetry* (1945). They are interesting reading, especially to those who find Auden's eclectic theology in these years instructive, but they cannot be said to be inspired as poems. There are no omissions from *Nones* (1951), and 'Gently, Little Boat' (from *The Rake's Progress*), which had been reprinted in *The Shield of Achilles* (1955), has been returned to the libretto where it belongs.

Notes

FOREWORD

1. *The Orators*, the plays, the libretti and *About The House* must be read in their separate volumes, and I have also referred the reader to the original edition of *New Year Letter* for material that does not appear in the *Collected Longer Poems*. My page references are to the latest edition in every case.

CHAPTER ONE

1. Quoted by Bloomfield, p. 3. The publishing history of *Paid* is as follows: *Criterion*, Jan. 1930; P30, P33; CSP50; CLP. An explanation of these and other abbreviations used in the notes may be found on p. 271.

2. Programme note to *The Dance of Death* (1933), quoted in Ashley Dukes, 'The English Scene', *Theatre Arts*, xix (Dec. 1935), p. 907.

3. The few place-names that can be traced point to the Durham area. There is a Rookhope Burn (cf. p. 14) in the lead-mining district of south-west Durham, and a Brandon (cf. p. 15) near the county seat. North Durham has a Lintz and a Lintzford (cf. 'Lintzgarth', the Nowers' house), both very near Allendale, the setting and title of an early Auden poem (see *New Verse*, Nov. 1937, pp. 4–5).

4. *Secondary Worlds* (1968), p. 101.

5. Compare 'following a line with left and right' with 'But left and right alternately/Is consonant with History' in *New Year Letter*, p. 155.

6. See *The Review*, No. 11/12, pp. 82, 89, for my comment on the MS. of this passage.

CHAPTER TWO

1. Captain Ferguson has not been identified. This might be a reference to some purely private though notorious schoolmaster (shades of Captain Grimes in Evelyn Waugh's *Decline and Fall*, 1928), or it might possibly refer to the Captain Ferguson who played Falstaff to the Marquis of Waterford's Hal in the nineteenth century (see *Notes and Queries*, 7th series, Vol. I, 1886, p. 46). As a practical joker, and the young Marquis's drinking companion, he would prove thematically suitable to the poem, though rather obscure.

2. The phrase from *Poems* (1928), 'The slow fastidious line/That disciplines the fell', would seem to have an even earlier origin in a poem dating from Auden's schooldays which describes 'the long slow curvings of the fells' on Alston Moor. See E. R. Dodds in *Shenandoah*, XVIII (Winter 1967), p. 9.

3. 'Cashwell' appears; and compare 'Greenearth Side' with 'Greenearth Fork' in 'The Engine House' (*Lions and Shadows*, p. 186) and with 'Greenhearth' in 'The Secret Agent'.

4. Most references to Carritt in *The Orators*, together with the Ode dedicated to him, have been dropped from the latest edition.

5. Page references to this work and to *Psychoanalysis and the Unconscious* are to the uniform Phoenix edition published by Heinemann (1961).

6. The notebook (Add. MS. 52430) was acquired by the Arts Council in 1964. Auden had given it to T. O. Garland thirty years before. Since the first seven shorts were first published by Auden in 1966, it would appear that he had an opportunity to see the notebook at the time of the Arts Council's acquisition, and to resurrect a number of pieces from it. See also 'Uncle Henry', CSP, p. 48.

CHAPTER THREE

1. 1932; 1934; 1966.

2. *The Old School*, ed. Graham Greene (1934), p. 17.

3. The speaker is an old boy, *not* the headmaster, despite the fact that he is given the mannerisms of one of Auden's old prep-school masters. See *Lions and Shadows*, p. 184.

4. See *Oxford and the Groups*, ed. R. H. S. Crossman (1934).

5. A 'tin-streamer' is one who gets tin by washing ore in a stream; a 'heckler' is a dresser of flax or hemp; and a 'blow-room major' is someone in charge of a tin-smelting house.

6. See Lawrence's *Fantasia of the Unconscious*, p. 119.

7. See *Racial Proverbs*, ed. S. G.Chapman (1938).

8. See *Lions and Shadows*, p. 214. She had visited Oxford on 7 June 1926

and given a talk at Christ Church (Auden's college). See *Oxford Magazine,* 10 June 1926, p. 564.

9. See *The Poetic Art of W. H. Auden* (1965), pp. 78–81.

10. *Runic and Heroic Poems,* ed. Bruce Dickins (1915), p. 28.

11. Pointed out by Kathleen Hoagland in *1000 Years of Irish Poetry* (1947), p. 23.

12. This book also provided Eliot with sources for 'Coriolan', a contemporary poem which it is instructive to compare with Auden's.

13. *The Poems of Wilfred Owen,* ed. Blunden (1931 edn.), p. 36. The allusion reappears in the last stanza of 'The Malverns' in *Look, Stranger!*

14. See J. G. O'Neill, *Ancient Corinth* (1931).

15. 'Hush! not a word of the beast with two backs/Or Mead and Muskett will be on our tracks!' may be compared with Lawrence's 'Innocent England':

> A wreath of mist is the usual thing
> in the north, to hide where the turtles sing.
> Though they never sing, they never sing,
> don't you dare to suggest such a thing
> or Mr Mead will be after you.

Frederick Mead was the eighty-year-old magistrate who, on 8 August 1929, handled the case of Lawrence's paintings seized by the police for obscenity.

CHAPTER FOUR

1. Auden knew no German before going to Berlin (see the *New Yorker,* 3 Apr. 1965, p. 190). Auden has said to Breon Mitchell that it would be wrong to isolate Brecht as a major influence (*Oxford German Studies,* No. 1, 1967, pp. 164–5).

2. Quoted by Ashley Dukes in 'The English Scene', *Theatre Arts,* XIX (Dec. 1935), pp. 907–8.

3. 1935; paperback 1968. The other two published plays on which Auden and Isherwood collaborated are *The Ascent of F6* and *On the Frontier.*

4. The range of critical attention may be gathered from Kenneth Allott in *New Verse,* Feb./Mar. 1936, and Ian Parsons in the *Spectator,* 28 June 1935.

5. See Isherwood in *New Verse,* Nov. 1937, and Bloomfield, p. xvii.

6. For a full account of the evolution of the published version, and of the authors' altercation with Faber and Faber, see Bloomfield, pp. 13–14.

7. See A. E. Wilson, *Christmas Pantomine* (1934), pp. 247ff. Auden has said that pantomime is 'the most important single influence' on *Dog* (Mitchell, *loc. cit.,* p. 169). Dick Whittington was a popular pantomime subject at the time (Wilson, p. 165).

8. Cf. Hegel, *Philosophy of History* (trans. J. Sibree, 1900), p. 414: 'Paradise is a park, where only brutes, not men, can remain.'

9. *The Listener*, 22 Dec. 1937, p. 137.

10. The idea of the diary may have come from J. Field's *A Life of One's Own*, which Auden reviewed and praised in *The Listener*, 28 Nov. 1934, p. viii.

11. One line of this chorus is based on a phrase of Winston Churchill's in *The World Crisis* (1923), his history of the First World War, describing Germany's March offensive: 'It was an hour of intolerable majesty and crisis.' See Auden's review in *Scrutiny*, Mar. 1933, p. 413.

12. 1936; 1937; paperback, 1958. The play was published before the acting text was finalized, so that last-minute revisions were not incorporated into the printed text until the second edition. For accounts of the revising process, see Bloomfield, p. 17, and Isherwood, *Exhumations*, p. 11.

13. *Hudson Review*, III (Winter 1951), p. 575.

14. See, for example, Kenneth Allott, *New Verse* (Nov. 1937), p. 19.

15. See *Poems* (1928), No. XII, 'The four sat on in the bare room', and *The Age of Anxiety*, where the faculties are represented by the characters Quant, Rosetta, Emble and Malin. See also *For the Time Being* (CLP, p. 141).

16. 1938; paperback 1958.

CHAPTER FIVE

1. Paul Haeffner has pointed out a similarity to Ella Wheeler Wilcox's 'The Arrival' in *Notes and Queries*, No. 207, Mar. 1962.

2. The last two lines are in fact a quotation from Lenin. See Auden's review of Basil Liddell Hart's book on T. E. Lawrence, *Now and Then*, No. 47, Spring 1934.

3. See E. W. White, *Benjamin Britten*, 2nd ed (1954), p. 22.

4. See Bloomfield, p. 24, for an identification of Auden's contributions.

5. For this imagery of North and South, frequent in Auden, see 'England: Six Unexpected Days', *Vogue*, 15 May 1954.

6. For instance, F. R. Leavis ('a pointless unpleasantness') in *Scrutiny*, Vol. IX (1940), and Kathleen Raine ('sniggers') in *Horizon*, Vol. III (1940).

7. Note prefixed to the Sermon from *The Dog Beneath the Skin* in CP, p. 242.

8. All six parts were originally published in JW and reprinted separately in CP and CSP50. 'The Ship' appeared in *The Listener*, 18 Aug. 1938, and 'A Major Port' was originally No. XXV of the sequence 'In Time of War'.

9. *College English* (April 1963), pp. 529–31.

CHAPTER SIX

1. 1941 (American title: *The Double Man*); CP and CLP (with some revisions) print the 'Letter' alone without the accompanying material, some of which is to be found in CSP, pp. 156 and 176–97. I refer to the original edition in order to make use of the line numberings and note material.

2. 'Traveller's Return', *Horizon*, Feb. 1941.

3. *Texas Quarterly*, Winter 1961, p. 81.

4. *Ibid.*

5. *Renascence*, XVI (1963), 13–19.

6. 'The Quest Hero', *Texas Quarterly*, Winter 1961, p. 83. See also 'K's Quest' in *The Kafka Problem*, ed. A. Flores (1946).

7. Titles are given in the *New Republic* and in CP.

8. Auden was reading Doughty as early as 1928, according to MacNeice (*The Strings are False*, 1965, p. 114).

9. Auden included the Humpty Dumpty poem in the *Oxford Book of Light Verse* (1938), p. 456.

CHAPTER SEVEN

1. Published in *For the Time Being*, 1944, 1945; CP, p. 407; CLP, p. 131.

2. Auden, in *Modern Canterbury Pilgrims*, ed. James A. Pike (1956).

3. In his introduction to *The Living Thoughts of Kierkegaard* (1952).

4. 'The Means of Grace', *New Republic*, 2 June 1941, p. 765.

5. Cf. Auden's remark about the history of the Church being strewn with its scandals in *Oxford and the Groups*, ed. R. H. S. Crossman (1934), p. 90.

CHAPTER EIGHT

1. Published in *For the Time Being*, 1944, 1945; CP, p. 351; CLP, p. 199.

2. The variety of form and style tempted a correspondent to *The Times Literary Supplement*, 13 Nov. 1948, to suggest, no doubt ironically, that it is a poem *à clef*, that Gonzalo is Eliot, and that other poets are parodied.

CHAPTER NINE

1. *Partisan Review*, VI (Spring 1939), pp. 46–51.

2. Quoted in William Willibrand's *Ernst Toller and his Ideology* (1946), p. 30.

3. CSP, p. 117. 'The Riddle' in fact borrows its initial phrase from an earlier version of 'As He Is'. See *New Writing*, Autumn 1937.

4. Cf. Spinoza, *Ethics*, Part III, 'Definition of the Emotions', No. VI (Everyman edn., trans. A. Boyle, 1910, p. 130).

5. See Daniel Hoffman, *Paul Bunyan: Last of the Frontier Demigods* (1952), pp. 144–5.

6. Cf. *New Year Letter*, 1. 1244 *n*, for an interesting elaboration of this in connection with psychology.

7. Cf. 'The Quest Hero', *Texas Quarterly*, Winter 1961, p. 84: 'I am conscious of myself as unique – my goal is for me only – and as confronting an unknown future – I cannot be certain in advance whether I shall succeed or fail in achieving my goal.'

8. Perhaps Auden had been reading Empson's *The Gathering Storm*, published the previous year, especially 'Aubade' with 'Leap Before you Look' resembles a little.

9. Discussed by Auden in his review of Denis de Rougemont's *Love in the Western World* in *Nation*, 28 June 1941.

10. Pointed out by John Bayley in *The Romantic Survival*, p. 174.

CHAPTER TEN

1. 1947, 1948; CLP, p. 253.

2. See Jolande Jacobi, *The Psychology of C. G. Jung*, 6th edn (1962), pp. 10ff.

3. A relevant discussion of the style may be found in Chap. 3, 'Baroque Art and the Emblem', of Austin Warren's *Richard Crashaw: A Study in Baroque Sensibility* (1939).

4. In *Gulliver's Travels*, Book One, the war between Lilliput and Blefuscu originates in their opening their eggs at different ends. In Book Four, the Anglican Swift ironically presents a perfect society of rational horses.

5. The form is mentioned by Auden in *The Dyer's Hand*, p. 47, and *Secondary Worlds*, pp. 67–68, and is described by E. V. Gordon in his *Introduction to Old Norse Verse*, 1957 edn., pp. 317–18.

CHAPTER TWELVE

1. Cf. *The Enchafèd Flood*, p. 21: 'The sea is no place to be if you can help it, and to try to cross it betrays a rashness bordering on hubris.'

2. Restituta (d. AD 284) is Ischia's patron saint; Epomeo its highest mountain, an extinct volcano.

3. See his 'Sirocco at Deyá'. Auden seems here to be almost deliberately imitating Graves, as in the latter's 'Lollocks'.

4. 'Comfy, that's it! Just reading the poems is ever so comfy' (Randall Jarrell, *Yale Review*, June 1955). The line has been picked on in this way by Howard Nemerov, Philip Larkin and others.

5. See Carlo Izzo, 'Good-Bye to the Mezzogiorno', *Shenandoah*, Winter 1967, p. 81.

CHAPTER THIRTEEN

1. The form that Auden uses here and in a great deal of this volume is the seventeen-syllable Japanese *haiku*. In several poems Auden builds on the form as a stanza in its own right. The virtuosity displayed in varying the tone and approach of this form is remarkable: the gravity of 'Elegy for J.F.K.' is answered by the intimacy of 'Lines for Elizabeth Mayer'; the syncopated reflective wit of 'Iceland Revisited' is supported by the discrete yet related epigrams of 'Symmetries & Asymmetries'.

2. See Auden's reply to a symposium on the poem in *Kenyon Review*, Winter 1964, p. 204: '*You's* age, sex, social status, profession, and persona-ego problem are those of whoever happens to be reading the poem.'

CHAPTER FOURTEEN

1. Texts of some of these poems are now not easy to get hold of. There are, however, two xerographic reprints of *Poems* (1928) by the University of Michigan (1961) and the University of Cincinnati (1964). I have also asterisked those poems which are still available in the first edition of the *Collected Shorter Poems* (1950). For everything else, the reader will have to go to the original collections.

2. Ciddy is a character based on Auden and Isherwood's prep-school headmaster. See Isherwood's story 'Gems of Belgian Architecture' in *Exhumations*, p. 176.

Bibliography

This bibliography is intended to be brief and selective. The first part, consisting of Auden's major works published in book form, is intended largely as a guide to abbreviations used in the text, and these are indicated where appropriate; the works are listed in chronological order. The second part consists of secondary material that is of general importance. There are many valuable articles on particular aspects of Auden's work, and some of these I have mentioned in the text where relevant. Anyone wishing to probe further should consult Bloomfield's admirable bibliography.

I. BOOKS BY AUDEN

P28	*Poems* (Oxford, 1928)
P30	*Poems* (London, 1930)
O	*The Orators* (London, 1932)
P33	*Poems* (London, 1933), second edition of P30
	The Dance of Death (London, 1933)
	The Dog Beneath the Skin (London, 1935)
	The Ascent of F6 (London, 1936)
LS	*Look, Stranger!* (London, 1936)
	Spain (London, 1937)
LI	*Letters from Iceland* (London, 1937)
	On the Frontier (London, 1938)
JW	*Journey To a War* (London, 1939)
AT	*Another Time* (New York, 1940)
NYL	*The Double Man* (New York, 1941), known in England as

CP   *The Collected Poetry* (New York, 1945)
                The Age of Anxiety (New York, 1947)
CSP50   *Collected Shorter Poems* (1950)
                The Enchafèd Flood (New York, 1950)
N   *Nones* (New York, 1951)
                The Rake's Progress (London, 1951)
                Mountains (London, 1954)
SA   *The Shield of Achilles* (New York, 1955)
                The Old Man's Road (New York, 1956)
HC   *Homage to Clio* (New York, 1960)
                Elegy for Young Lovers (Mainz, 1961)
                The Dyer's Hand (New York, 1962)
AH   *About the House* (New York, 1966)
                Marginalia (Cambridge, Mass., 1966)
                The Bassarids (Mainz, 1966)
CSP   *Collected Shorter Poems* (London, 1966)
CLP   *Collected Longer Poems* (London, 1968)
                Secondary Worlds (London, 1968)

II. BIOGRAPHY AND CRITICISM

Bayley, John. *The Romantic Survival* (London, 1957)

Beach, Joseph Warren. *The Making of the Auden Canon* (Minneapolis, 1957)

Blair, John G. *The Poetic Art of W. H. Auden* (Princeton, N.J., 1965)

Bloomfield, B. C. *W. H. Auden: A Bibliography* (Charlottesville, Va., 1964)

Everett, Barbara. *Auden* (London, 1964)

Hoggart, Richard. *Auden: An Introductory Essay* (London, 1951)

Isherwood, Christopher. *Lions and Shadows* (London, 1938)

———. *Exhumations* (London, 1966)

Jarrell, Randall. 'Changes of attitude and rhetoric in Auden's poetry', *Southern Review,* Vol. VII (1941)

———. 'Freud to Paul: The stages of Auden's ideology', *Partisan Review,* Vol XII (1945)

New Verse, November 1937

Scarfe, Francis. *Auden and After* (London, 1942)

———. *W. H. Auden* (Monaco, 1949)

Shenandoah, Vol. XVIII (Winter 1967)

Spears, Monroe K. *The Poetry of W. H. Auden* (New York, 1963)

———, ed. *Auden: A Collection of Critical Essays* (Englewood Cliffs, N.J., 1964)

Spender, Stephen. *World Within World* (London, 1951)

Index of Titles and First Lines

Page references in italics indicate the main treatment of each poem in the text, where details of publishing history are given in square brackets immediately after the title of the poem. I have not included any title where it is virtually identical with its first line. I have included alternative titles, and also variant first lines wherever difference in wording might make a poem difficult to find.

General Index

286